We regret very much a number of errors have appeared in the final work for which we apologise. For completeness then the following amendments should be noted:

Page 19/20 should read: This was necessary as GWR engines were banned from the Dock Company lines. Warning notices to this effect were placed at the actual boundary and also points to interchange.

Page 20/21 should read: The loading of the actual fish boxes into the fish vans was overseen by the checkers. There were a total of eight checkers and two foremen. All the checkers together with one foreman worked on one shift.

Page 61:   Full stop missing at end of column one.

Table Page 81 should read:

Payrolll Number	Fireman	Payroll	Fireman Number
41	J. F. Rushton	59	J. L. D. Richards
42	W. J. Spur	60	S. A. Parsley
43	P. J. R. Saunders	61	S. W. James
44	C. K. Bassett	62	B. G. Thomas
45	A. C. R. Lloyd	63	H. E. Orchard
46	A. C. G. Lewis	65	J. E. Davies
47	J. J. Pritchard	67	W. Bryant
48	D. J. Llewellyn	68	W. M. Williams
49	R. Bryant	70	J. E. Griffiths
50	K. A. Luff	71	W. J. Owens
51	I. C. Stone	72	D. S. Francis
52	G. F. J. House	73	R. L. A. Jenkins
53	W. G. Edmond	74	B. Phillips
54	D. M. Smith	75	A. E. Baker
55	G. Howell	76	O. A. M. Richards
56	S. J. Duignan	77	D. J. Day
57	R. Williams	79	R. J. Evans
58	F. C. H. Harriers	83	D. P. Jones

Payrolll Number	Driver	Payroll Number	Driver
1	K. G. Cannings	18	D. J. Vaughan
2	F. J. Vaughan	19	G. W. E. Simpson
3	L. C. Sweeney	20	A. Owen
4	V. J. Griffiths	21	T. Davis
5	W. J. James	22	J. H. Harnett
6	G. Lewis	23	T. S. Lloyd
7	W. J. Such	22	F. G. Morgans
8	A. G. Evans	25	F. Griffiths
9	I. J. Lewis	26	W. T. Harrison
10	W. G. Talbot	27	W. T. Hitchins
11	H. V. James	29	J. W. Davies
12	W. Evans	30	C. G. H. Morgan
13	F. H. Howells	32	V. C. Rowe
14	W. H. Vaughan	33	W. A. Glass
15	L. T. Lewis	34	K. E. Owen
16	A. Davies	35	N. J. Thomas
17	W. T. Llewellyn	36	J. W. Bevan

Table Page 84:

Siding No.	Used For	Capacity in wagons
1	Traffic for Carmarthen, Aberystwyth and Newcastle Emlyn	18
2	Traffic for Haverfordwest, Milford Haven and Neyland	33
3	Cripple wagons, 7. 00 am to 5. 00 pm and traffic for Clynderwen and Clarbeston Road	32
4	Traffic for Fishguard	32
5	Traffic for Whitland and branches	27
6	Traffic for Sarnau and St. Clears	23
7	General	10
8	Approach to cattle wagon cleaning sidings	10

Page 89/90 should read: The two buildings were 36 feet apart and between them was a fixed hand-crane.

Page 134 caption should read: ". . . The scene was recorded circa 1893."

To OUR FRIENDS

SVLYiA & PETER

Love from

Ruth BRyAN & IAN

2003

Neyland

a Great Western outpost

Richard Parker

KRB Publications

ISBN 0–9542035–3–4

Published by
KRB Publications
2 Denewulf Close
BISHOPS WALTHAM
Hants
SO32 1GZ

Printed by The Amadeus Press.

Front cover:

Neyland circa 1904.   *F.R. Burtt Collec. / N.R.M.. FB522*

The expanse of railway facilities at the Neyland Terminus and depicted in 1926. The sheltered position of the deep water inlet here and known as the Milford Haven, makes it easy to understand why the location was selected very early on as an ideal staging post for the lucrative Irish steamer traffic being sheltered as it was from the westerly gales. The land on the opposite side of the Haven was the location of Pembroke Dock.

National Railway Museum

— Contents —

© KRB Publications and Richard Parker 2002
ISBN 0–9542035–3–4
Published by KRB Publications
2 Denewulf Close
BISHOPS WALTHAM Hants SO32 1GZ

Printed by The Amadeus Press.

Neyland viewed this time from the Barnlake side of Westfield Pill. The photograph was taken soon after the turn of the century but before the construction of the Fish Market in 1908. Much of the town of Neyland was built on the hillside and accordingly gave rise to numerous steep gradients on the various roads and streets.

Collec. Desmond Davies

Preface, Introduction, Acknowledgements and Sources.

Why Neyland? I have frequently been asked. My wife having purchased for me a copy of *Behind the Steam,* by Bill Morgan and Bette Meyrick, inadvertently set me on the trail that has led to this book. Over the years I have derived much pleasure from re–reading the stories of Bill Morgan's early life as an employee on the Great Western Railway. Indeed for some time I had contemplated building a model railway based on Neyland to try and capture some of the flavour of its unspoilt Brunelian atmosphere, a unique survival of Victorian railways until its closure in 1964.

As a prelude to building of the model, and which has still yet to commence, it soon became clear that very little written material existed on Neyland's railway and that I would have to undertake the research myself to try and uncover what remained.

This commenced then in 1997 when the opportunity of a short holiday in Pembrokeshire allowed a visit Neyland and by dint of some detective work and good luck, I traced one former railwayman who in turn provided other contacts. From these beginnings has grown the work that is set before you.

I hope it will put on record for future generations the activities of Neyland's railwaymen and with what purpose they went about their daily tasks. Remembering that my endeavours began so long after Neyland's closure, I hope that it is not too wide of the mark. The recollections of necessity then are mainly of the latter years, but they would almost certainly be appropriate to previous generations as well. This is confirmed in that the working timetables show a constant pattern of services following the loss of the marine trade to Fishguard in 1906. Indeed it is obvious that had it not been for the coming of the railway, Neyland would certainly not have developed in the way that it did and in so doing shaped so many lives and destinies.

The work itself starts with an overview of the early history and the line itself from Clarbeston Road together with the branch to Milford Haven. Neyland, its traffic and infrastructure are then dealt with together with staff recollections. As no doubt applies in other parts, so much of the railway history of the area is of necessity intermingled although space within these pages precludes delving off at too many tangents. For those who require a history of the railways of Pembrokeshire as a whole there can be no better source than the late John Morris's book as recorded in the bibliography although at the time of writing, this is sadly out of print. Thanks especially to John Morris for permission to quote from his book on the marine activities at Neyland.

I wish also to record my sincere thanks to all who have helped me in any way in my research and especially the former railwaymen who welcomed me into their homes and spent time recalling their experiences. Not once was my request for information met with indifference. If material provided has not been included then this will be through oversight or, in the case of photographs, due to lack of available space. In this way some hard and often heart wrenching decisions had to be made. For this you may also blame the publisher for a book of this type has to be commercially viable as well as hopefully appealing.

Thank you then to, David Abbott, Aurora Imaging, Mike Bentley, Stephen Berry, Cyril and Mrs. Bevan, The late Jack and Mrs. Bevan, Rod Blencowe, The late Ray and Mrs. Bowen, Brinley and Mrs. John, Ron and Mrs. Brown, Roger Carpenter, Richard Casserley, Ray Caston, Paul Chancellor, Gordon Coltas, John Copsey, Di and Mrs. Day, Brian Davies, Desmond and Mrs. Davies, Edwin Davies, Ken Davies, Mike Esau, Douglas Francis, John Gilks, Simon Hancock, Charlie and the late Mrs. Harries, B.P. Hooper, David Hyde, Derrick Huddlestone, Mike Hughes, Morgan Hughes, Initial Photographs, Barrie Jacobs, Mrs. Hilliard James, Clive and Mrs. James, Ken Jones, Phil Kelley, Kidderminster Railway Museum and in particular Audie Baker and David Postle, Bob May, Alan Morgans, George Palmer, Mr and Mrs Perkins Castle Studios Haverfordwest, M.R.C. Price, Peter Radford, Bill Rear, R.C. Riley, Jim and Mrs. Rowell, Cyril and Mrs. Shortman, The Signalling Record Society, John Smart, Bernard and Mrs. Thomas, Denis Tillman, Adrian Vaughan, Mrs. Vaughan, Ken Vaughan, John Walter, E. Wilmshurst, Richard Woodley, The Western Telegraph – Haverfordwest, A.J. Williams, Roger Worsley, Henry Wilson and George Wright.

Thanks also to the staff of the Public Record Office at Kew, the County Record Offices at Haverfordwest and Trowbridge and also Haverfordwest Library. Almost the last word also to thank Mrs. Meyrick for permission to quote from *Behind the Steam.*

Finally to my wife Sandra for her support and encouragement and without which this work would not have been possible.

Richard Parker.
Bidford–on–Avon. 2002.

Bibliography:
Behind the Steam, Bill Morgan and Bette Meyrick. Pub: Hutchinson.
The Railways of Pembrokeshire, John Morris. Pub: H.G. Waters (Publishers) Tenby. With special thanks
The End of the Line, Desmond Davies. Pub: Pembrokeshire County Council.
Great Western Railway Travelling Post Offices, J.G. Hosegood. Pub: Wild Swan Publications Ltd.
Sir. Daniel Gooch Memoirs and Diary, Roger Burdett Wilson. Pub. David & Charles
History of the Great Western Railway, Mac Dermot. Pub: GWR.
The Great Western Magazine.

South Wales Railway Terminus & Hotel, from Hobb's Point.

Sailors from Pembroke Dockyard are in the foreground of this view of Hobbs Point on the opposite side of the Milford Haven waterway. Taken from what is either a contemporary artists rendition or a woodcut and dating probably prior to 1860, this must be one of the very earliest views, albeit distant, of the railway at what was at the time referred to as Neyland – several name changes occurring in later years. The South Wales Hotel stands imposingly on the opposite bank adjacent to the station whilst just visible to its left is the Station Master's, or to more accurate for the period, the Station Agent's house. The lack of housing on the hillside an accurate confirmation of the early period. As far as the station is concerned the shape of the train shed and used for arrivals is apparent, the departure platform to the left of the timber structure and perhaps not so obvious. To the right is the slipway at the end of which the ship could well be at anchor.

Desmond Davies

Chapter 1
NEYLAND
The Early Years – Setting the Scene

Before the coming of the South Wales Railway, Neyland was a small settlement on the shores of Westfield Pill in the parish of Llanstadwell having a population in the 1850s of less than 200 people. At this time it survived principally as a fishing and boat building community, one of numerous similar small areas of habitation in what was very much a country backwater.

In 1844 the South Wales Railway was formed to build a line into Pembrokeshire and with the intention of locating a suitable coastal staging post where a port could be established and a steam packet service operated to Southern Ireland. The South Wales Railway was supported by the Great Western Railway and in common with them, employed Isambard Kingdom Brunel as its Engineer Accordingly the civil engineering necessary was specified to accommodate the broad gauge. The GWR eventually absorbed the SWR. on August 1, 1863.

So far as is known there were initially no plans to build a line to Neyland. The original intention instead was to construct a line to Goodwick by Fishguard and there to form a harbour. Later an alternative site at Abermawr was considered but at each location minimal work was actually carried out because of a down turn in the general economic situation in this country and the Irish famine. Instead the directors of the S.W.R. decided to build their railway to a terminus on the banks of the Milford Haven estuary by way of Carmarthen, Whitland and Haverfordwest. These alternative proposals benefited much more the inhabitants of Haverfordwest, the County town of Pembrokeshire and who under the original plans would have been served by a mere branch line off the main route to Fishguard at a junction at what was later called Clarbeston Road.

Brunel had surveys carried out at various locations along the Milford Haven estuary and to the disappointment of those lobbying in favour of the town of Milford chose a site at Neyland point where the Westfield Pill flowed into the estuary. Had Brunel`s original plans of the period come to fruition then the harbour would have developed on both banks of Westfield Pill but in the event the objections of the landowner and the Royal Naval Dockyard at Pembroke Docks restricted development to the Neyland shoreline.

At what was then to be the site of the railway at Neyland, dwellings had been established on what was basically the only area of level ground on the shoreline. This though was also the position required for the new railway and so to enable construction to take place it was necessary to issue eviction notices to those inhabitants occupying this land. The majority of the properties that formally occupied the site were then demolished although some remained derelict for many years after the coming of the line. A new Neyland then grew up on the hillside with homes for the original Neylanders who had been dispossessed and also for the generation of railway workers. The railway company built eight homes in the High Street and ten in the appropriately named Railway Terrace as well as a house for the Station–Agent (sic). This latter building can just be discerned from the view on page 6. With the growth of the community established this in turn led to the provision of

An artists impression of the scene at Neyland on the opening day, April 15, 1856. The station building, train shed and goods shed are a good representation of the "temporary station" based on plans included in the contract between the South Wales Railway and William Lewis the contractor. Brunel and his staff had visited Neyland during March 1856 but were not present at the official opening. Despite the artists inclusion of numerous sightseers, the event was apparently a low key affair compared with the then more usual furore associated with contemporary new railway openings.

Illustrated London News.

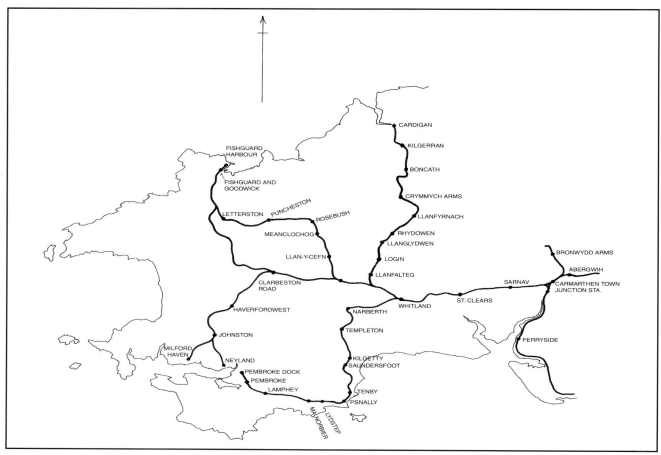

shops and other amenities thus providing further employment opportunities and further expansion of housing to accommodate these workers and their families.

At the time of public opening, April 15 1856, the station was known as 'Milford Haven'. Just three years later though in 1859, it was changed to 'Neyland' and shortly afterwards to 'New Milford', before reverting again to 'Neyland' in 1906. The route originally of just a single track was also doubled from 1 July 1857.   Seeing their neighbour starting to prosper in consequence of the new means of communication, it is not surprising that the inhabitants of Milford proper and located just a few miles on the coast westwards, were equally anxious to benefit from their own railway connection. Accordingly they formed their own railway company and on September 7 1863 that line was opened making a connection with the GWR near Johnston station. The Milford Company did not own its own locomotive or carriages and the line was worked from the outset by the GWR. To avoid confusion the station at Milford was known as Old Milford until 1906 when it was renamed Milford Haven.

Neyland's growth following the coming of the railway resulted in it being granted Urban District status in 1900 and by which time it could be aptly described as a railway town. However at this important time for Neyland, events taking place elsewhere would result in a decline in its prosperity. Not many of the inhabitants of Neyland in 1892 would have heard of Joseph Rowlands, but in that year he acquired a substantial interest in the North Pembrokeshire and Fishguard Railway Company. In 1895 this company successfully promoted a Bill in Parliament for a railway link between its company and that of the London and North Western Railway. This threatened the monopoly enjoyed by the G.W.R. in this locality and also that of the Southern Irish traffic. The G.W.R. hurriedly purchased the North Pembrokeshire and Fishguard Railway Company and resurrected proposals to construct a harbour at Fishguard. Thus when this harbour was opened in 1906 Neyland's fortune declined. However Neyland's railway station and yard remained active long after the transfer of the Irish trade to Fishguard because it continued to service the locomotive, carriage and wagon requirements of Haverfordwest and Milford Haven. Indeed the line to Neyland was still regarded as the main line whilst those to Fishguard and Milford Haven were referred to as the branches. (A description of neighbouring stations and their operational practices as affected Neyland follows in the next chapter.)

Returning though to the earliest days and a fortunate find was the report of the inspection of the line by Caption Tyler of the Board of Trade from April 12 1856 and which contains a remarkable amount of useful contemporary information.

"&.The route is a single line 9˘ miles from Haverfordwest to Neyland with one intermediate station at Milford Road. (*Authors note – this was the original name for Johnston*). The permanent way is of bridge rail 19 feet in length and 60 lb to the yard which is secured by fang bolts to longitu-

Neyland Staff. The photograph is not dated but is likely to have been taken circa 1880/90. The clerestory coach behind is to diagram E11, one of four composite vehicles of Lot No. 206 and built between May and November 1880. They were 46 feet 6˘ inches long and 8 foot and ∫inch wide. This particular vehicle is numbered in the series '658 to 661' – regretfully the gentleman's head is in just the wrong place to be more precise! Each vehicle had a lavatory and luggage compartment as well as first and second class accommodation. Lighting was by oil, as indicated by the oil pots on the roof and with most coaching stock on the GWR converted to gas lighting by 1892. The vehicle remained in service until the early 1930's. That reproduced also represents the total extremes of the print and there is no accurate clue as to the identity of the locomotive. Despite the print being one of the earliest so far located of Neyland or more accurately 'New Milford' as it was called when the view was taken, there are no details as to the names or occupations of any of the men present. Likewise there is no clue as to the reason for recording the scene although it could well have been in connection with a celebration to mark the 30th anniversary of the opening of the railway in 1886 or even the Golden Jubilee of the Monarch in 1887. Certainly it would appear that those present are either totally or primarily representative of the Traffic Department grades, although the station did of course also have a number of men in the locomotive, engineering and especially marine departments. Seated in the centre of the front row is no doubt the Station Agent (Master) whilst a point of interest is also to be found in the presence of the Railway policeman holding the stick on the extreme left. The other men are likely to be Clerical, Foremen, Guards, Porters and ancillary wages grades. The distinction between salaried and wages staff was represented by the GWR in that salaried men were officers of the Company whilst wages staff were Servants. The men are all gathered on the fish platform and with the station building some distance away to the left. That to the right is part of a complex of structures associated with the fishing industry.

Mrs G. Perkins

dinal sleepers placed at 11 foot intervals with transoms and strap bolts. The ballast is broken stone. There are three level crossings approached by gradients of 1 in 75 and require to be protected by signals at a considerable distance. At present there are three signals of a great height at a short distance. Lodges are required at the level crossings and clocks at the stations."

In reply the SWR agreed to provide lodges but commented that "...in the opinion of the Company they lead to neglect of attention at the gates". Capt. Tyler thought that at the very least a box ought to be provided and the gateman should not be "...unnecessarily exposed to the weather when not actively engaged in their duties". Perhaps not surprisingly the Board of Trade won the day and lodges were indeed provided together with the alterations to the signals as recommended. In respect of the clocks though, the SWR superintendent at Swansea replied that the clocks were at the stations and would be fitted when the stations were inhabited. The line was duly authorised and a public service commenced.

Numerous sidings were provided at the Terminus from the earliest days but such was the growth in traffic that expansion of the yard was necessary very early on. Because the railway already made use of the available land

between Westfield Pill and the hillside there was no inexpensive solution. During July 1876 Edwin Douglas, Contractor of Llanelly entered into an agreement to evacuate the hillside below Neyland woods and to use the material to form a new embankment on the Pill side. This had the advantage of providing land on which further sidings were laid at what became known as "The Rock" as well as on the new embankment later known as "Barnlake." To facilitate the work the GWR hired old rails to the contractor at £5 per ton so that temporary lines could be laid to allow wagons to transport the evacuated material from the hillside and so form the new embankment. The contract required that the material was to be removed and deposited at a minimum rate of 3000 cubic yards per week and that if he failed to do so a penalty of £20 each week was incurred. It is not recorded how this work was managed to minimise the impact of the train services, especially as the use of explosive material is indicated by the agreement and which stipulated that the store house for the powder had to be sited with the approval of the GWR.

Apart from the expansions mentioned the next major impact on the railway came in 1882 when the broad gauge line from Swindon Junction to Neyland was converted to standard gauge. This was a massive undertaking

and required elaborate and detailed planning. The work commenced on Wednesday 1st May and the following are extracts that relate to or had a bearing on Neyland.

It was stipulated that, "...the up line will be commenced from Neyland to Grange Court with the inner rail moved outwards throughout the entire length. That the ballast would have been cleared away previous to the commencement of narrowing and the transoms will have been marked to suit the narrow gauge."

The instruction directed that, "...the down line will be the first worked as a single line on the broad gauge from Grange Court near Gloucester to Neyland. On and from the same date the up line will be worked as a single line on the narrow (standard gauge) until the double line in the narrow gauge is opened. During the period occupied by the engineers the railway between Grange Court and Neyland will be worked as a single line by pilot engines in charge of a pilotman." The instructions provided for a special engine to leave Neyland at 10.00 pm on the 30th April with Inspector Langdon. It stated that "He will distribute notices to all concerned on the way up to Grange Court that the up line is closed and immediately after the passing of the engine and the receipt of such notices the engineers can take possession of the up line and the working of the down line as a single line will commence".

The pilotmen was also to wear a distinctive badge fastened to his right arm whilst on duty and the instructions further stipulated that when a man changed duties the badges must be exchanged only at the proper changing station and in the presence of the officer in charge of the station. It required him to record in a book the exact time at which the change is made to which his signature and the pilotman must be appended.

"Relevant" sections were ;–

No.	Section	Changing Station	Badge	Length
1	Neyland to Haverfordwest	Neyland	Red letters on white ground	9ˉ miles
2	Haverfordwest to Whitland	Haverfordwest	White letters on blue ground	17ˉ miles

The instruction provided for the continued working of two through goods trains which as far as possible should convey the Irish and other important traffic. The Irish traffic as well as the special fish traffic brought to Neyland by water had to be loaded and dispatched, "...with the greatest regularity during the whole period of the conversion".

It was stated that the change from the broad gauge to the narrow gauge will take place on a Sunday and following the issue of a special notice. This notice stipulated that as the broad gauge passenger trains on the Sunday night finished their journey they should be worked back as soon as possible to Swindon. The last of them must be dispatched from Neyland about 9.15 pm or as soon as possible after the arrival of No 10 down train. A "special engine" would follow the No 10 train with Inspector Langdon distributing notices to all concerned that the broad gauge

Opposite Page: Neyland in the late 19th century although the view has been seen elsewhere its historic importance certainly warrants a repeat inclusion. The 'temporary' station of 1856 how has an extension to the train shed in place. The pontoon, however, has not yet been provided with its corrugated curved roof. The curved departure platform can also be seen to the right and with its short platform and canopy, was no doubt suitable for the length of train that generally ran in the period.

On the opposite bank of the Milford Haven and less than half a mile in actual distance was Pembroke Dock, although the distance by rail was considerable. The tall wooden structure in the left middle ground is part of the hydraulic wagon lift. A 'Penfold' post box of a style constructed between 1872 and 1879 can be seen on the arrival platform. This was later removed to a site near the Station Master's house in Picton Road. The access to the cattle pens is across the departure lines and then through the gate in the stone wall just beyond the passenger brake van which stands in the foreground. Only one signal is visible towering above the coaches in the siding which lead into the train shed. This signal is of the 'disc' pattern and which style had largely disappeared by the 1890's.

The actual position of the departure platform away from the arrival side and separated by sidings would appear unique throughout the GWR and it's associated concerns. Little appears to have mentioned about this strange arrangement previously and there would certainly appear to have been no geological or operational need for such a separate arrangement. Indeed as referred to above when dealing with access to the cattle pens, operationally such an arrangement must surely have been less than ideal. Was it perhaps that Brunel was considering this as the standard design for a terminus? Certainly his ideas on some through stations and where a single platform served trains in each direction, were equally unusual at times. (Such as at Reading.) In the event the Neyland philosophy was not proceeded with elsewhere although the arrangement persisted here until the end.

Brinley John / National Railway Museum 880.51

stock had been removed and that the broad gauge line can no longer be used.

The first down train to traverse the up narrow gauge single line would be the 3.50 pm down mail from Gloucester on the Sunday and the first up train would be the 4.00 pm up mail from Neyland. After the up mail had passed Neath two trains were to leave for Neyland to provide narrow gauge stock for subsequent services from the terminus. Additionally provision was also made for a train of narrow gauge empty fish and goods wagons to be worked from Neath to Neyland on the Sunday night.

After the engineers had reported that the down line was ready for use as a narrow gauge line single line working was terminated by Inspector Langdon who would proceed, again by special train from Neyland to Grange Court distributing notices to all concerned.

The conversion of the branch to Milford (Haven) commenced on 1st May with an omnibus (horse–drawn) provided for through passengers. However the instructions stated that no local passengers between Johnston and Milford were to be carried. Goods traffic for Milford had to be carried to Neyland and "thence by Jackson & Co. ferry boat".

The South Wales Hotel and which was constructed for the South Wales Railway at a cost of £1850 and completed in 1858. At some time also it was extended and it is believed this turn of the century view records it in its final form. The Hotel was situated at the bottom of Neyland Hill with the road leading to the station in the foreground. Intended as a staging point for passengers travelling to and from Ireland, it was only really successful prior to the commencement of alternative ferry service via Fishguard in 1906. After 1863 it was taken over by the GWR but subsequently sold on, possibly around 1910. Certainly in that year it was recorded that the lease on the property had changed, this same document giving some useful contemporary information as to the facilities. These were recorded as consisting 28 Bedrooms including four for hotel servants, a Drawing Room, Dressing Room, Coffee Room, two Smoking Rooms, three Sitting Rooms, a Bar, Commercial Room, Billiard Room, two Still Rooms, Kitchen, two Scullery's, a Larder, Boot hole and a Linen room.

In the 1880's Sir Daniel Gooch, Chairman of the GWR was a visitor and commented that the rooms were comfortable. Despite the decline which occurred consequent upon the loss of the Irish Ferry traffic, the building remained as a Hotel, passing through several owners, but had closed by the 1960's. A motor bus service operated by Green's Motors also used the Hotel as one of its regular stops on a service running between Milford Haven and Haverfordwest. No GWR buses ever working in the Neyland area. During the 1940's and by which time the previous neat façade and been almost totally covered in ivy and other climbing shrubs, it played host to Winston Churchill and Vera Lynn. Later still the British Overseas Airways Corporation, better known by the initials BOAC, used the Hotel as a base for their crews and support staff on the flying–boat service to America. The flying–boats were based on the Milford Haven estuary. Such a renaissance though was to be short lived and following closure the premises were demolished during May 1970. To the left of the Hotel and immediately above the horse and cart, the building visible is the Station Master's house.

Bernard Thomas Collec.

The fact that the conversion took place without incident is all the more remarkable considering the almost total lack of communication available to the men as soon as their nearest colleague was out of sight or earshot.

A remarkable find associated with the conversion comes with the conditions of service for the gangers and packers carrying out the conversion and which required that ;–

"Each man to bring as much food as he can, consisting of tea, cocoa or coffee, sugar, bread, cheese and bacon (boiled). A suitable tin for warming drinks. Also a good supply of clothes enough to last one month at least. He should also bring one blanket or a good rug."

Further conditions of service dictated, "He is not to absent himself from the work. He is to make full time and as much overtime as required and to be diligent during all such time made. He is not to smoke in sleeping places. He is to agree the following scale of wages, a working day be 9 hours. 4d per hour to be paid for all overtime to packers and 5d to gangers. The wages to be as follows:–

Gangers one day of 9 hours – 4/– ration money 1s 3d
Packers one day of 9 hours – 3/– ration money 1s 3d.

Gangers presently getting more than 4/– will be paid their usual wage as well as overtime and ration money. In the case of men who are required to lodge in towns or not in places provided by the Company 6d per night to be allowed for lodging money.

1904, and two years before the good times would come to an end, and retrenchment was the order of the day. Partly hidden by the pontoon are either the SS Great Western or its sister ship SS Great Southern, then barely two years old and used on the Waterford route. SS Pembroke appears to be the ship moored inside the pontoon with a coal tip partly masking this vessel. A wagon turntable provided a connection to the siding leading to the tip and which allowed for bunkering facilities. The large wooden frame to the extreme right is part of the hydraulic wagon lift. Certainly from the view there appears to be a flourishing cattle trade and judged by the number of wagons alongside the cattle dock. (The marine department at Neyland is discussed in some detail in Chapter 3.) The stock of the mail train stands in the siding next to the arrivals platform and can be identified as TPO Coach No. 843 of Lot 521 and to Diagram L7. In 1903 this vehicle together with Nos. 844, 846, 859, 860 and 861 were specially allocated to the Paddington – South Wales Night Mail TPO service. Arrival at Neyland for this train was scheduled for 6.40 a.m. and the same stock then formed the 'up' service which departed at 6.30 pm.

National Railway Museum / F. R. Burtt FB522

A sub of £1.00 per week will be paid to each man. NB Each man is to bring his shovel and beater."

The programme of the work provided for 1 Inspector for every 2 gangs and that as a rule each gang consisted of 2 gangers and 20 men.

The line described – from an operational perspective, post 1920.

Neyland was situated on a level site being: – 285 miles 26 chains from Paddington on the old line via Gloucester, 270 miles 21 chains via the Bristol loop and 260 miles 12 chains via Badminton.

Shortly after leaving Neyland the route fell on a gradient of 1 in 396, the station site having been built up to assist in the exchange of passengers and goods from ship to shore. After this the single line hugged the banks of Westfield Pill. There was then one of several Permanent Way lineside huts used to store tools and the fixed distance signal for down trains (–to Neyland), 1512 yards from Neyland signal box.

Just north of Neyland and with the Westfield Pill at low water. Near this spot today is the Cleddau road bridge leading to Pembroke Dock. The railway hugs the waterway at this point and consequently did not require major work on this section save for the cutting seen in the distance. The signal is the advanced starter and stands 840 yards from Neyland box.

Brinley John

The north end of the station yard and looking towards Johnson some four miles distant. To the right are carriage sidings whilst the main line was single from the station, having first been converted to standard gauge in 1872 and then singled in 1917. This latter feature was probably intended as a wartime emergency measure to allow the rails be used for wartime emergency purposes but it was destined to become permanent. The building to the left is the oil gas house and to the right are the waters of the Westfield Pill.. The 55' turntable is also visible on the extreme left hand side. As is recounted in Chapter 5, this was replaced in 1939.

National Railway Museum / B.Box 161/22

Between Neyland and Johnston there were three level crossings over minor roads with gates which were normally closed against road traffic. These were known as Upper Rosemarket Crossing, Lower Rosemarket Crossing and Westfield Mill Crossing. At all of these the gates were hand operated, those at Westfield Mill not fitted with bolts to lock them in position. Each crossing was staffed by a crossing keeper and who was alerted to an impending train by the bell code sent by either the signalman at Johnston or Neyland and which could be heard on a bell located in the porch of each cottage. Additionally there was a repeating block instruments. Of necessity the crossing keeper's cottage stood close by their gates. In addition to the audible and visual reminders, the crossing keeper had to be familiar with the movements of trains by reference to the working timetable. Near to the crossing was a ground frame containing levers for the signals and except at Westfield Mill, bolts protecting the crossing gates. They were normally in the 'off' position allowing trains the right of way but could be set to stop as required. In addition, each set of stop signals was preceded by a distant signal. The close proximity of the two Rosemarket crossings meant that in each direction they also carried the distance signals on the same post as the stop signal.

The crossing gates of Westfield Mill, at mile post 283˘ guarded a minor road and from this point to Johnston

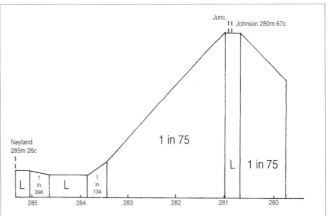

station, at 280 miles 67 chains the line climbed at 1 in 75 passing Lower Rosemarket crossing gates at 282˘ miles, and Upper Rosemarket crossing gates at 282 miles. Johnston station, also the junction for the Milford Haven branch, was on a short level section. From here to Haverfordwest the railway was double track and fell on a gradient of 1 in 75. The sectional appendices instructed enginemen of a fully loaded freight train, irrespective of whether travelling up or down the incline, that the minimum time allowed was 15 minutes. It however urged enginemen of lightly loaded trains travelling to Haverfordwest to take advantage of the

1027 'County of Stafford' still with its original single chimney passes the crossing keepers lodge at Westfield Crossing on its way from Neyland towards Johnston. The shadows cast suggest this was taken in the evening and is then likely to be the 7.50 pm Neyland to Cardiff parcels. The crossing keepers lodge survives today as a private residence

Adrian Vaughan

Upper Rosemarket Crossing and one of three such crossing on the line between Neyland and Johnson.

Adrian Vaughan

incline to run in slightly reduced times but cautioned them that incline instructions must be carried out, the train properly controlled on the falling gradient and all speed restrictions strictly adhered to. The instructions stated that where a passenger or a freight train running from Johnston to Haverfordwest was to be worked by 2 engines both engines had to be placed in front of the train.

In the down direction all services except passenger trains were required to stop at Johnston. Here the driver acting in conjunction with the guard had to ensure that sufficient hand brakes were applied on the wagons to ensure the train could be kept from running out of control when descending the gradient. The maximum load was 50 wagons in either direction.

Johnston, and the point of divergence of the of the line to and from Neyland – left, and with that to Milford Haven coming in from the right. Up to 1935 there had been a signal box controlling movements at this point and known as 'Johnson West'. Its duties though were taken over by the extended 'East' box at this time and which was also renamed without the suffix. The siding to the left was on the formation of the original double track route to Neyland and depicts well the extra width available from broad gauge days.

Adrian Vaughan

Chapter 2
AROUND THE PERIPHERY
The stations at Johnston, Haverfordwest and Milford Haven

In order to appreciate fully the workings at Neyland, it is necessary to peer slightly further afield towards the junction station at Johnston, the next station north at Haverfordwest and finally Neyland's near neighbour and to a great extent competitor on the coast, Milford Haven.

Dealing with Johnson first, this served as the junction for trains to Neyland and also for the branch line to Milford Haven, but was never provided with a platform dedicated solely for the branch trains. For some time trains to and from Milford Haven gained access to the main line by a junction situated near to the up platform. However, during the 1920's alterations were made to the track–work and signalling so that the original junction was used by trains from Milford Haven and a new junction, further along the line in the direction of Neyland, was installed for trains in the opposite direction travelling to Milford Haven.

At Johnston the main station buildings were situated on the up platform although just a waiting shelter sufficed on the down side. On arrival at the platform the branch train engine was uncoupled and run round its train and after coupling up, either pushed the stock into the up siding or ran into the down platform line. This allowed any main line services to or from Neyland free access to use the platform lines and so also to make a connection for Milford passengers. Coupling and uncoupling of engines on passenger trains were the responsibility of the traffic department.

Often it was necessary to detach a vehicle or vehicles from the rear of a down passenger train, in which case these had to be drawn over the trailing points on the down main line leading to the down siding and the points then set for the down siding.

A ground frame was situated at the east end of the yard and was electrically locked from Johnston signal box. It was operated by the checker or shunter and on completion of the work he was required to contact the signalman using the telephone at the ground frame. Special regulations also applied to shunting operations and which were to be suspended when a train was scheduled to pass in the following circumstances: –

The main station buildings at Johnston were on the up side of the line and with their characteristic tall chimneys. This particular view probably dates from the Edwardian period and displays to advantage a long run of what typical GWR 'spear' type fencing.

Collec. John Morris

57xx 0–6–0PT No. 9652 simmering in the sunshine at Johnston on a local service to Milford Haven. The coach is a former 'Toplight' 'slip', downgraded from its previous role and now ending its days on local workings.

Roger Carpenter

On the Down main: Shunting to and from the up siding and trains setting back on the up line.

On the Up main: Shunting to and from the down refuge siding and trains setting back on the down line.

West of the station an auxiliary token hut was situated on the down side of the down line. This contained two auxiliary token magazines for the Johnston to Neyland, and Johnston to Milford Haven sections, there was also a telephone for communication with Johnston signalbox. When it was necessary for a down train or engine to proceed to the advanced starting signal without a token from Johnston signal box, the fireman would, on arrival at the advanced starting signal obtain one with the co–operation of the signalmen at either end of the section and so allow the train to proceed further. Track circuits were also provided on both lines in the vicinity of the junction and telephones provided at the base of the signals affording direct communication with Johnston signal box.

Wagons arriving at Johnston for Milford Haven with empty fish boxes, coal for trawlers and fish plant were required to be kept together and put off in one shunt. Wagons for the station sidings at Milford Haven were, as far as possible, shunted by the main line goods train into the goods shed siding and formed next to the van of the branch goods train from Milford Haven. Where there was no room to deal with this traffic any empty stock or less important traffic was shunted out and worked to Neyland to allow the goods traffic to be put off. In the case of empty fish plant, Johnston after conferring with Milford Haven, could work these forward on the branch passenger trains.

When the shunter was off duty between 8 pm and 6 am, the guard of any down Neyland goods trains arriving at Johnston had to advise the signalman, by using the telephone in the ground frame at the top end of the yard, what, if any, Milford Haven traffic had to be detached. In later years most goods traffic arriving at Johnston in the down direction was bound for Milford Haven anyway and was then left in the down siding to be picked up and taken forward by a subsequent Milford Haven working.

Until the 1930's there was a goods shed at Johnston but this was removed, presumably because of a lack of local traffic. During the early crop potato season, Johnston served as a railhead for this traffic, with temporary office accommodation erected for the use of the potato buyers. The season lasted for about six weeks. Sugar beet was also

An interior view of the station and showing the down side platform. The signals in the background – and with arm clear for a train to approach bound for Milford Haven, may well be early Westinghouse type, a number of which existed in the area.

Collec. M.R.C. Price

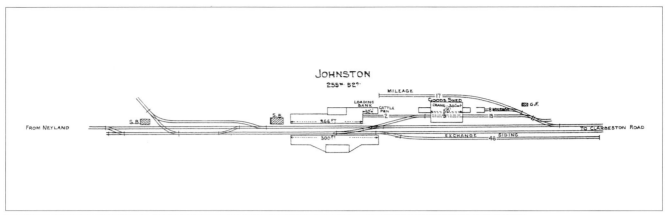

Johnston depicted on 2nd September 1959 with the waiting shelter on the down platform now devoid of foliage. The siding leading from the down main line was used to put off traffic for Milford Haven from trains to Neyland.

F A Blencowe F948B

5953 'Dunley Hall' allocated to 87H Neyland, heads the 6.50 pm mail and passenger to Paddington on 7th July 1958 and with GPO staff ready to load mails from the platform trolley. The junction of the lines to Neyland and Milford Haven lay some distance behind the train. station building. On the right a permanent way mechanical track vehicle stands in the cattle dock siding.

H.C. Casserley

loaded during that season and forwarded to the factory at Kidderminster. The branch engine performed any shunting required. In the event of a minor derailment of a wagon, re–railing ramps were kept at the station.

Johnston had a Stationmaster, three signalmen, a goods porter and three platform porters. The goods porter also undertook the shunters duties. The signal box was open continuously with the turns being 6 am–2 pm, 2 pm–10 pm and 10 pm–6 am, with rest day relief cover provided for the regular men. The signalmen recalled that at one time the points had been operated by wire rather than rods which together with the associated unusual lever action made them difficult to operate. Several signalmen thus suffered hernias as a result of straining themselves. Later the wires were replaced with conventional rodding and the levers by the standard pattern.

Beyond Johnston station in the direction of Haverfordwest, was a trailing connection on the up main line leading into Hook Colliery. This was operated by a ground frame electrically released by the Johnston signal-man. Coal was regularly despatched from here on a daily basis. Nearby was the appropriately named Coal Pit accommodation crossing and which requiring the driver of any approaching train to sound one long whistle as a warning to his approach. Further along the line, drivers also had to keep a look out for the crossings at Diamond Hill and Windsor and again warn of their train's approach by one long whistle. Compared with the public road, the railway took a different course to Haverfordwest and so avoided hilly ground, but road and rail came together again at Merlins Bridge on the outskirts of Haverfordwest, crossing the Western Cleddau it reached the station.

Working at Johnston

A number of trains departing Neyland went to Milford Haven via Johnston. Only one guard's brake van

was provided in the formation and it was necessary for the engine to run round its train and remove the brake van and put it on the other end of the train. If no wagons or vans came from Neyland this made the task much simpler. Any wagons or vans at Johnston waiting to be forwarded to Milford were added and the train went down the branch line to Milford. On the approach to Milford the train was halted at a stop board and the guard was responsible for pinning down a sufficient number of brakes to assist the engine in keeping the train under control down the gradient.

HAVERFORDWEST

The original station was a terminus until the line was extended to Neyland. The station occupied a cramped site some distance from the town and initially had only limited goods facilities for what was an important market town. Whilst a goods shed and cattle dock were provided, there was minimal provision for holding wagons when the goods shed was occupied and these often had to be worked down to Neyland and returned to their true destination when space was available. One curious feature of the layout in the early years was a goods siding provided between the up and down platform lines and as seen in the accompanying illustration.

Haverfordwest was extensively remodelled in the late 1930's with the provision of an up goods line in place of the former siding between the platforms and a goods loop behind the down platform. In addition a new and more substantial goods shed was built on land behind the down platform and four sidings were also provided in this area. These alterations were only possible by excavating the hillside.

The yard was frequently busy with goods traffic including, agricultural, cattle feed, livestock, household coal and fuel oil. The lack of a head shunt and the curvature

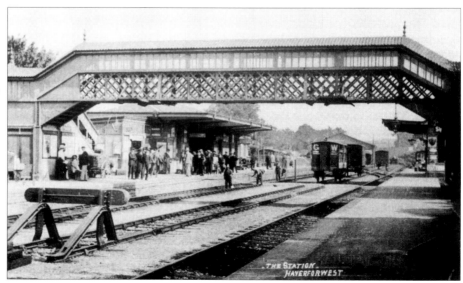

Haverfordwest Station, looking east, circa 1895. The multitude of persons present is typical of the golden era for rail travel when competition was almost nil and the railway had brought hitherto impossible travel within the reach of the masses.

Pembrokeshire Museums

The down platform at Haverfordwest recorded around the turn of the century. The buildings utilise local material whilst the plethora of advertisements are again typical of the period.

Collec. John Morris

of the site hampered visibility whilst shunting in the down sidings. To assist in these operations, a klaxon horn was fixed on the down advanced starting signal facing towards the station. Its purpose was to advise drivers of down goods trains requiring to be shunted clear of the down line points, that it was in order to push back. The horn could be operated from two locations, one by the telephone box and another on the retaining wall, both west of the station. To deal with minor mishaps a re–railing ramp was kept under the station

signalbox. No water cranes were provided so if water was required a trip to Clarbeston Road was required. However it was not unknown for locomotives to obtain water from the water hydrant at the cattle dock and via a temporary hose pipe connection!

A signal and telegraph linesman was stationed at Haverfordwest and whose area covered from Clarbeston Road to Neyland and also to Milford Haven. He was also responsible for the maintenance of the A.T.C

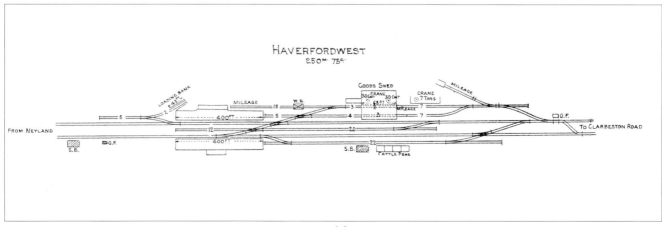

Haverfordwest in 1959. The substantial alterations to the station in 1939 allowed for a new goods shed and sidings to be provided and which are seen on the right, a section of the hillside being removed as a result. Despite the additional room a major drawback was restricted vision and there no adequate head shunt. The yard here was shunted by a pilot engine supplied from Neyland The train seen is entering the up platform and upon which was the main station building. From Haverfordwest the next stop will be at Clarbeston Road.

F.A. Blencowe

equipment at Neyland.

From Haverfordwest the line followed the Cartlett brook until it reached the junction of the line from Fishguard Harbour shortly before entering Clarbeston Road station. Before the opening of the Fishguard line the station served the settlement which had developed around it and the distant village of Clarbeston. The track layout was substantially altered when it assumed the role of a junction station with local services terminating here from Fishguard Harbour and making connections with trains off the Neyland line. The line continued to Carmarthen and beyond which is outside the scope of this work.

MILFORD HAVEN

The original station at Milford Haven was a modest affair with four sidings and a single platform and run around facilities sandwiched between the hillside and Hubberston Pill. By the 1890's the station had been rebuilt on land reclaimed from the Pill with a curving single platform and which remains in use today. A more substantial goods shed and further sidings were provided at this time as well as connections to the complex of sidings built in the docks. A single road engine shed was constructed nearby the rail served gas works.

Further expansion took place in the first decade of the 20th century. Amongst the work undertaken then was the provision of a loop siding next to the Pill side and three sidings beyond the gas works at what was known as the bottom yard. In the early 1930's major improvements took place which involved moving and narrowing the course of Hubberston Pill and slewing over the branch line as it approached Milford Haven station to accommodate four further sidings of a new yard known as, The Top Yard. These were used to form out–going trains. The loop line was then considerably extended and reclassified as the main

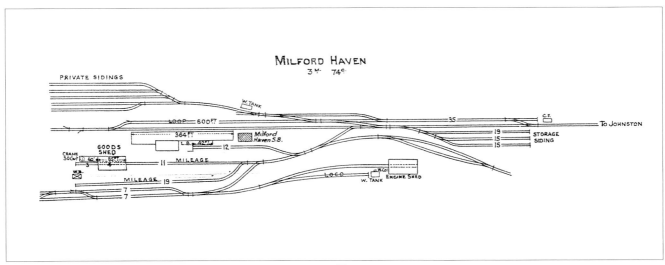

Milford Haven station building with the goods shed immediately to the right. The line to the junction at Johnston is beyond the station buildings. The station site lay between Hubberston Pill to the left and the town of Milford Haven on the hillside to the right July 7 1958.

H C Casserley

loop signalled for bi–directional working. During the second world war a further goods loop was provided next to the Pill side. All this development reflected the substantial part played by the railway in Milford Haven's rise to that of a pre–eminent fishing port.

A box factory – making fish boxes, was situated beyond the station limits and was served by the pilot engine. It was necessary to obtain the single line token to gain access to the siding and the shunting operations prevented any other train occupying the single line to Johnston until the engine returned to the yard limits and surrendered the token at the auxiliary token apparatus. The shunter would always accompany the engine on this working and assisted in the shunting operations.

Because of the substantial revenues generated at Milford Haven, by 1923 the Station Master was re–graded as a special class post and who was assisted by; two–three booking clerks, five clerks in the main goods shed, three–four clerks in the inward goods office as well as railway clerks in the Trawl Office. There were also two passenger porters, a goods foreman, three goods porters, up to thee lad porters and two shunters. In the 1950's the regular shunters were Joe Edmunds on the early turn 7 am to 3 pm, and Sid John on the late turn, 2 pm to 10 pm.

For many years one of the jobs of a lad porter here was to collect the wagon and van numbers for the purpose of collecting any demurrage due. Each day he would go around all the sidings in the docks and also the Hakin and Goose Pill and record the numbers of vehicles standing in a book. At Goose Pill the sidings held coal trucks to serve the needs of the local fishing fleet and which remained largely coal fired well into the 1950s.

Two lorries and their drivers were based at the goods shed for delivery and collection in the area whilst coal was brought in by rail to the town gas–works and which was situated near the single road engine shed.

The signal box was manned by two signalmen working an early and late shift and also a porter signalman working a short middle turn in the box. The box was a

Looking in the direction of Johnston in July 1958. The signal box dated from November 1890 and originally contained 27 levers. The frame size was doubled to 54 levers in 1932 and controlled a complex layout which had seen considerable expansion over the years as the terminus here grew into a major fishing port. The sidings in the far distance are the Top Yard, to their right was the Lower Yard.

H.C. Casserley

'Class 3' and closed after the last train of the day had cleared the single running line to Johnston.

If either of the signalmen were off work then the porter signalman would extend his turn to help cover the full day's work unless, of course, a relief man was available. The box itself was situated at the Johnston end of the station just off the end of the platform and was of brick construction with an exterior staircase to the operating floor. Normal practice as far as passenger trains were concerned, was for the signalman on duty to hand out or collect the token either from the top of the steps to the box or, from one of the windows. The telephone in the box was also used by the yard foreman to report the departure of all fish trains to the telegraph office at Carmarthen and with information on the number of vans, their weight and destination.

Engines of passenger trains arriving at the platform, would, after being uncoupled, run forward as far as the road bridge which crossed the station site. They did not go any further though as beyond this point was a stop board guarding the entrance to the Dock Company sidings. The

engine then ran round its train on the loop line and returned to the coaching stock.

The engine shed was a sub depot of Neyland. In 1954, three passenger guards were also based at Milford.

Milford Fish Trade

Neyland shed was responsible for supplying locomotives for the fish trains running from Milford Haven and also for the cleaning and stabling of the fish wagons and vans used in the fish traffic from the station. The procedure was for empty fish vans to be worked back to Neyland where the carriage and wagon department swept them out and then also hosed them down. The following day the vans were worked back to Milford Haven via Johnston.

At Milford Haven the train was usually brought into the goods loop next to the Pill. The engine then ran round its trains and pushed the fish vans into the exchange siding. Here the vans were collected by the Dock Company engine and worked to the fish market. This was necessary as GWR

change. Whilst originally this restriction had been based purely on operational or political needs, latterly the state of the track, combined with the greater weight of the mainline engines, made derailment a distinct possibility. Indeed on one occasion the tender of a 'Castle' class locomotive became derailed when the driver made a conscious decision to ignore the warning signs and ran a short distance on Dock Company lines. He did this only in order to help the Yard Inspector to expedite a loaded fish train, a problem having arisen when the Dock Company engine stalled and could not bring the train forward into the exchange siding. Despite acting in good faith, the driver had still to explain his actions and a written caution was administered. More serious disciplinary action would have been taken had his explanation that he was attempting to expedite the train because of the perishable nature of its cargo not been accepted.

It was not uncommon for three dock engines to be needed to bring the loaded vans from the fish market sidings ready to be handed over. The maximum load for a mainline engine from Milford Haven to Johnston depended of course on the locomotive class and was set at 370 tons for a 'Castle', 340 tons for 'Hall' and 'Grange' classes and 336 tons for a 'Manor' class engine. In calculating the load, the guard was required to total the tare weight recorded on each van and add a further three tons per vehicle. If the resulting total weight of the train exceeded the unassisted loading it would be the responsibility of the driver to judge whether to call for a banking engine. In making up his mind he would consider a number of factors such as, the amount of the overload, the condition of the engine, state of the track and weather conditions. Where it was necessary for one of Milford's pannier tanks to give banking assistance, this would buffer up to the rear of the train but not couple up to it. The single line token was carried on the banking engine and then surrendered at Johnston. In practice the use of banking engines was a regular feature.

The importance of the fish traffic to the GWR is reflected in the fish extract book for Milford Haven for the years 1936 – 48;

YEAR	TONS	NUMBER OF	RECEIPTS
1936	41,156	755,470	131,713
1937	43,459	855,527	141,486
1938	41,854	823,790	139,555
1939	37,370	734,728	122,376
1940	36,450	715,695	125,094
1941	1,228	27,195	4,994
1942	1,627	32,592	7,357
1943	29,197	43,295	131,525
1948	49,029	1,055,236	293,020

These figures are of particular interest bearing in mind the wartime situation as existed for part of the period and are even more remarkable when considered as just an example of fishing activity at a single location.

In addition, the coal consumed by the steam trawlers added to the value of the fish traffic. Whilst no specific figures are available for the total goods traffic, statistics for the Station show that coke and coal, and which amounted to the bulk of the tonnage received was;

YEAR	TONS	YEAR	TONS
1935	163,931	1938	149,705
1936	163,299	1939	116,524
1937	171,046		

Overall revenue from goods traffic in the same period was;

YEAR	TONS	YEAR	TONS
1935	£69,544	1938	£83,293
1936	£78,243	1939	£88,471
1937	£87,063		

For many years then there was a regular service of daily fish trains. The first of these, known locally as 'The Northern Fish' would leave at 3.20 pm and run via Carmarthen Town onto the LMS. After this came the 3.50 pm to Yeovil, known as 'The West of England Fish'. Additionally there was a timetable slot, or 'Q' path for a 5.10 pm to Paddington if required. These services were still in existence in the 1958/9 timetable although slight modifications had resulted in the 3.50 pm train now running to Severn Tunnel Junction and if needed, to the West of England whilst the Paddington service had been retimed to leave at 5.20 pm.

A roundabout working ensured the empty fish vans were returned to Neyland on two separate Class 'C' workings, the first arriving back shortly after midnight and the second just before 7.00 am. This then allowed time for the vehicles to be cleaned before their next duty. They were then worked forward to Milford Haven later the same morning.

Fish Market and Trawl Office

The Fish Market at Milford Haven was a covered building next to the docks. It was served by two sidings which ran adjacent to it and protected from the elements by a canopy. Equally spaced across the siding nearest the fish market were three planked lifting bridges and used to assist in moving goods from one platform to the other. The loading of the actual fish boxes into the fish vans was

M.R.C. Price

One foreman worked on one shift, from 9.00 am to 5.00 pm. The second foreman worked 7.30 am to 3.30 pm and so was able to visit the many fish traders and hopefully gauge their requirement for vans.

Armed with this information he would chalk a number on each van starting with No. 1 at the end of the fish market siding nearest Milford Haven station and working his way down the length of the siding as necessary. He then allocated each checker a number of vans, each van being destined for a specific location. Thus one checker would be overseeing fish for the West of England, whilst others would look after the North of England, Rhondda Valley, and Cardiff Valleys. Additionally two men covered London, one for Billingsgate traffic and the other the South of England including any fish destined for the Continent via Dover. Two men thus would be spare to assist if required.

The Fish Traders Association owned a number of Lister trolleys onto which up to 16 boxes of fish would be loaded and brought to the checker. The fish boxes had wire bindings and the loaders lifted them using a hook before slinging them with uncanny precision into the fish vans and in just the required spot. The boxes were loaded to a maximum of four high. As they were loaded the checker recorded the details and passed them to the Trawl Office.

The Trawl Office was situated by the steps that led down from the 'Lord Nelson' Hotel. It was staffed from Mondays to Saturdays inclusive by six clerks including a Chief Clerk. Consignment notes were prepared by the Fish Merchant who handed them into the Trawl Office via the Dock Foreman and who would insert the weight against the number of boxes recorded. Notes arriving at the office passed along the line of clerks who extracted the invoices that related to the fish train for which they were responsible. When the fish landings were heavy an additional train would be run.

As each clerk extracted the noted for his train he prepared, in duplicate, an invoice which showed the weight and the 'calculated weight'. This was determined by reference to a card that listed destinations alphabetically and the railway charge to convey it from Milford Haven. Details from the invoices were entered into a ledger account for each week and listed the amount due from each merchant. The merchant was then billed for the fish despatched accompanied by a copy of the daily invoices to enable him to check his account.

An example of the working of locomotives and serviced stock for the Milford Haven fish trains. The Pannier Tank is at the head of an afternoon goods trains leaving Neyland for Haverfordwest. Attached to the rear is a second train of 'bloaters' and passenger brake vans and with an unidentified 'Manor' class engine at its rear. At Johnston the train will divide. The 'Manor' will then work the 'bloaters and passenger brakes tender first to Milford Haven. Upon arrival the 'bloaters' will be worked into the docks there ready for the following days working. The 'Manor' taking a made up fish train later that afternoon. Such workings varied according to the years and could also comprise either a light engine(s) or engine and van dependant upon operational requirements.

Collec. Simon Hancock

Milford Haven as viewed across the waterway and to the docks. The edge of fish market is to the extreme right and with the wagons standing on the private sidings of the Milford Haven Railway and Dock Company. The station was located to the left hand side.
Authors Collec.

A further check took place with the details received from each checker of the number of boxes and which were then compared to the numbers recorded on the consignment note. If the numbers did not tally contact was made with the clerk assigned to that train to try and resolve and differences. If, for example, the consignment note recorded five boxes but only four were available to load, then the clerk issued a discrepancy note to the merchant to protect the railway's interest against a claim for loss in transit. Similarly if a station received a consignment of five boxes instead of four as recorded, they wrote to the Trawl Office, who in turn contacted the merchant. He was then billed him for the additional consignment! The waybills for each fish van were prepared by the clerks and taken up to the station by one of three lad porters who placed the waybill under the clip on the requisite van. The invoices were placed in an envelope and were sent away separately on a passenger train. The only time that invoices were handed to the guard of the fish train was to accompany a consignment going to the Continent. Regretfully all this fish traffic was lost to road transport in the 1960's.

Milford Haven Loco.

An engine shed was provided that housed two pannier tanks engines. The senior driver was in charge but overall control was exercised by the Foreman at Neyland. In the 1950's there were four drivers including: – George Russell as the senior man, Percy Edwards and Arthur Barras. There were also six firemen, including, George Day – later made up to a driver, Ken Mathias, Charlie Russell, Alan Bartlett and Edmund Davies.

At this time the shed labourer was Charlie Griffiths and who later became a fitter's mate at Neyland. He booked on at 10.00 pm to clean the fires and coal the two engines based here. On a Saturday night the fires were thrown out and a new fire prepared and lit on Sunday night ready for the duty on Monday morning. He also cleaned the engines.

The enginemen worked two early and two late turns. The senior driver being responsible for setting the duty rosters and for ordering stores. This included waste oil for cleaning and cotton waste. From time to time he travelled on the branch train to Johnston and from there to Neyland taking empty oil cans and collecting further supplies from the stores at Neyland shed. No repairs or boiler wash–outs were carried out at Milford and when this was required the engines were sent to Neyland.

The engine shed covered a single line and had an inspection pit inside the building. At the rear a door led to a cabin. This was gas lit and had lockers for the personal possessions of the drivers and firemen together with a desk on which the duty roster was placed. There was a coal fire for heating and boiling water. A tank was provided to store sand used in the sandboxes. Near the shed was the coal stage although the practice in later years was to coal the engine directly form the wagon rather than having to off–load the coal from the wagon to the coal stage as an intermediate step. A water crane stood near the shed together with an ash pit. Ashes from the engine were raked into the pit by the shed labourer who then also had the task of emptying the pit as necessary. This was a labour intensive and dirty operation. Firstly water was used to dampen down the hot ashes, next he shovelled the ash out of the pit into an old steel wheelbarrow, and then took these to a railway wagon positioned as near as possible to the pit before shovelling the ash from the barrow into the wagon.

The two pannier tanks undertook the pilot work in the yards and also worked the branch passenger trains that ran mainly to and from Johnston. However, some branch trains continued from Johnston to Neyland before returning to Milford Haven. The first engine on duty was at about 6.15 am and the driver and fireman for this booked on at 5.30 am. This allowed 45 minutes for preparation. When ready they took the engine from the shed to the platform line where the coaching stock was normally kept overnight.

At one time three coaches was the normal composition of the branch train but it was later reduced to two with a 'bloater' (fish van) provided in place of the third coach. This was used to carry parcels traffic including boxes of fish not carried by the booked fish trains.

The second engine was due off shed around 9.00 am and undertook shunting duties until 1.00 pm when it returned to the shed for water. After further shunting at Milford Haven it worked the branch passenger train at 6.30 pm to Johnston where it made a connection with a main line train before working to Neyland and finally returning to Milford Haven. The first engine also undertook any additional shunting at Milford Haven and Johnston as well as running the branch passenger trains.

Usually the goods shed by the station was shunted first with empties being taken to the top yard for sorting out and for the preparation of out going trains. After this the coal siding by the goods shed was dealt with and then the other sidings as required. The bottom yard, by the Gas Works, held

wagons waiting to be taken down to the Dock Company's sidings, crippled wagons, permanent way wagons and the sleeping coach in–between its turn of duty.

When goods trains arrived at Milford Haven they usually went into the 'water loop' next to the Pill side. At the lineside was an auxiliary token apparatus. When the train was safely in the loop the points were restored to the main line and the single line token for the section from Johnston was returned to the auxiliary instrument. In this way the line could be quickly cleared for the passage of another working if necessary. Departing goods trains would also obtain a token from the auxiliary instrument in the same way before proceeding.

When the Neyland Guard's depot closed in 1964, the turns that remained were transferred along with the former Neyland men to Milford Haven. The local branch trains ceased as did the guard's duties, but the depot remained open for a further six years. Other depots also worked into Milford Haven as well as Neyland and including in 1954 a turn from Fishguard Harbour.

Passenger Guards Duties	Milford Haven Depot	14 June to 19 September 1954
Duty No.	Times	Working
1410	2.00 pm to 10 pm	2.15 pm Milford Haven to Johnston 2.25 pm
		2.40 pm Johnston to Milford Haven 2.50 pm
		3.50 pm Milford Haven to Landore 5.55 pm
		6.22 pm Landore to Swansea (HS) 6.27 pm
		6.59 pm Swansea (HS) to Johnston 9.15 pm
		9.25 pm Johnston to Milford Haven 9.35 pm
1411	Goods Guard 6.00 am to 2 00 pm	ECS .20 am Milford Haven to Johnston 6.30 am
		6.45 am Johnston to Milford Haven 6.55 am
		8.10 am Milford Haven to Johnston 8.21 am
		8.42 am Johnston to Milford Haven 8.52 am
		ECS 10.45 am Milford Haven to Johnston 10.55 am
		11.35 am Johnston to Milford Haven 11.45 am
		1.05 pm Milford Haven to Johnston 1.15 pm
		1.30 pm Johnston to Milford Haven 1.40 pm
14.12	Goods Guard 3.00 pm to 11.00 pm	Assist with fish trains
		4.10 pm Milford Haven to Johnston 4.20 pm
		4.45 pm Johnston to Milford Haven 4.55 pm
		6.30 pm Milford Haven to Johnston 6.45 pm
		7.05 Johnston to Neyland 7.14 pm
		9.00 pm Neyland to Johnston 9.09 pm
		9.25 pm Johnston to Milford Haven 9.35 pm
		10.10 pm Milford Haven to Johnston 10.20 pm
		10.35 Johnston to Milford Haven 10.45 pm

0–6–0 Pannier tank No 3654 stands at Milford Haven platform with the 6.30 pm branch train to Johnston in July 1958. The vans in the sidings to the right of the train belong to BR but have a connection to the Dock Co. sidings. The fish market lies being some distance beyond the station. The roof of the goods shed is also just visible above the guards van in the siding behind the platform. On the skyline the houses in the area known as Hakin are prominent.

H.C. Casserley

From the docks area and viewed back towards the station. An obvious feature being the multitude of goods vehicle and apparent poor condition of track in the foreground.

John Morris Collec.

Around the periphery

Chapter 3
MARINE and FISH

It would be tempting to commence what was undoubtedly the principal source of revenue at Neyland (1) with an immediate account of the Irish traffic or even the fish market. To do so however would be to fail in the chronological sequence of events that apply to the marine workings and accordingly reference must be made to these even before the railway opened in 1856.

Records state that towards the end of 1855 the line was basically in a finished state and accordingly the directors of the SWR were no doubt delighted to receive an application in January 1856 from the owners of the vessel *Transit* for their ship to dock at Neyland and take on cargo destined for Australia. Pleased no doubt that some revenue might thus be accrued, a light engine trip was made over the line on January 6 1856, the first time this had been undertaken. It was reported also that Brunel himself was on the footplate. All was deemed well and the *Transit* docked on January 15 1856 taking on several hundred tons of coal and ore. In addition, from the opening of their line the SWR made provision to ferry goods traffic by lighters to the town of Pembroke Dock, then an important Royal Navy Dockyard.

Despite this initial success, variations in the tides allied to mud banks close inshore prevented ships from tying up at the jetty originally provided and it was quickly realised

some form of floating pier was required. As an interim measure an old sailing ship, the *Despatch,* was tied to the jetty and passengers to and from Ireland would first walk over the decks of this old vessel. Such an arrangement though was considered unsuitable for goods and livestock and tenders were therefore invited for ship to shore transfer. This contract was awarded to a local man, Mr. Briggs, who was thus employed on a temporary basis at a rate of £1 5s per week plus 2/– per ton of goods carried. Regretfully no detail of the means of such transfer appears to have survived.

Clearly though a more permanent solution was required, and this came in a design by Brunel for a floating pontoon to be connected to the shore by a landing bridge. It was ordered as early as the summer of 1856 and brought into use in spring 1857. Constructed of wrought iron and measuring 150 feet by 40 feet plus a connecting bridge 205 feet long it was a massive structure for the day. The specification for which also referred to the use of 9,200 cu. ft. of timber, 25 cu. ft. of hardwood, 112 cwt of wrought iron and 14 cwt of cast iron. Moving forward slightly, but following the completion of Brunel's Saltash Bridge over the Tamar near Plymouth, the four pontoons used in that construction were also brought to Neyland for permanent use. These were secured to stout timbers sunk into the sea bed although there

Right: Pontoons from the construction of the Saltash Bridge in use at Neyland to form an additional floating landing stage. These were secured against the ebb and flow of the tide by wooden dolphins anchored in The Haven. They are depicted on this occasion on a tranquil day and with a low tide. As is well known, the weather was not always so favourable in the area.

NRM B.Box 161/3

Left; Broad Gauge days at Neyland, Pembroke is on the opposite shoreline. The landing stages visible were principally involved with the landing of fish, hence the hundreds of boxes visible and also the raised wooden platform alongside the line of wagons. Likewise the vessels moored against the jetties. This whole area would be extended somewhat in later years and as can be seen from the other photographs in this chapter. The purpose of the two rectangular timber buildings on the edge of the dock is uncertain although they may have been trawl offices. Further along can be seen the covered pontoon and with ships berthed either side. The paddle wheel steamer is interesting and could be the 'Waterford,' 'Limerick 'or 'Milford'. Notice also the blurred image of the man crossing the tracks towards the fish stage.

NRM 987/51

Reported to be the launch of the pontoon for the 'Great Eastern' at Neyland.

Collec. Bernard Thomas

remained only the single connecting bridge onto dry land referred to earlier. The resultant size of the extended pontoon was now 500 feet by 40 feet. Steamers could now tie up either side of this pontoon whilst a further technological development for the period was the provision of a hydraulic wagon lift which enabled rail wagons to be raised from the level of the pontoon to the jetty. The principal use of this lift appears to have been for wagons of coal used by the actual ships and which could then be tipped directly into ships bunkers.

From the jetty to the pontoon was a bridge known as 'The Tube' constructed of wrought iron and measuring 205 feet by 12° feet. The Tube had two passageways, one for passengers which led to a covered way to the station building, whilst the other was for livestock which were driven through to the extensive lairage available in the station yard. Perhaps not surprisingly with the juxtaposition of people and livestock, complaints were received of both the smell and the mess. However nothing appeared to have ever been done to remedy the situation.

Aside from the wagon lift, cranes, capstans and hoists were provided for the docks, power being provided from the hydraulic building. Railway lines were laid down to and on the pontoon. The wagons and vans worked down with the aid of capstans as these lines were connected to the sidings by a series of wagon turntables and so precluded the use of locomotives. Two running lines were laid on the pier. One of the lines continued to the pontoon pier where a substantial covering, 300 feet by 30 feet, was later provided. Through the shed ran a siding connected to the line on the jetty by a wagon turntable. Parallel to it and connected by a wagon turntable at each end of the shed was a siding running almost the whole length of the pontoon.

Moving back in time though and with the opening of the railway to Neyland it did not take long for the then existing Milford Haven and Waterford Steam Ship Co. to realise that their operation would be best served by transferring their base to Neyland and where improved communication was now on offer. This arrangement would obviously suit both parties as although it might have appeared obvious there would appear to have been some initial reluctance by the SWR Directors to become involved in shipping operations. They were destined to completely

Captain Thomas Jackson of the partnership. Born in Yorkshire in 1810 he had a number of other interest aside from shipping including being a JP and Deputy Lieutenant for the County of Pembrokeshire.

Prof. James Gaddarn / Simon Hancock

change their opinions in later times.

Sea communication between Pembrokeshire and Southern Ireland had in fact existed for some time prior to the coming of the railway, the first record of this in 1824 with a Steam Packet service operating from Pembroke Dock and also Milford to Dunmore. Mail that had also previously used this route was though lost to the Hollyhead ferry consequent upon that town being rail connected. Even so some services did still continue from Pembrokeshire, as well as Bristol, but were very much dependant upon both weather and tides.

The Milford Haven and Waterford Steam Ship Co. was operated by two partners Captain Thomas Jackson and Captain Robert Ford, the new port arrangements seen to benefit both parties in the form of extra traffic. The railway able to offer a safer and more regular means of conveyance for both passengers and goods to and from the port.

This arrangement with Jackson and Ford commenced formally in August 1856 but was almost immediately in trouble due to the condition of the vessels used by the partners. It would appear these were all paddle steamers of varying size and condition and with Jackson and Ford forced to borrow £7,500 from the SWR in the opening month of operations for repairs to one of these, the *Malakhoff.*

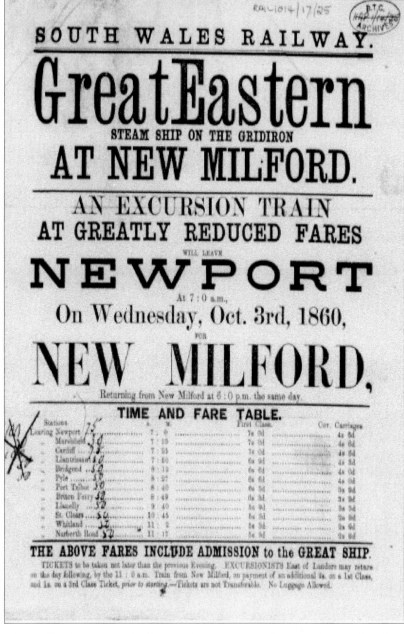

Sailings were twice a week in either direction, leaving Neyland at 7.15 pm and Waterford at 3.15 pm. Advertised as being able to accommodate 500 passengers and 900 head of cattle, pigs and sheep, at the very least conditions must have been cramped. The crossing of 118 nautical miles took in the order of eight to nine hours and meaning arriving passengers from Waterford were landed at Neyland around midnight and compelled then to wait for the first Paddington train which did not leave until 8.15 am. This arrangement continued until around June 1859 when a night service, the 2.45 am Neyland – Paddington service was instigated. Even so the rail journey time was in the order of eight to nine hours and so conditions for the passengers were far from ideal. (Sleeping cars were not introduced on the GWR until about 1871.) Such travel was though no different to contemporary journeys elsewhere and both the ferry and connecting rails service increased in popularity. (A rail service was also available in Ireland to and from Waterford.)

Moving back in time slightly and this increasing popularity had involved Jackson and Ford in the provision of an additional vessel the *City of Paris* from around the spring of 1857. The third vessel, and which had been in use from the start of the service was the *Courier* and whose Captain was the brother of the Master of the *Malakhoff.*

In 1858 a further addition to the fleet came in the form of the *Griffin,* chartered by Jackson and Ford and who, now with four vessels under their control, were able to commence a daily Monday – Saturday service. Despite the

The Pontoons

or New Milford and its Shipping Accommodation

by John Mathias, Johnston.

Old Cymry, the land where the minstrels of yore
Sang loudly the praises – we here them no more;
Thy muses are dead, and their harps they are all still,
There's no bard left to praise thy mechanical skill.

Could our ancestors now from their slumbers arise,
Our modern improvements would cause them surprise;
Every harp would be strung, every bard would unite,
To praise thee, New Milford, from morning to night

Thy splendid hotels – they would visit them all –
Thy cattle–sheds praise, and thy noble sea wall,
The telegraphs, and its intelligent wire,
Would, with songs of delight, the old heroes inspire.

But never again will the minstrels return;
Alas; they are gone and 'tis folly to mourn;
Let the living endeavour thy praise to rehearse,
And all thy grand beauties to picture in verse.

There's the well known hydraulic – the best in the land;
All strangers that wait for the train, let them stand,
For a moment or two, and at work they shall see,
This jolly hydraulic – astonished they'll be.

They shall see the large trucks, with the greatest of ease;
Lifted up from the vessels – as high as they please,
Without any trouble, they slide up and down,
On the noble pontoons – the New Milford renown.

Yes, the noble pontoons in verse I will praise –
They surpass all inventions our fathers could raise;
Just half—way across the old Ferry they stride;
Unmoved by the torrent, the tempest or tide.

The Waterford Packets of Johnson & Co.
There safely discharge the pork and lingo;
And Paddy is seen, with shillelagh so gay
Whacking up his great cattle, all parts of the day.

And Pat is astonished, and seems at a loss,
When from Erin he makes his first voyage across,
And New Milford pontoons appear to his sight,
His heart is so full, and he sings with delight&&....

additional revenue the partners were no doubt accruing, this additional service was only made possible by further loans from the SWR. Jackson and Ford had wished to operate a Sunday service as well, although unspecified objections from the Neyland Customs staff precluded this.

Meanwhile the SWR had also attracted sailings by a unrecorded operator on a Neyland to Cork service. This is believed to have commenced in 1856/7 but was withdrawn as early as February 1857 consequent upon the vessel used, the *Troubadour,* becoming damaged. How, what and where this damage occurred is not reported. Jackson and Ford then took over the service in may 1857 using a new vessel the *Pacific*, but again it was to be short lived and despite protests by the SWR it was withdrawn in the summer of 1858.

It would appear that between the summer of 1858 and the summer of 1860 the Cork service was reinstated on several occasions and it was not until the latter date that a more permanent arrangement was reached with the establishment of the 'Milford Haven and Cork Royal Mail Co'. This time the SWR openly backed the venture a total opposite of course to the reluctance of just a few years previous.

The first vessel used on this route was the 283 ton *Talbot* and which arrived at Neyland on August 2 1860. The maiden voyage to Cork though did not take place until September 8, after which sailings were thrice weekly. A second vessel, the *Shelburne*, arrived to supplement the service just eight days later, but even so the venture was destined to be short lived.

No doubt now bolstered by this initial success, the SWR hoped to attract regular shipping destined for distant ports, such desires being raised when the mighty *Great Eastern,* designed by Brunel arrived in Neyland in August 1860.

Launched in 1858 the *Great Eastern* had made her maiden voyage from Liverpool to New York. She then returned to Britain with 63 passengers and disembarked them at Neyland. The *Great Eastern* was at Neyland for repairs and repainting and the opportunity to capitalise on her presence was not missed as she was made open for inspection on payment of an entrance fee. This interest was so great that numerous excursion trains were run. During September she was placed on the gridiron specially constructed for her and the required work undertaken. The *Great Eastern* sailed for New York in May 1861 but returned in February 1862 for further repairs that were completed in May of that year. She returned again to Milford Haven but the transatlantic business never materialised.

Meanwhile at Neyland, Jackson and Ford had established a yard downstream of the railway and occupying some six acres of shoreline near to the South Wales

Hotel. A siding connection was made to the station and accessed via a wagon turntable. Wagons were horse drawn over this distance. Slightly out from the shoreline, a grid was put down for maintenance and overhaul of the vessels. (It is not certain if this grid was in fact the one taken over from when the *Great Eastern* had visited.)

Following the GWR takeover of the SWR in 1863 shipping matters at first continued as before, the new owners as similarly reluctant as the SWR had been some years earlier to expand the port facilities although keen to take advantage of the ferry traffic. This reluctance was seen also later in the same year when a meeting was held at Neyland to consider the construction of a dock to be used solely for the export of coal. Plans were prepared by R P Breiton and which would have provided for an area of 20 acres of enclosed water behind a lock gate. Without outside financial support though, such an ambitious scheme could only hope to succeed with the backing of the GWR. Paddington though were ambivalent, preferring instead to back development in the docks at Neyland's neighbour, Milford Haven and in which the company had a financial interest. Taking a brief moment to consider this and it appears that right from the outset the GWR were not prepared to speculate everything on a single location. History would prove this was also the correct decision, the fortunes of the town of Neyland destined to be sacrificed at the alter of commercialism.

All this though was years in the future and no doubt as a means of first 'testing the water', the GWR established an Irish Traffic Committee and which is recorded as having its initial meeting

on March 1 1866. Not surprisingly the question of the Cork service was again immediately raised. Jackson and Ford, by this time, appearing to have yet again slipped into financial insecurity although relations with the GWR remained amicable.

With the financial support this time of the GWR, the partnership now ordered two replacement vessels, named the *Great Western* – but despite the name the property of the partnership, and the *South of Ireland*, they entered service in April and July 1867 respectively, *Courier* and *City of Paris* taken in part exchange by the builders, W. Simons & Son. Both these vessels were capable of making 10 knots and could carry 50 first class, 30 second class, and an 'unspecified' number of third class passengers. Presumably the maximum number of the latter would be squeezed in as required! A complement of some 30 crew was carried.

No doubt to ensure the partnership lived up to its own expectations, the GWR signed a fresh agreement with Captain Jackson on May 1 1867 and to last for seven years. One of the conditions of this being that the vessels were to maintain an average of 14 mph across the Irish Sea and also that a minimum of three vessels be available. As a concession to the partnership, the GWR would carry coal for bunkering as a 'reduced rate'. In addition Paddington sent a reminder that 'good sleeping accommodation' was required for 1st class passengers. Nothing is mentioned for 2nd class travellers, but for third class the operative word is 'ought', in that '...covered

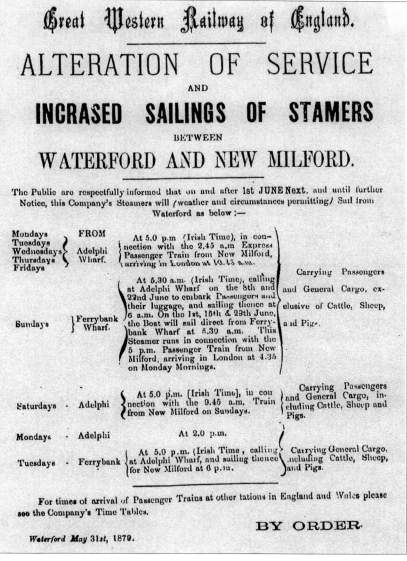

Great Western Railway of England.

ALTERATION OF SERVICE

AND

INCRASED SAILINGS OF STAMERS

BETWEEN

WATERFORD AND NEW MILFORD.

The Public are respectfully informed that on and after 1st JUNE Next, and until further Notice, this Company's Steamers will (weather and circumstances permitting) Sail from Waterford as below:—

Mondays Tuesdays Wednesdays Thursdays Fridays	FROM Adelphi Wharf.	At 5.0 p.m (Irish Time), in connection with the 2.45 a.m Express Passenger Train from New Milford, arriving in London at 10.15 a.m.	
Sundays	Ferrybank Wharf.	At 5.30 a.m. (Irish Time), calling at Adelphi Wharf on the 8th and 22nd June to embark Passengers and their luggage, and sailing thence at 6 a.m. On the 1st, 15th & 29th June, the Boat will sail direct from Ferrybank Wharf at 5.30 a.m. This Steamer runs in connection with the 5 p.m. Passenger Train from New Milford, arriving in London at 4.35 on Monday Mornings.	Carrying Passengers and General Cargo, exclusive of Cattle, Sheep, and Pigs.
Saturdays - Adelphi		At 5.0 p.m. [Irish Time], in connection with the 9.45 a.m. Train from New Milford on Sundays.	Carrying Passengers and General Cargo, including Cattle, Sheep and Pigs.
Mondays - Adelphi		At 2.0 p.m.	
Tuesdays - Ferrybank		At 5.0 p.m. (Irish Time, calling at Adelphi Wharf, and sailing thence for New Milford at 6 p.m.	Carrying General Cargo, including Cattle, Sheep, and Pigs.

For times of arrival of Passenger Trains at other tations in England and Wales please see the Company's Time Tables.

BY ORDER.

Waterford May 31st, 1879.

Courtesy: David Hyde

accommodation ought to be provided for 3rd class'. The need to maintain three vessels – *Malakhoff* was still working at this time, was no doubt the reason why another vessel, the *Vulture* was acquired in 1870. At the time some six years old this was a larger ship, at 793 tons, than the earlier acquisitions. She was though also sluggish by comparison and appears to have gained a poor reputation.

Behind the scenes the GWR though, to quote John Morris, appeared to acquire, "...a sudden burst of enthusiasm for nautical matters&", and which eventually resulted from February 1 1872 in the take over by the GWR for £36,500 of the Jackson and Ford partnership together with the vessels, *Great Western, Malakhoff,* and *South of Ireland*. This purchase had followed various deliberations by the GWR and no doubt came about due to ever increasing involvement with shipping matters at both Neyland and Weymouth and at which port there was a packet service operating to the Channel Islands.

Jackson and Ford appear to have been none to unhappy at parting with their business, it having previously run at an annual loss in the order of £2,000 and mainly due to heavy capital and interest repayments due, not least of which were to the GWR for earlier loans. *Vulture,* the final Jackson and Ford purchase dating from 1870 was also bought by the GWR under a separate arrangement of April 1872 and, despite her poor reputation, cost the GWR a further £9,000. As an interim measure, Captain (Thomas Thompson) Jackson agreed to remain at Neyland as temporary 'Manager'.

Neyland was now to enter what can only be described as its golden age in so far as maritime operations were concerned. A period that would last until 1906 and after which its demise would lead to a terminal decline. Before that unhappy period though a lot was to occur and commencing in July 1873 when Captain RN (later Admiral) William Henry Haskell was appointed the first Marine Superintendent of the GWR. at New Milford – as Neyland was then called. The port was now the headquarters of the GWR Marine Department and with the whole of that Department's clerical staffed based there. It was also the Port of Registry for all GWR vessels including those operating out of Weymouth.

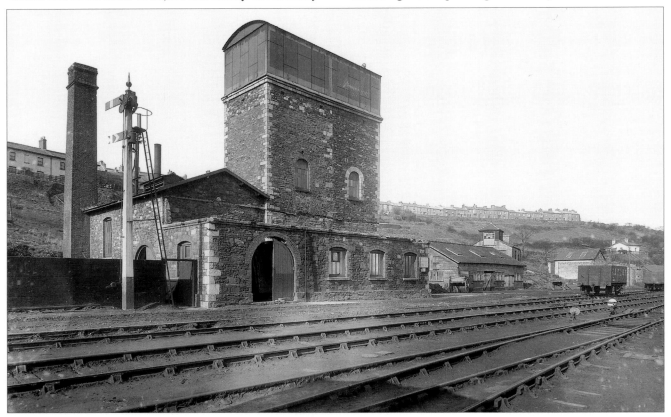

Standing some 50' above rail level was the hydraulic tower and pump house in Neyland yard and from which power was obtained for the wagon lift, cranes, capstans and hoists. Years earlier this had been the hiding place used by Joe Jenkins, the shed cleaner, to hide his beloved wheelbarrow, brush and shovel. Joe was determined that during his enforced first week of paid leave no one would have access to his equipment. They had remained suspended high off of the ground within the hydraulic tower and defied all attempts by the shed staff to locate them.

NRM B.Box 161/21

The hydraulic wagon lift at Neyland depicted by the official photographer around 1930. Originally wagons of coal and other goods were dealt with on the lift, but could also reach the pontoon via a series of wagon turntables and capstans onto the actual landing stage. In both cases the final positioning of a wagon was by hand. It is not clear how much use was made of the wagon lift after the demise of the Irish Ferry traffic although with vessels still predominantly coal burning it is possible some fishing vessels would have continued to be serviced. Certainly there would appear to be small heaps of coal on the pontoon..

NRM B.Box 161/31

The acquisition of the Jackson and Ford operation had really been a matter of time. In true businesslike fashion, the mighty GWR had slowly bled the partnership dry through the latter's financial obligations in loans and other repayments and so was unable to invest in new vessels. It was a situation repeated up and down the system in so far as competing services were concerned. Counter the romantic notion in which the GWR was perceived for many years with reality, and the result is a ruthless business empire, and which very success and longevity was founded on harsh economics.

Back at Neyland, James Grierson, the GWR General Manager, made a personal visit and which included the arrangements at Waterford. His findings appear to been generally good in so far as Neyland was concerned, although it was mentioned there was at the time no cover to the jetties and cargo being brought ashore was thus exposed to the elements. At Waterford Grierson

interviewed Mr. Downey and who had been the Agent employed by the former partnership, probably from around 1858. Downey, although 'of advancing years', was well placed at Waterford and he remained there, although now under the employ of the GWR and at an annual salary of £400.

Assisting Downey were a staff of some four clerks and 14 men. Ten of these were porters and who had up to that time supplemented their wages with tips. When advised by their new employer they were no longer to "solicit gratuities', they instead promptly applied for an increase in wages! Three ships butchers were also taken over at the same time and whose job had been to deal with and dress any carcasses of pigs that died en–route. These carcasses were then taken back to Waterford to be sold as bacon. The arrangement was hardly ideal as on further questioning it was quickly established that some of this bacon was often "spoiled" on the return journey

An unidentified fishing vessel tied up alongside what was formally one of the landing points of the fish stage. The coaching stock also worthy of a second glance. Mud banks at low water level could make loading and unloading difficult for ferries and fishing vessels and dredging was necessary on occasions.

NRM B.Box 161/29

and ended up being thrown overboard. A more obvious solution then was for the butchers to be employed at Neyland and the carcasses dealt with there.

A similar situation was endured by cattle travelling from Ireland, the conditions for the transport of live animals at the time being very poor. It was not uncommon then for dead cattle to be seen littering decks of vessels arriving at Neyland and they too would be sunk on the return journey usually off St.Annes Head loaded down with weights. Records indicate that Grierson also spoke to the Captains of the vessels who spoke of difficulties with space on board, a need for signal guns to assist in navigation at the respective ports during foggy weather and also that steam winches should be provided. Whether by intention or design some of the passengers were also canvassed, and from them came a complaint over the presence of Irish Cattle Drovers in the saloons. Grierson's report on this

latter issue would recommend that, "...only the better class of dealer&", be allowed in the saloon – the remainder being herded into the fore–cabin!

So far though Neyland had only achieved port status for Irish traffic, the one known exception to this having been in 1856. The GWR though were anxious to develop the port into a location dealing with traffic destined for further afield and this opportunity came in late 1872 when a public meeting was held at the South Wales Hotel to discuss the 'Anglo–Australian Mail Packet Co.'. With no less a personage as Sir Daniel Gooch lending support it would have been expected that the venture would have been a success although shortly afterwards the local Member of Parliament, J.H. Scourfield effectively scuppered development by pointing out that Neyland was on a lee shore. This though had not stopped the *S.S. Africa* calling in 1872 whilst en route to the Continent of the same name from Liverpool, Neyland dealing with mails from this vessel whilst its cargo of gold, some monkeys and a small alligator attracted much local interest. Sadly the latter creature died, it is said of cold, whilst the vessel was at Neyland. Subsequent to this the principal time other vessels would use the port was when coastal traders would call and the very occasional ship destined for foreign climates.

In 1874 the GWR invested in three new paddle steamers and which arrived in 1874. *Milford, Waterford,* and *Limerick,* were all in the order of 344 tons to 349 tons and brought the compliment of ships to seven. Their arrival was also somewhat fortuitous for *Vulture* had collided with

dock at Waterford and damaged a paddle wheel in February 1874, while in the summer of the same year *Malakhoff* was out of service requiring a new boiler. The accident involving *Waterford* would also appear not to have been unique, for records show *Milford* had rammed a smack off St. Anne's Head on 23 July and in October the same year *Limerick* collided with a schooner. To conclude a bad year *Vulture* was also laid up with boiler trouble and leaving *South of Ireland, Limerick* and the now repaired *Milford* running the service with *Great Western* as spare.

Despite these obvious setbacks operationally, revenue from the Irish traffic was displaying a healthy in-

Contemporary postcards of Neyland. In the top view the 'Innisfallen' is moored against the pontoon and to the right is the mouth of the Westfield Pill which separates Neyalnd from the village of Burton. Between Neyland and Barnlake a row boat ferry was operated. 'Inisfallen' was owned and operated by the City of Cork Steam Packet Co. and was used on the Neyland to Cork route. Launched in 1896 she survived until sunk by a German submarine on May 23 1918.

Lower view; Seen from the Pembroke side of the Milford Haven and the expanse of Neyland is clear at what was the peak of its marine activity. Behind the steamer - unfortunately not identified and with the South Wales Hotel as a backdrop, is the GWR Marine Factory. The building to the right of the factory was used as offices for the Marine Department. The rear of the station building, train shed and goods shed make for an interesting profile as does the view of the 'Tube' which led to the pontoon. Houses on the hillside show the growth of Neyland resulting from the railway and Irish Ferry service.

Both – Simon Hancock Collec.

Although referred to on the postcard as the pontoon, what is highlighted is in fact 'The Tube', the twin passageways were simultaneously used by both passengers and livestock during the period the steamers plied to and from Southern Ireland. (The pontoon is to the right and end of 'The Tube' and where the vessel is moored.) Not surprisingly complaints were received about the smell and it seems incredible that it was not until 1876, some 20 years after the ferry service had commenced, that a man was specially employed to clean the pontoons of cattle and no doubt other 'discharges'. This may well have been an individual made redundant when the GWR had ceased operations at Cork. The structure remained in – situ until October 1930 when it was removed as part of improvements in connection with the short ferry journey between Neyland and Hobbs Point (Pembroke Dock).
Top; Collec, Brinley John   *Lower, NRM GWR B.Box 161/34*

Views of the vessels used on the Irish ferry services in the 19th century are perhaps understandably if sadly rare. This though is 'Great Western' depicted in 1904, and the second vessel to carry the name. Launched in 1902 she would survive until 1934. When not in use steamers were tied up either at an Admiralty Buoy in the Haven or at Neyland Pill. The steamers would, as necessary also use old rails as ballast. Captains and crews would also interchange as necessary and with both male and female stewards carried on board. Some difficulties could also arise at the ports over demarcation in that ships' crews would not unload baggage stating that this was the job of the shore staff.

Desmond Davies

crease and whilst regretfully figures for 1872 and the year the take over of Jackson and Ford occurred are not available, a comparison between 1870 and 1874 reported a 20% increase in revenue over the period much of this attributable to a vast increase in the movement of horses, cattle and sheep.

Having now increased the size of the fleet and although it is not stated as such presumably maintained to a reasonable standard, the GWR once again began a service between Neyland and Cork. This was twice weekly and commenced from June 1 1875. Additionally *Vulture* was given over exclusively to cattle on the Cork route presumably then sailing empty on the outward journey from Neyland. The GWR sailings to Cork though lasted just one year, for in 1876 the City of Cork Steam Packet Co. took over the route. Again it is not mentioned, but presumably with the blessing of the GWR for the service continued, thrice weekly this time, for some years, aside that is from a brief period in 1882 when there was a temporary dispute over rates. The railway still benefited of course through connection boat trains run to and from Paddington.

Redundant from her role as a cattle boat to Cork, *Vulture* took on a similar role on the Waterford route. It is believed that other of the vessels were also used to provide a separate means of transporting livestock alone. This was perhaps a long overdue arrangement for there had been

many complaints over the smell when beasts were carried as cargo on the passenger sailings. Complaints over the movement of cattle at Neyland though would continue, and are referred to in the accompanying caption.

Three vessels were all that was required now to operate the Waterford passenger service and these were the *Milford, Limerick* and *Waterford. Malakhoff* seeming to spend most of its time under repair.

Despite the ending of the Cork service new employment was found for two of the vessels, the *Great Western* and the *South of Ireland* which transferred to Weymouth in 1878 ready for the Cherbourg route from that port. *Vulture* followed in 1879. *Great Western* would return again to Neyland in later years although of the other two, *South Of Ireland* ran aground in 1883 and which resulted in her Captain being dismissed and *Vulture* was broken up at the end of 1885. *Malakoff* was sold in 1881, and subsequently broken up three years later.

With just three vessels remaining at Neyland, the GWR invested in their last paddle steamer and the only one ever built of steel. *Pembroke* at 927 tons was also the largest and would achieve the distinction of being the longest running of all the vessels in the GWR fleet.

A seemingly backward step too from March 1 1880 was the reintroduction of mixed passenger and livestock transport on the same vessel. This could have been due to a general downturn in the market around this time but was not assisted by the previous restricted number of sailings the livestock only vessels offered.

The following year Paddington commissioned an audit of the general facilities at Neyland, and which provides for a useful snapshot of contemporary thinking as well as detail of traffic. Various headings were given including one on:

Steamship arrangements. "The SS Pembroke was alongside the pontoon and ready for work. If she is put on the Waterford service she will invite unfavourable comments. It might be desirable to run her to Cork taking alternative turns with the City of Cork Company boats as we are likely to be able to increase traffic to Cork than Waterford."

Cattle and livestock. "The disadvantage of conveying livestock by the daily service is recognised and the unpleasant smells have necessitated the closing of the ships hatches before the cattle are put aboard. The cattle have therefore to be shipped at the last moment and sometimes this leads to rough treatment that is annoying to passengers. The cattle occupy space that could be better used for our increasing traffic in perishables. On being loaded at Neyland the passengers leave the pontoon to cross the line of livestock to gain access to the gangway. Each person on being questioned thought the steamer service should take everything on offer. Traffic in livestock is increasing with an additional £4,900 in 1880 compared with 1879. Traffic in horses accounted for £1,400 of the increase."

Returning again to the vessels, and *Great Western* returned to Neyland in 1885 after which she was deemed as the spare vessel for either Neyland or Weymouth. She was sold in 1890 and survived under a new name sailing in the West Highlands of Scotland until 1904, the last also of the former Jackson and Ford fleet. *Pembroke* in the interim had eventually settled down on the Waterford route

despite initial reservations that she was too large!

Although it could not have been known in 1890, there would be but 15 years left for Neyland as the headquarters of the GWR Marine Department. Several of these would pass without incident although when situations did occur they could be dramatic. One of these came in December 1898 when a fire occurred on board *Pembroke* enroute for Waterford. Fortunately it was quickly dealt with, the cause suspected to be a flammable substance in the mail she was carrying. In February the same vessel ran aground in fog, although fortunately this time her Captain retained his Masters Ticket and his position, unlike his unfortunate compatriot on the *South of Ireland* some years previous.

Further development of the GWR Marine Department at Neyland was planned for 1895 including a massive sea wall as a replacement for the pontoon together with an extension to the Marine Workshops. Both of these would have cost some £250,000 but were never proceeded with. At the time the reasons were not made public although it is likely Paddington were already beginning to doubt the suitability of the venue as a long term port. With the resignation then of the Marine Superintendent, Captain Thomas Lecky and who had been in post since 1883, the GWR took the opportunity to re–organise the Department and much of the clerical work from the department was transferred to Paddington in 1898. The Marine Department now came under the direct control of the GWR General Manager supported by an Officer and with Nautical Assistants at Weymouth and Neyland. Even so it is clear from contemporary records of the importance still placed in the Irish Traffic. Ships Master's on the Neyland to Waterford route receiving considerably more in pay than those in an equivalent role sailing out of Weymouth. The weekly rates specified as £5 15s 6d for a large vessel and £3 17s for a small steamer.

Opposite page, top; The ferry service from Neyland to Hobbs Point had commenced in 1858 and was first operated by row boats or sailing boats and was initially under the control of Captain Jackson, the cost per passenger being then 2d per head.. Eventually the operation was acquired by Frederick Lee in 1933 and operated by 'Alumchine'. She was built in 1923 being 80 feet long and 17° feet in the beam and despite her Isle of Wight name had previosuly been used in North Wales. She was licensed to carry 216 passengers, four crew and six cars. For some time it was hoped she would be preserved by the Paddle Steamer Preservation Society but this did not come to fruition and she was scrapped in 1962.

R.C. Riley

Oppsite page, lower; 'Cleddau Queen' was introduced when the ferry service from Neyalnd to Hobbs Point was taken over by Pembrokeshire County Council in 1950. She was the last paddle wheel ferry constructed in the UK and had a capacity for 250 passengers and 16 motor cars. Initially steam powered she was later converted to diesel. She was joined on the crossing in 1965 by the larger 'Cleddau King' capable of carrying 350 passengers and 24 motor cars. They continued in service until March 1975 when the ferry service was withdrawn following the opening of the Cleddau Road Bridge. After leaving Neyland, the 'Cleddau Queen' was sold to a North of England engineering firm whilst the 'Cleddau King' went to Northern Ireland and was renamed 'Portaferry' and used on Strangford Lough.

Phil Kelley

Around the same time there is the first detail of the of the GWR Marine Workshops which existed at Neyland and which had developed following the take over of the much smaller facilities of Jackson and Ford in 1872. Necessary repairs to the increasing number of vessels operated by the GWR had resulted in a sizeable workforce, details of which can gleaned from a record of the week ending November 6 1897 when it was stated that 246 men were employed just within the Marine Workshops and which equated to a weekly wage bill of £279. In the two following years however, this workforce would see a marked decline so that in the same week of 1897 just 177 men were involved at a cost of £214. The last date for which information is available is the week ending October 28 1899 when the figure had dropped to 107 at a cost of £120. These figures also raise a number of questions over which a century later there can only be speculative answers. It is not known for example whether the 1897 staffing level represented the peak employment figure and likewise why the rapid decline in subsequent years although one possible example may be the increased reliability of the screw driven vessels compared with the earlier paddle steamers. There is no record also of the Neyland workshops being involved in other than repairs – perhaps also for vessels belonging to other parties. New vessels acquired by the GWR were never built at Neyland.

Moving ahead in time slightly, but the Marine Department continued to offer engineering apprenticeships based at Neyland and which were eagerly sought after. Company Minutes of July 26 1900 recording the premiums

to be paid by an apprentice, Marine Engineering £30, Fitters and Turners £20, Other Trades £10. The record states that the premium was deliberately intended to restrict the number of applications, but also that it, "was to be returned to the apprentice in the form of a wage in such weekly sums that the entire amount received by the Company was refunded during the first year or two of the apprenticeship". Wages though paid to apprentices at the time were modest even for the times. As an example an apprentice Marine Fitter, Fitter or Turner could expect to receive 5/– after two years rising to 12/–in the 6th year and 20/–in the 7th year. Despite the reference to the decline in the workforce between 1897 and 1899, contemporary reports refer to the Factory continuing to provide about 200 jobs until it closed in 1906 and when the new facilities were opened at Fishguard Harbour.

Meanwhile two new twin–screw driven steamers entered service in 1902, *Great Western* and *Great Southern*, they could carry 680 passengers and 500 cattle. Pembroke, and which had also been converted from a paddle steamer to a twin–screw steamer in 1895, was now the reserve. *Milford* and *Limerick* were taken out of service in 1901 and 1902 respectively, and *Waterford* in 1905, the latter the last paddle steamer operating for the GWR.

1. As is referred to in Chapter 1, the name Neyland was used in the earliest days and then again in the 20th century. It is by this designation though that it is of course best known. To avoid confusion Neyland is used throughout this chapter.

The Importance of Fish

As was referred to in Chapter 1, the Town of Neyland had its origins as a small fishing community long before the coming of the railway. The railway though allowed for catches to easily reach markets further afield and so it followed that commensurate with the development of the railway network so the fishing industry would likewise prosper.

Regretfully information on the fishing industry over the years is scant, useful snippets and facts though do occur from time to time although it is naturally difficult to built up a complete picture just from these. What is known is that the 1881 GWR audit report referred to earlier also mentions the 'Fish Traffic Arrangements', and with the following reference, "Smart and efficient with the limited accommodation at the command of the traffic officers. New jetties and lines for fish traffic, not available for the season. Work was in progress."

The following year, 1882, there is a reference to an enquiry into the regular late running of the 2.45 am express from Neyland. The report explained that the express carried passengers, fish (other than fish for London which was sent by the 6.45 am train), poultry, dead meat, parcels and similar traffic. It was stated the express was often delayed by more than 30 minutes due to the late arrival of the Irish boat because of adverse weather conditions. When this occurred it was the practice for the express to be sent on it's way without the boat traffic. The report concluded that the delay to the express cannot easily be reduced even if an additional checker was provided and this would only save about 15 minutes. It stated there was insufficient passengers to regularly run two trains.

Returning though to the latter part of the 19th century and running north from the ferry pontoons along the mouth of the Westfield Pill were two jetties with a wooden platform between them, this facility was used for fish landings. Contemporary photographs show large stocks of fish boxes stored nearby. A fish office was also provided. A substantial mackerel trade developed reaching a peak in 1884 with 19,000 tons dispatched by train. Fishing was seen as a possible means of also negating the loss of the Irish traffic and resulted in the GWR seeking additional ways to make Neyland viable. The GWR must have been delighted when "The Neyland Steam Trawling and Fishing Company" was formed in January 1906 and approached the GWR with plans to develop the fishing industry. The Managing Director was Captain Davies who had for many years been in command of one of the GWR steam packets on the Waterford route. Seizing the opportunity, the GWR entered into an agreement with the Trawling Company dated 6th September 1907 to build, at its expense, a corrugated building for the fish market. For an annual rent of £100 the Trawling Company had the use of the fish market, land and the fish jetty. The agreement also provided for the use of the gridiron at a further payment of £100 per day or part day. For a payment of 3d per ton of coal loaded, they could also use the coal tips for bunkering their boats. The agreement required the Trawling Company to send and receive goods by the route most favourable to the GWR who in return undertook to carry such goods at a rate no worse than generally available at the time.

The official opening of the fish market took place in November 1908. It was built partly on the foreshore and partly on a jetty, which allowed the transfer of catches from the trawler to the market building with the aid of four 30–cwt cranes. The market building measured 100 feet long by 57 feet wide and was constructed with corrugated sheets for the sides and the roof. The roof was partly glazed to give some illumination other than from the gaslights provided. A fish stage, some 460 feet long, was available opposite the fish market.

An ice factory was also constructed across the Westfield Pill at Barnlake and had a maximum daily output of 35 tons and a storage capacity of 600 tons. The crushed ice was passed by a conveyor belt and chute into the trawler's ice room. The trawlers moored against a jetty at the ice factory 180 feet long by 60 feet wide.

Initially the Neyland Steam Trawling and Fishing Company provided the men to load the fish trucks but this soon lead to dissatisfaction amongst the fish buyers. To overcome this the Trawling Company asked the GWR to undertake the loading at an agreed rate. In 1910 they asked the GWR to be relieved entirely of this payment contending that the rate charged for the conveyance of the fish included a terminal charge. Whilst not accepting this view was entirely correct, the GWR agreed a rebate of 6d per ton applied retrospectively. Probably because there were few other taker, the railway also offered a substantial reduction for the use of the gridiron. The GWR were keen to foster the fish traffic which brought in much needed revenue and it was reported that in 1914 £41,828 of wet fish was landed and sold through the market.

Even so it was unable to compete with its larger neighbour Milford Haven and closed in 1919 when nine trawlers transferred to Milford Haven. The Trawling Company formally returned the fish market, land and the jetty to the GWR on 24th June 1919. Subsequently the fish market was removed and the jetties fell into disrepair. The fish market was demolished in the 1920's and the cranes removed.

The ice factory continued to operate until 1935 supplying ice to trawlers using Milford Haven. Thereafter it saw no further use and was not demolished until 1974.

Opposite page; A heavily retouched contemporary postcard that pre–dates the fish market. On the quayside are offices used in connection with the fishing industry.

Collec; Desmond Davies

Above; The piles of fish boxes dominate the scene in this view that pre–dates the opening of the fish market in 1908. At the time some 30,000 empty fish boxes were stored in the yard together with a reserve stock of 700 tons of coal. A fatal accident in April 1887 involving a youth employed on the fish stage was in part attributable to the large number of fish boxes stored and which thus obscured visibility. Aside from personal injury there was considered also to be a real risk of fire, so much so that in the same year 1887, Commander (Later Captain) Lecky, the GWR Marine Superintendent, wrote to the Chief Constable of Pembrokeshire because certain Policemen were in the habit of smoking on or near GWR territory. When challenged the response had also often been abusive. The original station signal box is just visible on the right hand side and partly obscured by smoke drifting from one of the complex of buildings in the foreground. Although undated, the style of coaching stock would suggest the view was taken in the latter part of the 19th century.

Due to the fish market at Neyland having ceased to operate from 1919 recollections of the method of working are not generally available. Bill Morgan however does refer to it in his rendition, and which due to a shortage of packers unloading the mackerel boats onto the railway wagons saw two engine cleaners drafted into help. "We would be paid one penny for every four crates we loaded. Charlie and I were delighted at this sudden stroke of good fortune, and we lost no time in making ourselves known to the checker, who duly entered our names on his board. Every time we passed him with a crate he would put a mark against our name and at the end of the session they would be totted up and we would be paid accordingly. We started off at a great rate, dragging and humping the heavy crates. Back and forth we went, mentally ticking up the strokes, dividing by four and counting the pennies, until our dreams of riches were rudely shattered by a swarthy fish–smelling packer who told us, in no uncertain terms, that we were loading his wagon and that ours was a good fifty yards down the line. He didn't look the sort of man we could argue with, far too muscular and ill–tempered so we walked meekly away. All the wagons seemed to belong to huge, burly fish packers, until we came to the fifth one. We took a quick look around and as there did not appear to be any aggressively–minded owner about, we started again, humping and dragging and clocking up our ticks&.". The story continues with the lads being told off again, until eventually they are forced to load the correct wagon after all. There was though a sweetener as they subsequently hid one of the boxes for themselves, and later retrieved it to sell the contents door to door in the town for a profit of 24/–!

Collec. Desmond Davies

Left; Inside the new market building of 1908 and which was some 100 feet long by 57 feet wide. The view is one of a series of official photographs fortunately taken by the GWR around 1910 all of which are of such superb quality they are reproduced within these pages.

NRM GWR A.1380

Great Western Railway.

LIST OF THROUGH RATES

FOR THE CONVEYANCE OF

TRAWL FISH, MACKEREL & HERRINGS
FROM MILFORD HAVEN & NEYLAND

TO STATIONS ON AND BEYOND THE

GREAT WESTERN RAILWAY.

1.—The Great Western Railway Company have two Rates for the carriage of Fish Traffic from Milford Haven and Neyland; One the Ordinary Rate when the Company accept the ordinary liability of a Railway Company with respect to the carriage of perishable merchandise by Passenger Train, the other a Reduced Rate adopted when the Sender agrees to relieve the Company and all other Companies or Persons over whose Lines the Traffic may pass or in whose possession the same may be during any portion of the transit, from all liability for loss, damage, mis-delivery, delay or detention, except upon proof that such loss, damage, mis-delivery, delay or detention arose from wilful misconduct on the part of the Company's servants.

2. The Rates given herein, which apply also from Fishguard, are calculated at the Reduced Rate, and are those which are now in operation.

All Fish not expressly consigned at the Reduced Rate will be carried and charged at the Ordinary Rate which can be obtained on application.

3. The Rates include delivery in London but not at any other place. The Birmingham Rates apply to the Great Western Stations at Snow Hill, Bordesley and Hockley, to the London and North Western Station at Curzon Street and to the Midland Stations at Lawley Street and Camp Hill.

4. No rebate or drawback will be allowed off the Rates.

5. The Fish, whether packed in boxes, barrels or baskets, will be carried and charged at the actual gross weight; minimum charge as for one cwt. per consignment.

6. Special Trains will be provided upon special orders being given when there is a load of not less than 30 tons for the Station to which the Special Train is required to be run, or when the Carriage charges as for that quantity are paid. Smaller quantities will be sent by the first available train.

Dealers and Shippers should see that their Traffic is plainly addressed and consigned by the Great Western Route.

GENERAL MANAGER'S OFFICE,
PADDINGTON STATION, *March*, 1912.
FRANK POTTER.

(2000—U 21—3.12)

Above; Because there was no room for the Ice Factory in Neyland Yard, it was built on the opposite bank of Westfield Pill and opened by Lady Phillips of Picton, the wife of the Chairman of the Neyland Steam Trawling and Fishing Company. Having landed their catch the trawlers would travel the short distance to the Ice Factory to take on fresh supplies. Vessels from Milford Haven also used the factory and which outlived the Neyland fish market.

Collection; Desmond Davies

Opposite page;

'Great Western Magazine' for March 1910 carried a single page article dealing with the future of Neyland as a port consequent upon the demise of the Irish services. Principal amongst the topics covered was the fishing industry, two of the wonderful glass plate views taken at the time accompanying the piece. In the same year there were also a number of articles on the blossoming trade from Fishguard and proof, if it were needed, that the eyes of Paddington were looking forward rather than back.

Overleaf;

Although clearly posed for the camera, there is nevertheless a hive of activity recorded here. Railway staff are visible amongst the fish porters and buyers whilst fish boxes attributable to John Gibson and E. Davies can be seen together with those belonging to a merchant from Fleetwood in Lancashire. In 1909 nine boats were sailing from Neyland and weekly catches could exceed £1,000. Thirty–one men and ten boys were employed by the, 'Neyland Steam Trawling and Fishing Co.' in 1912.

NRM GWR A1386

The Goods Department

The Future of Neyland.—Upon the opening of the Fishguard and Rosslare route to Ireland in August, 1908, and the consequent withdrawal of the Company's Irish steamboat service from Neyland (or New Milford, as it was then called), the thought must have flashed across the minds of many : " What use will now be made of the pon-

market, which has been erected by the Great Western Company on the platform level. The advantage of such an arrangement can readily be appreciated, as the fish, after it has been sold, can be wheeled direct from the market to truck for conveyance to the centres of consumption. The market is so situated that trawlers can come alongside at any state of the tide and land their catches. Having landed fish and taken in ice, the boats

Neyland Jetty and Fish Market.

toons and other apparatus at Neyland ? What of the future of that place ? "

Any misgivings upon these points have long since been removed. No sooner was the Fishguard route opened than the Company were approached on the subject of opening up a new industry. The outcome was the establishment of the " Neyland Steam Trawling and Fishing Company."

The new concern determined to start business fully equipped in all branches. In addition to a fleet of nine steam trawlers, it possesses an up-to-date ice factory capable of turning out 35 tons of ice per day, with a warehouse adjacent with a capacity of 600 tons.

Directly opposite the ice factory is the new fish

move down to the pontoon, where coal is shipped.

Neyland was opened as a fishing port in November, 1908, and is already doing a very good trade— in every sense quite a new industry, while, side by side, the fish traffic at Old Milford continues to show a steady increase. It is pleasing to record that the turn of events has enabled such excellent use to be made of facilities which, in the absence of enterprise, might to a large extent have become redundant.

The Fish Company have as their managing director Captain Davies, who was for many years in command of one of the Great Western Company's steamers running between Neyland and Waterford.

W. DAVIS.

A commercial postcard dating from about 1904, most of the vehicles depicted no doubt involved in the fish traffic. The wagon turntable gave access to two other lines leading to the pontoon, and with the right hand set of rails in front of the camera heading off to the wagon lift which is behind the photographer. The goods shed and original train shed are dominated by the later extension to the train shed. (See also view on page 121).

Simon Hancock

The fish market at Neyland opened in 1908, an official ceremony being held at which Mrs. Kingsford, wife of Rear Admiral Kingsford of Pembroke Dockyard officiated. The event was also attended by a number of local dignitaries and who were then entertained to dinner at the South Wales Hotel. The view was taken to record the opening and although the Irish Traffic had ceased two years earlier there are still a considerable number of cattle wagons in the sidings, suggesting perhaps that they may have been pressed into service as temporary fish wagons. Despite the loss of the ferry traffic the yard gives the impression of a hive of activity.

Collec. Simon Hancock.

The interior of the fish market, part of which view was also reproduced in the 1910 GWR Magazine article. The quantity of fish seen here was by no means uncommon for the period and meaning the ports of Neyland and its neighbours were destined to be a principal source of supply to a number of markets.
NRM GWR A1387.

Opposite page; Stages in the unloading of a trawler. The dock crane is being used to unload what is probably a full fish box after which empty wooden barrels will be loaded. Although not confirmed it is likely there was a box factory and cooper's shop at the Port around this time.
NRM GWR A1382 & A1381

Above; One of the nine vessels of the Neyland Steam Trawling and Fishing Co Ltd. positioned alongside the jetty at the Ice Factory. It is not known if this figure remained constant over the years. Fishing Smacks from Brixham, and possibly other locations were also regular visitors to Neyland where their catch would be landed.

NRM GWR A1384

Previous page; Icing of a fish container – one man seen making use of an empty fish box to gain additional height. The container has been loaded onto a vacuum fitted wagon labelled to work between Milford Haven and Paddington only. There were eight vehicles of this type having the running numbers 42510–17 and of size 14'8" x 7'1°'' x 7" having been altered from timber trucks at Swindon circa 1911. All were also branded as seen. Their subsequent history is of interest as in February 1918 they were converted once more this time to Match–Trucks before being reverting finally for fish traffic once more in November 1920. They were finally condemned in 1935. *NRM GWR A1385*

Opposite top; Viewed from near what was the cottage occupied by the Manager of the Gas Works, the buildings are the Ambulance room and with what was shown on the plans as a Store Room. The structure with the frame is likewise shown on the plans but without a description, it may well be housing accomulators used in connection with the hydraulic process – the hydraulic tower is just out of sight. On the far shore is the village of Burton. Here for some years the Trininty House Service had a base and private jetty.

Pope/Parkhouse Collection

Lower; 'Fish and Ships' 'Hero' of the Neyland Steam Trawling and Fishing Co. Ltd. was built in 1907 and registered at 226 tons. She is moored alongside the jetty with the fish market immediately behind. The engine shed building stands beyond the empty fish boxes. Nowhere in contemporary records is there any record of complaints from passengers over what must have been an all pervading smell of fish. Possibly then this was an accepted aspect of what was for the time a busy fishing port.

Fish Loading Stage & Ice Factory, Neyland.

Standing to the left of the station approach the building in front was occupied by Mr. Mends the Permanent Way Ganger. Before this it had been used as offices for the Trawling Co. and earlier as the GWR Marine Superintendents Office when Neyland was the base of it's shipping operations. The building immediately behind still carries the coat of arms of H.M. Customs and continued to be used by the Customs Officer operating at Milford Haven after the loss of the Irish Ferry service to Fishguard.

NRM GWR B.Box 161/13

Located to the rear of the 'Customs House' this particular structure is thought to have once been used as a slaughter house around the time of the cattle trade. Plans also show it as lairage with the fencing incorporating former broad gauge rail. Later still it was used as a garage by a local coal merchant. *NRM GWR B.Box 161/14*

Chapter 4

NEYLAND
Development at the station

A General Description of the station site

Opposite the Customs House were the original station buildings, which stood under an overall roof on the arrival platform. The land in front of these buildings in Neyland's heyday had been used as cattle lairage, which cannot have been pleasant for the passengers. Later this land was used as allotments and finally as a car park.

Looking down the curving departure platform on the right hand side stood the former cattle pens 360 feet by 40 feet with 14 pens and 6 water hydrants. Following the demise of the cattle traffic, this area was used to store coal for the locomotive department. The carriage and wagon department used the cabin on the dock. On the embankment almost opposite this cabin was a water tank measuring 32 feet x15 feet x 7 feet with a capacity of 19,500 gallons. This tank fed the water cranes in the engine shed via an underground pipeline. Further down the yard on the same side stood two distinctive buildings. The first of these was the hydraulic building whose brick tower was surmounted by a water tank measuring 30 feet x 14 feet x 9 feet having a capacity of 22,312 gallons. The complex included, a stationary boiler which had raised steam to operate the hydraulic equipment in Neyland's heyday and in front of this was the accumulator house measuring approximately 47 feet by 14 feet and which by the 1930.s had fallen into ruin. Next to the tower was the final location for the turntable and following alterations made in 1939, these are described more fully later on. The ambulance building lay close to the turntable and was distinctive because of a cupola in its roof. The upper room was used by railway staff for first aid training and who would also use a room in the annex of the South Wales Hotel. In addition to first aid training this upper room was used by the locomotive and traffic departments for their mutual improvement classes. The ground floor room was used for storage including uniforms and was known as the sail room. The name suggests that this building survived from the original Neyland fishing community.

Behind the signal box was an unofficial access to the yard used by railwaymen that branched off the footpath leading down from Railway Terrace over the 160 foot iron bridge spanning the railway tracks to the shore by Westfield Pill. Here the rowboat ferry crossed the Westfield Pill to Barnlake near the Ice factory.

Beyond the signal box and the Iron Bridge was the Gas works built by the GWR and used to supply gas to the station buildings, including the engine shed, and to the railway owned houses. Two gasometers were situated further down the line in the direction of Johnston. Next to the gasworks was the permanent way departments' cabin and

storage area. Sidings known as the 'Rock' lay beyond the P.W. cabin and here until 1939 was the site of a 55 foot over-girder turntable. This was the second turntable site the original position having been next to the engine shed. Opposite the Rock sidings was a further group of sidings known collectively as Barnlake. Returning towards the station, there were further sidings next to the water known as the 'Pontoon' sidings and following extensive in filling in the middle 1950s, additional sidings were laid on what was known as the NATO quay. In the area between the arrival line and the line leading from the departure platform was situated the engine shed. This comprised two separate buildings upon a stone footing and originally with slate roofs. Two cabins stood in front of the top end of the shed. The first of these was used by the engine cleaners and the other by the shunters. Between the bottom end of the engine shed and the arrival platform was a primitive coaling stage and beyond this was a cabin used as office accommodation by the carriage and wagon chargeman fitter and the boiler smith. The carriage cleaners` had a cabin next to the coal store.

Station

The layout of the station was unusual in that the departure and the arrival platforms gave the appearance of following on one from another, albeit the departure platform curved away from the other platform. No other terminus of this design existed in the UK. It is interesting to speculate that it may have been a development owing its` concept to Brunel`s design for through stations an example of which existed for some years at Reading,

A contract of January 15th 1856 provided for William Lewis of Carmarthenshire, to constrict a "temporary station" at a cost of £1,038 with an additional £90 pa for maintenance. The main building were formed in timber and carried on creosoted sills and roofed with Bangor Duchess slates. The contract stipulated 20/- grates to be used for the 1st class waiting room and 30/- grates for the superintendents, booking and goods office's. The station buildings measured approximately 75 feet by 17 feet and provided the following accommodation:- Stores, Urinals, Lamp Room, Porters Room, Guards Room, Telegraph Room, 1st Class Ladies Room, 2nd Class Ladies Room, 1st Class Waiting Room, Superintendents Office, Booking Office, and a Lobby.

The station building stood on the arrival platform and passengers were given some protection from the elements by an overall roof 121 feet by 36 feet. Later the roof was extended.

A goods shed 66 feet by 47 feet was provided adjacent to the arrival platform. A covered walkway linked

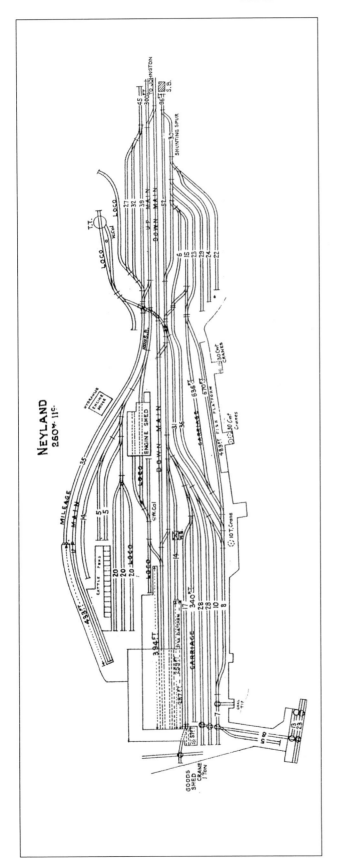

Top; Taken from official GWR sources and although undated likely to the early 1920's. The figures on the sidings refer to the capacity of each siding in so far as 4-wheeled vehicles were concerned. Sidings designated for carriages however, are just shown with their actual length. The whole area appears generally cramped and where every last bit of space has been used to the full.

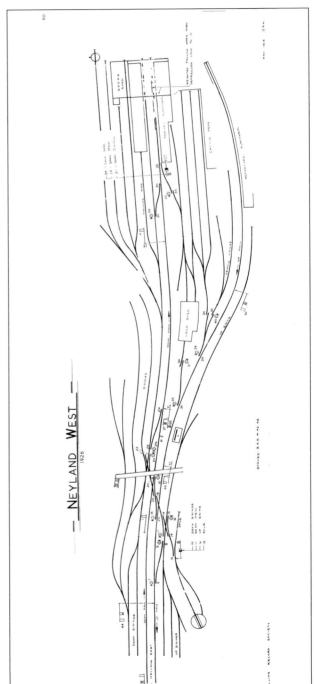

the arrival platform with the departure platform. The facilities were improved when the original timber station building was replaced by a brick building. This measured 72 feet long by 25 feet wide and had the following: Gentlemen's toilets, Ladies` waiting room incorporating a toilet, Booking hall with a fireplace and two serving windows for selling tickets, Booking office with a central stove, Station-Master`s office which had what was described as a book room leading off it.

The masonry station building was demolished in the late 1930`s along with the covered walkway linking the platforms, the overall roof and the goods shed. Also the canopy over the departure platform was removed and the platform wall reduced in height and a new entry formed. It

In 'Behind the Steam' Bill Morgan refers to the prize winning First Aid team at Neyland although not all of whom were employed by the GWR. Bill (then a fireman) is pictured in the middle of the back row in this 1920's view. When Bill moved to the bungalow on the promenade he lived next door to Mr. May a Passenger Guard seen on the 3rd row. Dr. Douglas who supervised the team three times each week is between Mr. Parnell the Shed foreman and Mr. Winters the Stationmaster.

Top row left to right; Billy Bowen - Carriage Cleaner, George Nicklas - Goods Guard, Dan Evans - Goods Guard, Teddy Parnell - Shed Fitter, B. Rogers - Passenger Guard, J. Lloyd, Ben Higgons - Signal & Telegraph, Jack James - Carriage & Wagon Examiner, Third row; M. Lloyd, Hugh Morgans - non railwayman and brother of Bill Morgan, B. Rogers - son of Guard B. Rogers, Owen Davies - son of a Neyland Driver, Bill Lloyd - Engine Shed Clerk, Charlie May - Passenger Guard, Second Row, Di Thomas - Hydraulic and Shedman, Phil Phillips - Passenger Guard, J. Kirby - Fitter, Mr. Parnell - Shed Foreman, Dr. Douglas, Mr. Winters, Ben John - Shunter, ? Folly, Bert Jefferies - Fitter. Front row; J. Thomas, George Perry - Fireman, Charlie Lewis - Cleaner.   *Courtesy: Desmond Davis*

The departure platform at Neyland the track at which was 443 feet in length. From the photograph it would look as if the railway has been foreshortened at some stage although this was not the case. Passengers would enter the station through the booking hall at the arrival side and then after purchasing their ticket would walk via a covered way to the departure side. Originally this wooden covered area had extended the total distance between the arrival and departure buildings although it was cut back to that seen here sometime before the view was taken. The porter using a sack truck as a temporary step ladder has made an entry on the chalk board headed "GWR Cheap Trips". The notice continues "Ask for pamphlets and bills giving particulars". He appears to have written "Sundays June", but the rest of the message cannot be read. The posters in the background include, Holiday Season Tickets for West Wales 15/-, Corona Fruit Drinks, a GWR Track Topics poster featuring the Royal Albert bridge at Saltash. and another extols the beauty of Devon. The LMS poster is of "The Matlocks" Derbyshire. Finally there is a poster on the West Highland line. From the view the actual passenger facilities would appear to extend both sides of the coach although this did not continue for the entire length. It looks as if the carriage cleaner may also be busy soon judging by the mop and buckets! The vehicle is a 70' 'brake third' to diagram D83/5 and Lot No. 1321, and dating from July 1924.

NRM LGRP 3846

is said that certain drivers timed their final brake application to coincide with the engine entering under the overall roof. Luck ran out for one driver who on returning to Neyland did not realise that part of the roof had been removed and in consequence failed to stop in time and demolished the buffer stop.

When the masonry station building was demolished alternative accommodation was provided in a building already standing on the arrival platform. It measured 96 feet long by 12 feet wide and was brick built with a slate roof. This building had formerly provided the following accommodation: Lamp room, Oil store, Unspecified, Porters room and two separate store rooms. After the alterations in 1937 / 38 and at a cost of £560 it provided for a Stationmaster's Office, Parcels Office, Booking Office, Waiting Room, Ladies` Waiting Room, and Guard's Room.

Station Master's Office

This was a small room with a single door from the platform. There was a screen on the left-hand side on entry, which afforded some privacy and protection from draughts. The room was sparsely furnished with a desk and chair there was a fireplace for the coal fire. The room was gas lit and there was a telephone linked to the railway's internal system.

Parcels Office

The office was entered by a single door from the platform. Opposite this door were double doors leading to the rear of the building. A counter was provided on one side of which was an area used to store parcels awaiting collection or delivery. There was a hatch between the adjoining booking office as well as a door. The office was unheated The GPO telephone was sited here, Neyland 307, together with an omnibus telephone. A large Pooley weighing scales was provided, outgoing parcels were charged according to the rate set down in a book provided and which was updated as required by the clerk.

Booking Office

Entry was through a door from the parcel office, which was kept, locked for security reasons. There were two desks and chairs for use by the senior clerk and the junior clerk. The room was gas lit and had a fireplace for heating and for boiling a kettle. A safe was situated next to the senior clerk's desk. Opposite the door in the wall of the booking office and the waiting room was a hatch through which the clerk conducted business with the public. On this wall above and to each side of the hatch were racks holding tickets set out by pre-printed destinations or containing blanks with their current prices chalked on a slate. The tally

The station area depicted circa 1930, the fish market buildings now disused and the sidings used to store coaches. The extension to the train shed has also been removed and the pontoon has lost its roof. Notice the coal merchants using the siding behind the signal box whilst the turntable is still situated at the Rock.

Collec. Simon Hancock

From the west side of the Westfield Pill and with the railway to the right. The 1893 footbridge which spanned the complete site is visible as are the steps that led down from it to the foreshore. No covered accommodation was provided at any time for intending rowboat passengers and who were no doubt considered to be well used to the vagaries of Pembrokeshire weather.
NRM. C14001

Lower; The actual row boat ferry in use on its way from Neyland to Barnlake over the Westfield Pill. The cost for many years being set at 2d. A similar row boat ferry had been provided from the station across to Hobbs Point by Pembroke Dock and was the scene of another attempted means of making money by a young Bill Morgan. On that occasion he made it across with a number of sailors but the return trip saw the current carry him some distance downstream. The line of private owner wagons appear to be from W.R.Willis of Cardiff.
Collec. Desmond Davies

of sales made was also recorded on this slate to assist in the daily balance and cash reconciliation. There was another hatch from the parcel office wall to which the weekly paid men came to collect their wages.

Booking Hall

Access was through a single door from the platform or from a door opposite. In the middle of the room was a large table and there were wooden benches around the walls on three sides. A fireplace was situated on the rear wall although otherwise this room could well be described as spartan.

Ladies Room

Opposite the doorway from the platform was a fireplace, the two toilet cubicles were to the left-hand side. For those ladies who preferred not to sit in the booking hall, seating was provided. In the 1950s the ladies room was hardly ever used.

Guard`s Room

This had a large table and latterly a big green settee. It had a fireplace, wash hand basin, lockers and a gas ring for boiling a large kettle.

Gentlemen's Toilets

Were situated on the arrival platform some distance from the station building. They were decidedly careworn by the 1950s. During the Royal visit in 1955, in common with the station building, they were adorned with buntings to mask their run down appearance.

General

On the wall of the building were fire buckets that the porters ensured were filled with sand. At one time a bell was provided to warn station staff of the arrival of the ferry from Hobbs Point so that they could hold the train to allow ferry passengers time to board. Taxis were based in the town rather than the station the telephone number was kept in the booking office and made available on request.

Yard

After the demolition of the goods shed it was replaced by a goods platform equipped with a lock-up shed and a crane to handled traffic to and from Neyland and surrounding area. Nearby was the machine road, so called because underneath a section of track was a weighing machine for weighing wagons. Next to this siding was a brick building housing the scales. This building remained in situ until the station closed although the weighing machine had long before been removed. A 280-foot wooden ticket platform had originally been provided to assist in the inspection of passenger tickets prior to trains arrival at Neyland. This had stood only a few hundred feet from the station platform being close to the engine shed and was fenced off from it as a safety precaution. It was though out of use by early 1905

The remains of the GWR pattern fencing remained though long after the ticket platform was removed.

Before the coming of the railway Neylanders' had enjoyed unrestricted access to the foreshore at Westfield Pill and on Milford Haven. Row-boat ferries had been established over the Haven to Hobbs Ferry by Pembroke Dock and over Westfield Pill to Barnlake. The development of the railway infrastructure and the consequent restrictions to shipping imposed near the pontoons then used by the Irish ships, brought the railway company into conflict with some of Neyland's inhabitants. Petitions were sent to the Board of Trade in London objecting to these restrictions and to the company enforcing the laws on trespass. In a fatal accident report the yard was considered dangerous to cross because of the piles of fish boxes. However the most controversial matter related to the railway company denying local access to the Barnlake Ferry over railway land, whilst at the same time not providing a footbridge over it. This matter led to a long running legal dispute which was finally settled in the High Court in favour of the townsfolk and against the GWR. who were obliged to provide a bridge over its land. The Iron Bridge spanning the railway tracks was opened in 1893 and remained for some time after the closure of the station in 1964.

There were plans in 1923 to provide a mileage yard on the site of the former lairage area in the station approach

The arrival platform and train shed and with the stock on the left standing at what used to be the fish platform. The main station buildings are to the right and with the locomotive - unfortunately not identified, standing on the loco siding which led from the engine shed. The broad gauge origins of the station are clearly identified by the gap between the platforms.
NRM GWR B.Box 161/17

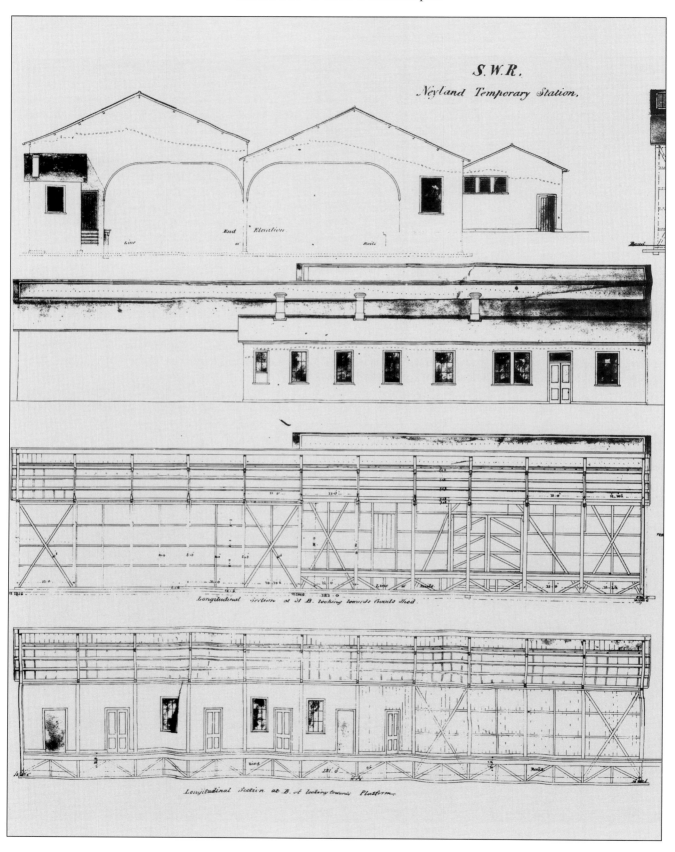

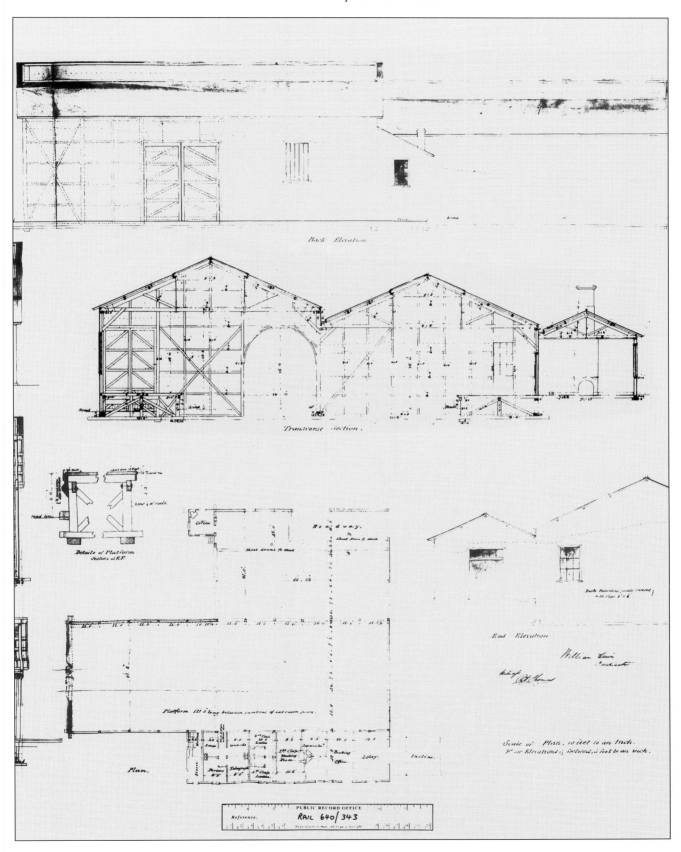

Above; The carriage and wagon department used the wooden platform to clean coaching stock and some of their long handled brushes and a bucket are on view. The building immediately behind the brushes became the third and final station building when the second building to the left was demolished. Posters on display include, Buchanan's Black & White Whiskey, Pear's Soap, Wright's Coal Tar Soap, and Sutton's Seeds - free by post and rail direct from Sutton and Son Reading. Above the row of buckets on the station building the notice reads, "The fire buckets must not under any circumstances be used except in the case of fire".

Lower; The "second" station building replaced the temporary wooden structure provided at the opening of the station in 1856. The train shed is that originally provided with the large extension having been removed. The "arced" opening sandwiched between the station building was the covered walkway leading to the departure platform. A sign hanging inside this opening points the way to the parcels office and cloakroom.

NRM. B.Box 161/18 and 161/19

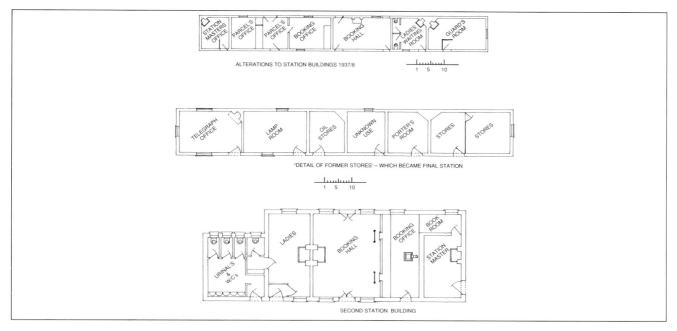

ALTERATIONS TO STATION BUILDINGS 1937/8

1 5 10

"DETAIL OF FORMER STORES' – WHICH BECAME FINAL STATION

1 5 10

SECOND STATION BUILDING

Circa 1926 with the "second" station building immediately on the right and which was demolished in the 1930's. The land in front of the station building had formerly been used for cattle lairage, later as allotments and finally for car parking. The departure platform is behind the wall at the far end of the station approach. The hipped roof affording parcels access to the departure side is also seen. One noticeable feature must be the total lack of road orientated transport.

NRM. B.Box 161/12

Above; A few posters grace the approach to the parcels entrance to the departure platform - passengers were encouraged to enter the station via the arrivals platform, but do little to hide the shabby appearance. The building with the chimney was at one time used as the station master's office.

NRM LGRP 3847

with three sidings, a cart weighbridge and carriage and horse landings. In addition it was intended to provide a goods platform with accommodation for goods clerks and a lock up store and to move the one ton crane from the original goods platform which would have been removed. None of these proposals came to fruition.

In 1928 a substantial removal of surplus sidings took place including those leading down the pontoon and a siding next to the goods shed together with two sidings each at the Rock and Barnlake. The mileage siding next to the hydraulic building was also shortened. In 1933 the siding that had once served Messrs. Jackson and Ford, later the G.W.R. marine workshops, was removed. Since 1926 this had been the subject of a private siding agreement with a Mr

Hitchen. It was accessed by a wagon turntable off the goods shed siding.

Before the Second World War there were 4 coal merchants receiving coal at Neyland station including Messrs. Lewis, Lloyd, Warlow and Davies. None of the firms had their own private wagons. Mr Lloyd specialised in culm coal. This was in effect coal dust that was difficult to burn unless mixed with another ingredient to form a ball. Often seaweed was used as this was readily available. No coal yard was provided. The merchant's off-loaded coal from the wagons, normally placed in the pontoon sidings, on to their vehicles although photographic evidence would also tend to imply that unloading also took place on the siding at the rear of the signal box.

Opposite page; Top - The departure platform looking towards Johnson. The double doors gave access to the platform but passengers were encouraged to use the covered walkway from the arrivals side. The platform furniture includes a cigarette / sweet dispenser, chocolate bar dispenser, two GWR platform seats a platform trolley and barrow. The notices boards have the legend, Rhonda and Swansea Bay, London Brighton and South Coast - with a poster of Eastbourne, Midland, and two GWR examples giving details of weekend tickets available. Although there is no reference to any difficulties it could well have been that the presence of the uprights may have caused inconvenience to loading on occasions.

Lower - 70' Toplight First to Diagram A10 and constructed in 1910 for the Fishguard Boat trains stands in the departure platform. A weighing scale is almost hidden under the canopy. One of the posters proclaims, "The Best Cooks Cook best By Bovril"

Top; NRM GWR B.Box 161/15, Lower NRM LGRP 3845

NEYLAND - Development at the station

Taken in the late 1920's and seen from between the departure and arrival areas and in front the large cattle dock that had not been used for about 20 years. The sidings were used in locomotive disposal operations by the shed men. The loco shed is also visible to the right. In the distance can be discerned the hydraulic building.

NRM. GWR B.BOX 161/16

Chapter 5
THE LOCOMOTIVE DEPARTMENT

Unusually the shed was situated between the arrival and departure running lines. Its location prevented any enlargement without major alteration to the station site. The access to the two–road end was known as the bottom end and the single road the top end. At the top, end the exit led almost immediately to the departure line and was provided with a trap point as a means of preventing entry on to the running line without the permission of the signalman. The walls of both buildings were constructed of wooden planking on a timber frame which in turn stood on dwarf walls three feet above ground level.

Double road building

This was 105 feet long on the side next to the departure line and 106 feet long on the side nearest to the arrival line. The side next to the arrival line had eight windows each being 8 feet 6 inches high by four feet wide and set one foot above the top of the walls. The planks were set horizontally and a smoke vent 85 feet in length surmounted the slate roof. The building was 39 feet wide and the smoke vent was set 28 feet above floor level.

Inside the building on the fitters road there was a pit between the rails commencing 12 feet from the bottom end and terminating 10 feet from the wall of the stores room which formed the end wall of the double road building. The pit was not parallel to the wall being eight feet from it at the bottom end and 10 feet at the top end. Eight wooden posts supported the roof in this section. On the wall facing the departure line there were two lean–to buildings. That by the bottom end being 10 feet by 7 feet and is shown in drawings dated 1935 as a store for fire bars. Adjoining this with stone walls under a single roof and measuring 11 feet wide by 66 feet long was a building divided off to provide the following; a tool store 11 feet wide by 8 feet with an exterior window and with a door leading to the inside of the building, the driver's cabin, which was also shared with the firemen and which had gas lighting, a gas cooking ring, a coal fire, a long wooden table and wooden seats and a wash hand basin. Some lockers were provided for the drivers, with the firemen either sharing these or making use of others provided in another lean–to near the foreman's office.

Next to this was the fitting shop, 11 feet wide by 33 feet long with three exterior windows. An internal door led to the inside of the building and another door led to the adjoining boilersmith's room. This was 11 feet wide and 22 feet long having two exterior side windows and one on

A line up of private owner wagons outside the shed, most of which are probably waiting to be returned to the various collieries. Of the various buildings on the outside of the shed, these are (L to R), stores, Clerks office, Foreman's office and finally the Engineman's cabin. The ice factory is also visible across the Westfield Pill. *Brinley John*

the end wall facing in the direction of Johnston.

Single road building

This building had originally stood at Chepstow but was dismantled and brought to Neyland in time for the original opening of the line. It gave the appearance of two separate buildings that adjoined the double road, being 48 feet long by 15 feet wide with vertical planks on a wooden frame standing on walls one foot above ground level. There were three windows each 6 feet 6 inches by 4 feet wide under a slate roof with a smoke vent running most of its length. The other building also had vertical planking on dwarf walls with seven windows each 5 feet 9 inches wide by 6 feet and having nine separate panes of glass, unlike the other side windows which just contained a single glass sheet. The roof was replaced around 1932 and latterly was formed of asbestos sheeting without any external smoke vents. On the building adjoining the double road was an 'L' shaped lean–to 79 feet overall. The bottom of the 'L' was used as the storeroom with three exterior windows accessed by a door from inside the shed. Next to this was an office for the two clerks with an exterior window and an internal window to which the weekly paid shed staff came to collect their pay. Adjoining this room was the shed foreman's office. This could be accessed from the clerk's office or through an exterior door, which led out to the side by the departure line. Beyond this were two more lean–to buildings one of which was used by the engine drivers and firemen. Access was from a door inside the shed and each had an exterior window. Next to this was another room, which in 1935 was used as a stationery store. Beyond this was the firebrick store, 23 foot long. At the bottom end next to the arrival platform was the primitive coaling stage. This was a small wooden structure, which originally had a roof but was later removed.

Outside the engine shed at the bottom end, the first turntable of 40–foot diameter was installed. The turntable was the means of access to shed road, the fitter's road and a short siding. Earlier plans show that the access to the fitter's road was from a siding in the cattle dock area with no short siding provided. This turntable was removed and replaced by a larger one situated next to the sidings, known as the Rock, some distance from the shed and at the Johnston end of Neyland yard. The replacement turntable was 55 feet in diameter of a standard over girder pattern with two lines leading to it. A water crane was sited between these two lines. In 1939 this turntable was again replaced at a cost of £5,525 by a Ransom and Rapier 65 foot 'under girder' table and which had a working load of 149 tons. It was installed on a new site by the hydraulic tower and close by the shed. This table, like those previously, was hand operated, unlike some others on the GWR that used vacuum power from the engine or were electrically driven. Just one line now led to the turntable and this was provided with a 60–foot inspection pit and a water crane. Three short holding sidings were also accessed from the turntable. To enable the new facility to fit the site, it was necessary to remove some of the embankment and to provide a vehicle crossing over the line leading to the turntable to maintain a lorry route to the buildings beyond the turntable site. The former mileage siding was also slewed over and shortened in length and was then used to hold engines waiting their next turn of duty. The track layout was altered so that engines could access the turntable line from the former cattle dock sidings where the coaling and disposals roads were situated. An AWS testing ramp was later installed on the exit line from the turntable.

An unidentified Pannier Tank, complete with 'Not to be Moved' board, awaits the attention of the fitters. The gas lighting is visible whilst the one through road of the shed appears to be totally empty. The structure remained basically unaltered until closure.

Brinley John

Lower view;

A 2–6–0 Mogul inside the single road section of the engine shed and which had originally been erected at Chepstow. Beyond is the double road shed. The roof of the building is clearly in need of repair and indeed at a later stage was re–clad with asbestos sheets. The store room, shed Foreman's office and Clerk's office are all located to the right hand side. (– see also view on page 70).

NRM. 04

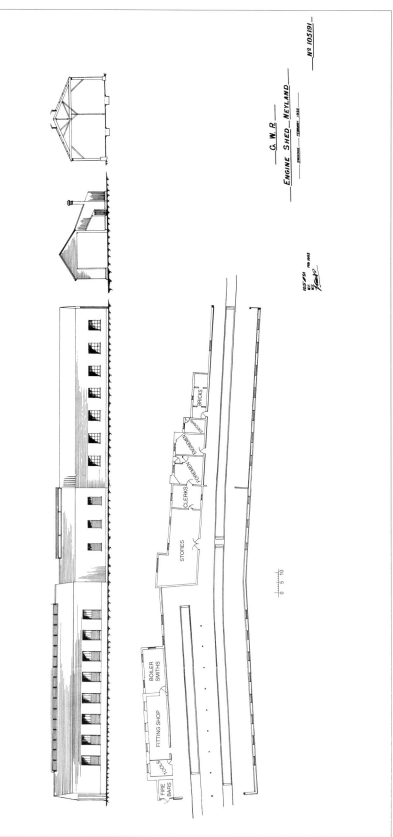

In May 1913 plans were prepared for a new engine shed in the area known as the Rock. Had the plans come to fruition the existing turntable then situated at the Rock would have remained and the new shed buildings built immediately beyond and next to the gasometers. Part of the hillside would have had to be removed in order to give necessary additional width to the site and a running loop next to the main line would have been removed. A raised coaling platform was to have been provided and the two lines feeding to the turntable retained. A new line from the table would have led to a siding behind the coal platform and the shed building. The shed was to have measured 280 feet long by 75 feet wide and provide four dead end sidings under cover. Because of the restricted nature of the site and as a safety measure the office accommodation was to have been on the side of the shed furthest from the running lines. The new proposal would certainly have afforded a much needed improvement.

A final proposal for a new engine shed was also prepared as late as September 1952. Again the original shed would have been demolished and the sidings in the immediate area altered. This time the alteration would have provided seven sidings between the cattle dock area and the arrival platform and these would have been used for carriage storage. It is not known if this would have resulted in rationalisation of carriage sidings elsewhere at Neyland. The existing 65–foot turntable would have been retained and a new siding installed leading under the Barnlake footbridge to serve a coal store area. The line running behind the signal box was to have been truncated and used as the breakdown van siding. The new coal stage would have been served by a ramped siding, as in the traditional GWR style and with the coal stage building housing a 1 ton electric hoist. This was

The second Neyland turntable, located at an area understandably known as 'The Rock' It could accommodate engines up to 55' in length and was installed around the turn of the century replacing a smaller 40' turntable located nearer to the shed.

Brinley John

The final turntable at Neyland was this 65' under girder type and necessary as engines sizes increased. Installed in 1939 it had a life of just 24 years. Depicted making use of the facility is County Class 4–6–0 No. 1020 'County of Monmouth' and which for the present retains its single chimney. In the can are Driver 'Teddy' Morgan. and Head Shunter, Reggie Thomas.

R.C. Riley

to have run on an overhead railway with the tubs having a capacity of 8–10 cwt and equipped for side discharging. They would have run on a 2–foot gauge track and four ash tubs would have been assigned. This alone would have been a considerable improvement on Neyland's coaling facilities. A cycle shed and coalman's cabin were featured in the plans and would have been sited between the coal stage and the coal stacking ground, the latter occupying the site of the former turntable at the Rock. The coal stacking area was to accommodate up to 1,400 tons of locomotive coal. A new engine shed would also have been built in a similar position to the 1913 proposals except that this time three through roads were envisaged and which, after passing through the shed building, would come together to form a headshunt from which a line passed back

alongside the shed building in the direction of the coal–stage. Because of the restricted nature of the site and also for safety reasons no doors were to have been provided on the side of the shed by the running lines. The proposed accommodation on the opposite side of the shed would have provided offices for: the foreman, clerk's, train crews' lobby, duty room, stores, ambulance room, workshop, locker rooms, washroom and lavatories and a mess room.

The work would also have necessitated the removal of part of the hillside. Out in the yard a boiler house was to have been provided with its own coal storage area and a separate sand drier with a coke store. Inspection pits running 60 feet would have been provided on the lines leading out from the engine shed on the Johnston side of the building. The overall dimensions were shown as 215

A raised wooden platform with a simple crane operated by hand served the engine shed from the earliest beginnings until almost the end of steam. Coal was off loaded from a coal wagon placed on one side of the platform and then re–loaded into tubs. These were then raised to the level of the engine and moved into place – the tub was then tipped to empty the contents. This was a two–man operation and also very hard and dirty work. Later the steam crane and depicted in the lower view, was used to hoist the coal tubs.

Brinley John.

Old and new coaling facilities are in view. The covered shelter afforded some protection from the elements for the coalmen off loading coal from a wagon into the coal tubs. The former coal platform was now out of use.

H.C. Casserley, 7–7–1958.

'Bulldog Class 4–4–0 No. 3345 – later 3333, 'Perseus' alongside the shed. The Bulldog type had once been the mainstay of locomotives on express passenger workings from Neyland and a number were allocated to the depot including , 3303, 3315, 3326, 3378, 3382, 3397, 3400, 3408, 3422, 3432, 3435, 3437, 3447 'Jackdaw', 3453 'Seagull', and 3454 'Skylark', most though had disappeared from the area by the end of the 1930's.

Roger Worsley

feet long by 70 feet wide. Inspection pits would also have been provided on each line within the shed and running the full length. As with the 1913 proposals it would have provided vastly superior accommodation and improved working conditions but it did not materialise and the original shed remained in use until closure in 1963.

Loco Fitters

In the final 30 years of Neyland's existence there were four fitters, each of them had a mate, who were under the control of a chargeman. The chargeman was Ron Shorey although later Billy Conway took over. Men known to have been employed as fitters include; Bert Jeffries, Tommy Davies, Abbey Lloyd, Norrie Roach and Harry Steward. The mates included; Bertie John, Walter Howell; Tubey Davies and Tommy Harris. All the fitters were time served apprentices. The training lasted five years, part of which involved a requirement to move away from their home shed. In addition it was not uncommon for the men to attend the mutual improvement classes. Locally these were organised by the drivers, with the fitters finding that they could learn from the practical experiences of the drivers, whilst also contributing to the footplate crews knowledge from their own technical ability.

The fitting staff worked one of three shifts, 6 am to 2 pm, 2 pm to 10 pm, and 10 pm to 6 am. Additionally there was a day turn from 8 am to 4 pm. Each turn had a fitter and mate allocated to it. The day turn was used to undertake larger jobs with the shift fitters tending to carry out running repairs and other less time–consuming tasks.

The fitters occupied an area of the engine shed on the left–hand side of the dead end road. Here they had their benches with storage for small loose tools above the benches and for heavier tools below. Typically the tools held included spanners of different sizes, screwdrivers, hammers of different weight, hacksaws, hand drills and special tools for specific jobs, the latter often made by the fitters themselves. An example of a special tool was one to separate the piston from the crosshead. This was cylindrical and had a nipple at one end. It fitted into the crosshead after the fulcrum pin had been removed and came into contact with the end of the piston. A wedge incorporated into the cylindrical tool was then used to drive the piston out. Different size tools were required for each class of engine.

Each bench had a vice and a lathe that was turned by hand – no electricity was available. No personal lockers were provided but the men did have coat pegs. They also had chairs but no mess table. A round coal fired stove was provided which boiled their kettle and was used for cooking as well as for heating. Gas lighting illuminated the work.

The charge–man fitter had a small office next to the fitter's area in which he had a "counting house" style high desk with a hinged sloping top giving access to a storage area beneath. A high stool was provided. Two trunks were used to store the records he was required to keep and no form of heating was provided. Access to this office was from the fitter's area and which was separated from the dead end road by a partition wall. Nearby was a stacking frame used for storing superheater tubes and which were supplied in varying lengths. There was also an area where discarded brake shoes were stored. The pile of shoes was prevented from spilling out by planks that formed a temporary wall. Worn shoes were kept for emergency use in the event that replacement new shoes were unavailable from stores for a particular class of engine. One reason why brake shoes wore unevenly was due to the nature of the action of the vacuum brake on application. Engine drivers reported faults to the fitters by completion of a card describing the fault. A good driver was often able to record exactly what was required to remedy the fault. In common with other depots each engine not otherwise stopped for repairs was subject to a daily inspection which was carried out by the chargeman or the fitters. The results were recorded on a card kept for each engine and signed by the person who carried out the inspection. Typically this inspection involved a visual examination and also a sound test on certain parts using a hammer. One side of the engine and then the other would be examined and if applicable, the tender.

Of the examination itself, the connecting rods would first be checked for excessive side–play, if found to be in need of attention this would either be done when the engine was next due for a boiler wash out or immediately if the condition was judged detrimental to safety. This same policy was adopted for all faults that did not require to be urgently dealt with. After dealing with the connecting and coupling rods, the crosshead was then checked for side play and the integrity of the gudgeon pin confirmed. The gland nuts were checked, as were all other nuts. The underneath of the engine was also examined to check for any loose fittings and the springs inspected to ensure the leaves were free from cracks. The inside motion parts were likewise examined for signs of wear or damage. The wheels were then tapped to listen for faults that would become apparent by the sound that the hammer made. The tyres and flanges were checked by eye–sight and if any doubt existed of their worthiness then they were checked by a gauge. Again a specific gauge was required for each class of engine. Brake–blocks and the brake–rods were similarly inspected. On a tender loco similar checks were carried out on the running gear. The examination

then moved to the cab of the engine to check the injectors and gauge classes.

To assist the fitters and other men crossing over the pits between the rails they made use of wooden planks. To reach the upper parts of an engine ladders were not provided and instead the men made use of an open wooden frame that had a passing appearance to a wheelbarrow but without the barrow or wheel. Standing or sitting on it enabled them to work on the engine.

As well as daily inspections there were additional inspections based on mileage or time in steam. This ensured that each engine was subject to a comprehensive series of planned maintenance. To ensure this routine maintenance took place each engine had a history card. These cards were kept up to date by the chargeman fitter. Work carried out on an engine based at another depot was entered on a card and sent on to the home depot chargeman fitter to add to his history cards.

Most fitting and repair work was carried out in the shed but occasionally a fitter would be called to carry out running repairs at the platform line. In the dead end road in the engine shed was also a pit used to allow work under the engine or tender. This road was officially designated for repair work and it's access was controlled by the foreman fitter. Time–consuming jobs were always carried out on the dead end road. Work on valves and pistons and associated jobs could take 3 days whereas changing an IR (India Rubber) band in the vacuum cylinder took perhaps eight hours. Repair work was also carried out on the through road in the engine shed but usually only because it was convenient to do so as the engine concerned had perhaps been stopped for a boiler washout. The shed carried a variety of spare parts which were required on a regular basis such as brake

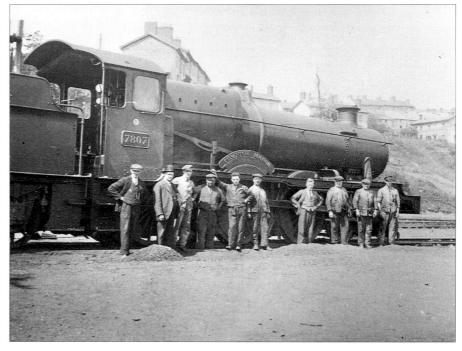

Neyland staff depicted alongside No. 7807 'Compton Manor', circa 1938/9 and which arrived new from Swindon in March 1938. Neyland also received 7803 'Barcote Manor' and 7816 'Frilsham Manor' in February 1938 and February 1939 respectively. The engines being replacements for the 'Bulldog' type. Alongside their new machine are left to right; Billy Conway – Foreman Fitter, Alf Jenkins – Shed Master, Sid Davis – Shed Chargehand, Evan Jones – Coal Stage. Sid Davies – Fitter, Charlie Griffiths – Fitters Mate, Mr. Lloyd. Timekeeper, Jim Davies – Fitters Mate, Wally Hansford – Fire Dropper and Bowen Griffiths – Engine Cleaner.

Brinley John

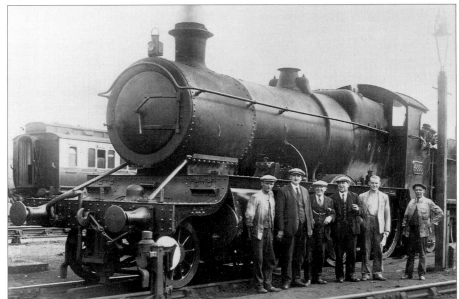

Mogul 2–6–0 No 4335 of Lot 194 was built at Swindon in October 1913 and withdrawn from Pontypool Road shed on November 14 1936. Some parts from this engine were incorporated into 4–6–0 No 6826 'Nannerth Grange'. Grange class engines were not allocated to Neyland but were visitors from Carmarthen, Llanelly and Fishguard. The men are left to right, W. Conway – Fitter, George Morgan – Driver, Jack Thomas– Clerk, Stanley Perkins – Clerk, Bill Rudge – Boilersmith, Bert Davidge – Carriage and wagon, in the cab are Ted Rees – Driver and Dan James – Fireman.

Brinley John

Inside the shed during BR days and with Neyland allocated engines 1029 'County of Worcester' on the fitter's road and 22xx No. 2283, the latter stabled where boiler washouts would take place. A hosepipe used in these operations is connected to a hydrant and water came from the hydraulic building via pipes laid underground. The fitters used the bench in front of 2283 as a platform when working on the tender or engine.

B.P. Hooper

shoes – different sizes according to the class of engine, washers, seals and steel packing for vacuum pumps. Asbestos would also be stocked as this was regularly used as a sealant on the outside steam pipes. Certain repairs could not be undertaken at Neyland because it was not equipped with any heavy lifting gear such as an overhead crane or sheerlegs. Thus it was not possible to remove wheels or replace axle–boxes and work of this nature was undertaken by prior arrangement at Carmarthen or Landore. Where possible the engine was also worked there under sometimes on a revenue earning turn, but there would also be occasions when the recourse had to made to it being towed 'dead'.

The lack of power tools or heavy lifting gear was often overcome by ingenuity and technique, but with the task understandably taking longer in the process. In this way springs could be removed from the engine or tender just using steel bars. To do so the engine or tender was placed over a pit and with the aid of a sling hung from the roof supports it was possible to lift the frame sufficiently for the spring to be eased out. Repairs to axle boxes were carried out using lifting jacks. Coupling rods were also rebushed with new bushes being ordered from Carmarthen and fitted at Neyland. The lack of equipment and the very heavy nature of the work often required close co–ordination between two men, hence the fitter worked closely with his mate. Some mates also took a closer interest in the work than others, accordingly although not formally trained they could undertake the more routine work of a fitter from having observed what had to be done. Working in tight spaces it was useful if the fitter or his mate were of slim build and not too tall.

An example of this was with the '1000' or 'County' class, of which several members were based at Neyland in the 1950's. Despite their large engine size there were a number of awkward areas in which it was often necessary to work,

'Dean Goods' No. 2413 circa 1930. The men are, left to right, Ben John – Shunter, Gilbert John – Carriage Cleaner, Bert Davidge Carriage Cleaner and Albert Blackmore – Driver.
Collec, Brinley John

including when access was required to the steam pipes at the front end. Unlike other classes this access was not through the smokebox door, but instead via a trap door between the frames of the engine and which was recalled as being a very tight squeeze.

The fitters were also responsible for checking for wear on the shoe of the Automatic Train Control equipment on engines. This was in addition to an electrician based at Carmarthen who visited Neyland at regular intervals to carry out inspections and any electrical repair work on the engine.

The fitters would also do straightforward maintenance work on the turntable at Neyland if required. Typically this would be to remedy a problem with the chain winding gear. Water crane repairs were not their responsibility, but they were responsible for maintaining the pumps at Westfield Mill. This equipment required minimal attention apart from packing the piston glands.

Mail vans forming the South Wales mail service await their next turn of duty and forming part of a train in the mileage siding. The two four–wheelers are the breakdown train vehicles. When required for emergency use any available locomotive would be used to haul them to the particular location. The lean too section of the engine shed was occupied by the fitters. The sand house and toilets are partly hidden by the 2–6–0 'Mogul'. On the opposite side of the building are a 'Manor' and another 'Mogul'. Behind this is a former 'ROD' 2–8–0.

Collec. D.K. Jones

The fitters also manned the breakdown train based at Neyland, which in common with other small depots was not provided with a crane. The breakdown train comprised two vehicles one fitted out with seats to carry the men but without messing facilities or sleeping accommodation. The other carried the tools and equipment, which remained on the vehicle ready for use. This equipment included hand operated jacks and suitable packing together with various steel sheets. In later years oxyacetylene cutting equipment was also provided. The breakdown vans carried a supply of small paraffin hand lamps that were placed around the site of work for necessary illumination. At Neyland, as other small depots the fitters and their mates were 'on call' as were the shed labouring staff and cleaners to form the breakdown gang. A gang usually comprised eight men although unless it was a major derailment only one fitter and his mate were normally required amongst the eight. If a gang could not be raised from the men on duty then a callboy was dispatched to find sufficient off duty men to make up the numbers. In spite of the difficult and dirty nature of the jobs undertaken no overalls were provided nor any eye or face protection.

Boilersmith

Neyland had one boilersmith and for many years this was Londoner, Billy Rudge. After Mr. Rudge retired Morgan Hughes took on the role. The boilersmith was also provided with a 'mate and for many years this position was occupied by Ivor James.

The boiler–smith also worked with, rather than under the control of the engine–shed foreman being instead answerable to the chargeman boilersmith based at Carmarthen Aside from care of the boilers of the engines allocated to Neyland he would also work on engines allocated to other depots, as directed. The normal working day commenced at 6 am and concluded at 2 pm but he was also on call to deal with any emergencies. On duty with him in addition to his mate, were two boiler washers, a man who looked after the boiler tubes, and two fire droppers.

At the start of the shift the boilersmith would examine the log of Neyland engines requiring boiler attention either because their periodic inspection was due or from a list of faults reported by the driver. For visiting engines requiring attention a list was provided by the

6309 and 3382, the latter an un–named 'Bulldog' at Neyland in 1936. The 'Bulldog' is also coupled to one of the 'intermediate' tenders and which looks somewhat out of place. The Bulldogs were the pride of Neyland shed before the advent of more powerful engines. Before the working day was reduced it was common practice for a driver to be allocated the same engine on a regular basis. In 'Behind the Steam' Driver John Thomas who was described as short in stature but a man of grim determination, had 3303 'St Anthony' as his regular engine. It is therefore of no surprise that in GWR minutes concerning the Strike of September 1918 the following was recorded, "On September 25th a large consignment of fish was dealt with at Milford Haven and Neyland and a special fish train ran to London. The exemplary conduct and work of engineman John Thomas in connection with this train is worthy of special mention. It appears that the Fish Merchants had offered either of the enginemen on strike at Neyland £20 to run the fish train. That was later increased to £40 without result. Engineman John Thomas of Neyland who had worked the down Mail train into Neyland at 2.16 pm volunteered to work the train after completing his own turn of duty. He refused any special reward from the traders and left working the fish turn at 4.40 pm." A considerable sum of money to turn down..   *Brinley John*

chargeman at Carmarthen. He then directed the men under his control to their tasks and later returned to inspect what had been done. Verification of work carried out was also undertaken by the Carmarthen chargeman who would visit on Wednesdays.

Where it was necessary to stop an engine for repair, or the repair overran its expected time, the boilersmith had to alert the shed foreman in order that the foreman could arrange for a replacement engine if required.

The boilersmith shared accommodation with the chargeman fitter. This consisted an old grounded carriage body near the coal stage. On entry there was a locker room and storage area with the coach partitioned to form a second room with a single large desk. This room was lit by electricity and was, in so far as Neyland railway facilities, unique in this respect. There was also a wash hand basin and a stove for heating as well as to the means to boil the all important kettle.

Engines requiring boiler examination were placed over the pit on the through road in the shed to allow access beneath the engine. They were first examined cold after the fire dropper had removed the fire and the steam exhausted from the boiler. If the engine also required attention from the fitters this work was undertaken when it was convenient to do so. The boilersmith had to ensure that the boilers were cleaned and in sound mechanical condition, in particular that the copper stays which held the inner and outer firebox passages apart were intact, the fusible plugs sound and the brick arch in good order. This required him to inspect each engine by going into the firebox through the firebox door. The procedure for this was to place a canvas sheet in front of the door and which then allowed him to slide his body through the narrow opening. He then reached back for his tools, principally a tapping hammer and which was used to check the integrity of the copper stays. When the hammer struck the stay and produced a dull sound this was a sign that the stay was damaged and needed replacement. Frequently the loss of a stay put pressure on the others and it was necessary to replace several of them at the same time. This was an awkward job with the old stay having to be drilled out to allow a new one to be fitted. It was also made more difficult when working on one side of the boiler because it was necessary to work "wacky–handed". The boiler–smith had a mirror on a pole to help to inspect awkward areas and a lamp. The lamp was carbide, and the beam of light was emitted from the end of a flexible tube, in this way it could be directed into the tubes and around the corners of the boiler.

The tube cleaner cleaned each boiler tube by first passing a long steel rod the length of the tube and then blowing them through using a steam pressure hose. He could tell if they were clear by the ease or otherwise of the rod passing down the tube or the action of the steam in the tube.

Confirmation was by a visual inspection. Hot water for boiler washing was obtained from the hydraulic building via underground pipes to valves in the shed. The hot water was introduced through the mud hole doors on the engine and then drained out carrying with it the scale and debris from the dirty boiler. The mud hole doors were then resealed and after inspection by the boilersmith, the covers bolted down. The boiler washer also removed the fusible plugs and after cleaning, these were refitted and inspected by the boilersmith. All in all a dirty and far from glamorous but nevertheless essential part of steam locomotive operation.

Where on inspection the brick arch was found to be faulty or had been reported as unsound by the driver this was pulled down and rebuilt. The firebricks were of different size and shape and fitted together in a set order being secured in place by a 'key brick' and fire cement which was mixed in a bucket to a prescribed consistency. Firebricks, stays and the ingredients for the cement were always available to be drawn from stores. Boiler tubes if not held locally, were ordered from Carmarthen by the depots stores clerk. The fitting of a replacement tube required two special tools as the tubes were held in plates at the firebox and smoke box ends. These plates contained holes through which the tubes were inserted and which held them in place. The tubes had to pass through the holes yet be a tight fit and so once fitted it was necessary to expand both of the ends. The tool required for this was barrel shaped with rollers. The ratchet action of the tool expanded the end of the tube until a tight fit was achieved and there was a protrusion of a quarter inch at each end. Another special tool was then used to form a lip flush with the throatplate and tubeplate. To remove a tube this lip had to be chiselled off at the throatplate end. A cold chisel was used to split the end and a special tool then used to knock the tube out and through to the smokebox where it then could be withdrawn.

Coalmen and Firedroppers

Coal was shovelled by hand on to the coal stage from a 20–ton loco coal wagon placed adjacent to it. Until 1938 this wagon was placed on the side nearest to the arrivals line but after this date on the opposite side. The coal was then shovelled from the stage into tubs. When loaded these tubs weighed half a ton and had to be winched by hand using an antiquated crane to the height of the tender or bunker where the other coalman had to man handle the tub into position before tipping its contents out. This was hard dirty work made somewhat easier in the last few years by the provision of a steam–powered crane. In 1938 the two coalmen worked 48 hours each week on each of two shifts 6 am to 2.30 pm and 5 pm to 1 am.

After an engine had completed its turn of duty it went to the sidings by the former cattle dock. At this location pits where provided for use by the fire droppers. If the engine was to be stopped for washout and inspection all the firebox

7811 'Dunley Manor' depicted in 1963. This engine had been allocated to '87H' – Neyland on March 4 1963 and was moved to Whitland on September 7 1963. Reading left to right the men are; on the footplate, Jim Warlow – Shedman, Ivor James – Boilersmith's Mate, standing, Hilliard James – Driver– acting Shed Foreman, Hubert Townsend – Coal stage, Fred Etherington – Shedman, Percy Evans – Driver, Albert Lloyd – Fitter, George Morgans – Driver, Harold Roberts – Shedman, W. Nicholls – Boiler Inspector Carmarthen, front, William Hughes – Shedman, Benny Gwilliam – Crane Driver coal stage and Billy Lawrence – Guard.

Aurora Imaging

contents would be removed, otherwise in was just the clinker and ashes. The cleaned fire was retained behind the fire box door for the fire raisers to use to build the fire ready for its next turn of duty and was known as saving the fire. The coal, ash and clinker which had been raked from the ash pans into the pit had then to be thrown from the pit up to ground level and then on to a wagon. Once the wagon was full it was sent away for disposal.

Engine Shed Foremen and Clerks

The shed foreman's office had a coal fired stove, a table, chair, a railway omnibus telephone, a wash hand basin and was gas lit. On his office wall was a large map showing the GWR. system extant in the 1930's. The foreman, who normally worked 8 am to 4 pm, prepared the daily roster sheets, arranged for cover in case of sickness or other absence and was responsible for conduct and discipline. With the chargeman fitter and boilersmith he ensured his allocation of engines received maintenance on a periodic basis and that locomotives were available for the booked turns of duty allocated to the Neyland's engines. He was also in charge of the sub sheds at Whitland, Pembroke Dock, Cardigan and Milford Haven although the day to day responsibility was delegated to the Chargeman at

Whitland and to senior drivers elsewhere. In later years the Foremen included Mr. Lovejoy and later Sid Tipton. At Neyland they were assisted on the running side by a chargeman working on standard eight hour shifts commencing at 6 am. If a chargeman was unavailable through holidays or sickness, his turns were either covered by the other chargemen working 12–hour turns or by drivers acting as relief. Latterly the chargemen were, Hilliard James, Sid Davies and Tommy Mount and assisted by Charlie Harries.

The foreman had two clerks, Jack Thomas, later Cyril Shortman, whose responsibilities were pay and stores, and Billy Lloyd, later Granville Roach, who saw to all other correspondence. The clerks occupied an office next to the foreman with the pay clerk working 7.30 am to 2 pm and his colleague 9 am to 4 pm. Each clerk had a desk and chair with the room heated by a coal–fired stove and illuminated by gas lamps. A window, opening out into the running shed, was situated behind one of the desks. It was to this window that the men employed in the locomotive department came on a Thursday to claim their weekly pay. Next to the clerks office was the storeroom and in charge of this latterly was Victor James. In the storeroom were drums of oil for cleaning and lubrication. Some of the drums were placed on horses (benches) to raise them off the floor which made it easier to draw off supplies. In the storeroom there were bales of waste for cleaning together with soap, emery paper and other regularly used items. When stores were required, the clerk made out a requisition note which was sent via the internal mail service. If an urgent requisition was necessary he would telephone his requirements using the omnibus phone. The code for the clerk's phone was 2 rings followed by 4.

Every Wednesday a stores van came by train and the storekeeper replenished his stocks from this. One important item always kept in stock was the footwear for the fire droppers. These were clogs having leather bodies and a wooden sole and which gave the best protection when walking on the hot coals.

The work of the pay clerk involved collecting the engine driver's tickets from a box located in his office. These tickets showed the time that the driver and his fireman booked on and off duty. The clerk recorded the details on a payroll order form 779, which was sent to Swindon where wages due were calculated and prepared pay packets forwarded to Neyland to be distributed each Thursday. The men were paid one week in arrears. A notice board on the shed wall by the clerk's office displayed the daily and weekly notices including the driver and firemen's rosters and speed restrictions both permanent and temporary.

In 1956 members of the GWR Enginemen and Firemen's Mutual Assurance, Sick and Superannuation Society based at Neyland were as listed

Engine Shed

Newly employed cleaners would learn their duties from the more senior cleaners and until reaching 18 years old they were not allowed to do night work. When cleaning engines the routine was to go to the stores to draw cotton waste and an allotted amount of engine oil, this together with brick dust and tallow was used in the cleaning process. Two cleaners were put on to an engine one either side of the footplate. Each cleaner worked to one of the three chargemen who showed them how to use a fireman's shovel, which on the G.W.R. had a blade longer than its handle, to prepare a fire and raise steam. W h e n raising steam from cold, firelighters would be used with coal being added until the fire was made. If it was necessary to raise steam quickly then live coals were taken from the sand house furnace. This required two men, one using a long handled scoop perforated round its circumference and who first dug the scoop into the fire. He then turned his back to the fire and with the handle

resting on some cotton waste on his shoulder removed the scoop and carried it to the engine. He then handed the scoop to a colleague waiting for him on the footplate who placed the contents into the firebox enabling a substantial fire to be rapidly built up.

A 10–ton truck of sand was left alongside the sand house which was a brick built building near the bottom end of the shed building. It was the duty of a cleaner to unload the sand from the wagon and into the storage area. Below where the sand was held was a large arched fire place and the cleaner had to ensure that a fire was maintained in good order to dry the sand used in the engine's sanding equipment. It was especially important to have a substantial fire available early on Monday morning, as it was the practice to use live coals to raise steam on the early turn engines. Adjoining the sand house were toilets; one section of which was divided off and used by the foreman and the shed clerks. The access door was kept locked.

Prospective cleaners were taken on at age 15 (before the 1930's the age limit was 14) and they had first to go to Swindon to undergo a medical examination.

Payroll	Driver	Payroll	Driver	Payroll	Fireman	Payroll	Fireman
1	K.G.	18	D.J.	41	J.F.	59	J.L.D.
2	F.J.	19	G.W.E.	42	W.J.	60	S.A.
3	L.C.	20	A.	43	P.J.R.	61	S.W.
4	V.J.	21	T.	44	C.K.	62	B.G.
5	W.J.	22	J.H.	45	A.C.R.	63	H.E.
6	G.	23	T.S.	46	A.C.G.	65	J.E.
7	W.J.	24	F.G.	47	J.J.	67	W.
8	A.G. Evans	25	F. Griffiths	48	D.J.	69	W.M.
9	I.J. Lewis	26	W.T. Harrison	49	R.	70	J.E.
10	W.G. Talbot	27	W.T. Hitchins	50.	K.A.	71	W.J.
11	H.V.	29	J.W.	51	I.C. Stone	72	D.S.
12	W.	30	C.G.H.	52	G.F.J.	73	R.L.A.
13	F.H. Howells	32	V.C. Rowe	53	W.G.	74	B.
14	W.H. Vaughan	33	W.A. Glass	54	D.M.	75	A.E.
15	L.T. Lewis	34	K.E. Owen	55	G. Howell	76	O.A.M. Richards
16	A.	35	N.J.	56	S.J.	77	D.J. Day
17	W.T.	36	J.W.	57	R.	79	R.J.
Shedmen 126 T.G. Perry ? S.A.G. Davies				58	F.C.H. Harries	83	D.P. Jones

Providing they passed they were then appointed.

Inevitably as a new cleaner they were given the worst jobs to start with, such as cleaning inside the firebox but as they gained experience they graduated to cleaning the exterior of engines and giving general assistance around the shed filling in for the shed labourers. They would also undertake callboy duties knocking up drivers and firemen for booked turns as well as when men were required to substitute for absent colleagues or for special workings. As cleaners they were encouraged to take an interest in the working of steam engines and eventually they would be allowed to undertake firing turns on the pilot engine that shunted the station and sidings at Neyland. An unusual duty performed was when each year some cleaners travelled to Westfield Mill to clean out the weeds from the millpond. This was necessary to prevent weeds fouling the pumps that supplied water to the reservoir on the hillside. Coal was delivered to the coal fired boilers for the pump house at the Mill by lorry from Neyland every two weeks.

At one time promotion to fireman was based on seniority but from the 1940's cleaners were considered for promotion on reaching their 17th birthday. This entailed a further visit to Swindon and another stringent medical examination, including an eyesight test and an examination on the rulebook. If successful this normally meant moving away from Neyland. Those wishing to return to Neyland then had to wait for a suitable vacancy.

Promotion to driver was based on seniority and it would help if a firemen had a sympathetic driver who would allow them to act as driver and so gain practical experience. Firemen would also be expected to attend the mutual im-

provement classes in their free time. When the time came they would be again called to Swindon to undertake a medical examination and a stiff examination on the rules by a locomotive inspector. This oral test also covered the working parts of an engine. If successful the advice often given by the inspector was to buy a reliable timepiece and always remember that the safety of passengers was in their hands. They were now classed as a passed fireman. This allowed them to be in charge of the engine and to undertake driving duties. For the hours they were acting as a driver they received a drivers rate of pay. These hours also counted towards seniority and a chance of being later promotion. Locally at Neyland there was little opportunity to take on driving duties unless covering for sick or holiday absence or special workings. Passed fireman then continued firing duties relying on a sympathetic driver to allow them to act as the driver and thus build up experience albeit on a fireman's rate of pay. Often passed firemen who were not able or prepared to move from Neyland had to wait years for promotion.

At Neyland the enginemen were formed into three links, Passenger, Fish, and Pilot. In the late 1950's or early 1960's firing turns recorded in a diary of a former fireman shows the following: 7.30 passenger, 2.40 passenger, 7.45 shed, 2.25 as passengers, or 6.00 am shed duties.

The turns worked also included covering shunting at other stations such as the Haverfordwest pilot which was a 7 am turn. The men on this were later relieved by a crew who rode in the guards brake van attached to the engine for the 2.15 pm Haverfordwest to Carmarthen Junction freight. This engine was on the front of the train as far as

Neyland allocated No. 1001 'County of Bucks' on the turntable and with the hydraulic in the background. Fitter Tommy Davis is walking towards the photographer. On the hillside are the railway owned properties in Lower High Street and Railway Terrace. In 1901 the rents at Neyland were 5/– per week and were amongst the cheapest on the GWR.

P. Chancellor

Johnston being banked by the engine, which took the 12.30 pm train to Milford Haven. The early turn Haverfordwest pilot men returned to Neyland as passengers. Other duties recalled are the 12.20 pm fish empties to work the 12.30 pm to Milford Haven and then 3.20 pm Fish, the 10.40 passenger returning to shed at 3.00 pm. There was also a turn for the sleeper from Milford Haven as far as Carmarthen.

In the pilot link, which covered shunting at Neyland and Haverfordwest there were at least seven turns including spare turns each lasting a week. Duty sheets were posted on the shed notice board each day and showed the following days work. On spare turns the men could be fetched to work by a callboy two hours either side of their booked starting time. Spare turns were booked at 6 am, 8 am and 2 pm. Drivers were required to undertake any job providing they had signed that they had the knowledge covering the route of the train for the time that they would be in charge of the engine. This knowledge had to be mastered in daylight and at night. To gain this a driver was given a set number of weeks to learn each route and would do so by travelling on the footplate of an engine, in addition to the normal engine crew, noting and learning the position of all signals along the route and critically the position of all trap or catch points. They had to understand the route each signal arm controlled and the track layouts at stations or yards. Where the track layout or route was complex they would walk the route as this gave them more time to study it in detail. In addition they had to aware of the gradient of the line and the position of whistle boards and level crossings.

The furthest travelled by Neyland crews on goods

Neyland Engine Turns March 1938

Engine type	Duty	Engine type	Duty
Grange	Goods	43xx	Pasgr.
Grange	Goods	43xx	Goods
Manor	Goods	43xx	Goods
Bulldog	Goods	43xx	Goods
Bulldog	Shunting	43xx	Goods
30xx	Goods	43xx	Goods
26xx	Goods	43xx	Goods
43xx	Passgr.	43xx	Special
43xx	Passgr.	Note; Not all involved allocated to	loco turns engines Neyland.

workings in the 1950's was Llanelly, whilst with fish trains it was Landore. On passenger turns Carmarthen was their normal limit except for the Sunday Mail train which they worked to Swansea High Street station. Here they turned their engine on the turntable and worked home light engine. Before the 1940's Neyland footplate men had regular passenger turns to Swansea and double home turns had taken them as far as Gloucester on fish trains but such turns had ceased during, or just after the end of the Second World War.

Based on the working time table for 1958 and the recollections of the men the turns booked for Neyland crews or other depots are shown as follows: –

8.00 am Class 'A' Neyland to Paddington arr. 3.10 pm.
On this turn the Neyland engine and men worked to Carmarthen. Here another engine and crew took the train forward. The Neyland men turned their engine and waited the arrival of the 6.20 am Newport passenger train. They took this train to Neyland where on arrival the fireman uncoupled and after the coaches had been removed by the station pilot they took the engine to the shed. The fire–dropper cleaned the fire while the crew took the opportunity to make tea in the driver's cabin. They returned to their engine and took on further coal ensuring that large lumps were broken up and trimmed the tender to ensure the load was safe. The driver oiled round the engine and once the preparation had been concluded they turned the engine and took it to the departure platform and coupled to the coaches forming the 2.30 pm train to Paddington. They were relieved at the platform by the crew booked for the 2.30 pm working. The driver then completed his ticket giving details of the work that he and his fireman had undertaken and if necessary filled out a card reporting any faults on the engine. The crew worked this duty for a week and often retained the same engine unless it had to be stopped for its boiler washout.

9.55 am Class 'B' Passenger to Milford Haven
The Neyland engine and crew worked to Johnston where they uncoupled and ran round their train. They hen re–coupled and working tender first, took the train to Milford Haven. Arriving at 10.35 am they uncoupled and ran round the train and re–coupled. They departed at 11.10 am and took the train as far as Carmarthen. Here they were uncoupled and a fresh engine and crew took the train to Paddington for arrival at 5.00 pm. After turning the engine on the triangle at Carmarthen Junction they took over the 8.55 am Paddington to Neyland passenger train from Carmarthen at 2.30 pm arriving back at Neyland at 3.58 pm.

10.35 am Class 'B' Passenger to Carmarthen due at 11.58 am.
This was the return working for a Carmarthen crew and their engine off the 5.34 am Yeovil fish empties and often worked by a Hall class engine.

11.00 am Class B Passenger to Milford Haven arrive 11.32 am depart 12.05 pm to Paddington arrive 7.20 pm
Neyland engine and men worked this turn as far as Carmarthen
2.15 pm Neyland men with engine to Milford Haven arrive 2.42 pm. Depart 3.20 pm Fish Train to Carmarthen
Neyland engine and men to Milford Haven via Johnston. Fish train with a goods guard brake van taken as far as Carmarthen Town where the train less the guards brake van handed over to the LMS (later LMR). The Neyland men with their engine and the brake van then proceeded to Carmarthen Junction where they cut the brake van off and turned their engine on the triangle and under the guidance of the shunter entered the complex of sidings. The down sidings at Carmarthen were numbered consecutively from the

Siding	Used for	Capacity
1	Traffic for Carmarthen, Aberystwyth and	18
2	Traffic for Haverfordwest, Milford Haven and	33
3	Cripple wagons, 7.00 am to 5.00 pm and traf-	32
4	Traffic for Fishguard	32
5	Traffic for Whitland and branches	27
6	Traffic for Sarnau and St. Clears	23
7	General	10
8	Approach to cattle wagon cleaning sidings	10

down goods running loop line as follows:–
Having coupled, they worked the 5.55 pm Class 'J' to Neyland which allowed the men and their engine to return home.
2.30m Class 'A' Passenger to Paddington arrival at 10.05 pm
This was booked for the same engine as the 8.00 am turn. Neyland men worked as far as Carmarthen Town, uncoupled and a fresh engine took the train forward with the Neyland crew turning their engine on the triangle at Carmarthen Junction and returning to the Town station. They then awaited the arrival of the 11.55 am Class 'A' passenger to Pembroke Dock which arrived and its own engine uncoupled. Once this had drawn clear and the road was set, they coupled–up and departed with this train at 5.21 pm as far as Whitland where their engine was uncoupled and pulled forward to allow the engine of the Pembroke Dock portion to couple up and to depart at 5.54 pm. The Neyland crew then backed their engine down onto the remaining coaches and departed to Milford Haven, this time as a Class 'B' working, arriving at 6.57 pm. Here they uncoupled their engine and ran round the coaches and coupled back up. At 9.00 pm they departed running tender first to Clarbeston Road arriving at 9.31 pm. They uncoupled their engine and ran round the coaches and coupled up. They were booked to make a connection with the 3.45 pm Paddington to Fishguard Harbour passenger train due at 10.00 pm. They departed at 10.17 pm and arrived at Neyland at 10.46 pm. This train was known to the local railway men as "The Cork", harking back to the days of the Irish Ferries. If there were spare men at Neyland they provided relief at Johnston and worked the train to Milford Haven and to Clarbeston Road etc.
3.30 pm Class 'C' Engine and Passenger brake van to Milford
This ran as required with a Neyland engine and crew via Johnston to Milford Haven. They departed at 5.20 pm with the Class 'A' fish train for Paddington due at 1.20 am. The Neyland men worked as far as Llanelly and left the engine coupled to the train upon arrival at 7.08 pm. They reported to the foreman at Llanelly engine shed and were booked to prepare an engine. After this they telephoned the control office at Swansea and if there was no available return working they returned to Neyland as passengers on the 3.55 pm Paddington arriving at Neyland at 10.46 pm where they booked

off.
3.50 pm Milford Haven to Severn Tunnel Junction Class 'C' Fish Train
Neyland men worked the train as far as Landore due in at 5.55 pm. A fresh crew was waiting and took the train onwards with the engine returning the next day as a light engine working if no balancing work could be found. The Neyland crew would then hitch a lift on an engine from Landore to Swansea High Street station. Here they telephoned control and if there was no work for them returned as passengers on the 1.55 pm Paddington to Pembroke Dock departing Swansea at 7.01 pm and arrived at Neyland at 9.35 pm on what was known by local railway men as "The Cheap". Prior to 1940 and in the days of double home working, this duty had involved a Neyland crew working the train as far as Severn Tunnel Junction before coming off and running light to Cardiff. Here they booked off and went to their lodgings. Next day they worked back to Neyland with their engine.
4.25 pm Class 'B' Passenger to Cardiff General arriving at 9.36 pm
Neyland engine and men worked this service to Carmarthen Town arriving at 5.59 pm. Here they uncoupled and turned the engine on the triangle or sometimes used the turntable at the engine shed. Their return working was on the 1.55 pm Paddington to Pembroke Dock due at 7.59 pm. The Neyland engine coupled on to the rear of the coaching stock and departed at 8.05 pm arriving at Whitland at 8.28 pm. The Whitland shunter was waiting and uncoupled behind the engine which then drew forward and allowed the engine of the Pembroke Dock portion to back down and couple up It departed at 8.36 pm after which the Neyland men backed their engine on to the remaining coaches and after being coupled up departed at 8.52 pm arriving at Neyland at 9.35 pm.
4.35 pm Class 'C' Parcels to Paddington booked to arrive at 3.20 am
This was worked by a Neyland engine and crew with the men working to Felin Fran due to arrive at 8.17 pm. They awaited the arrival of the 12.45 pm Class 'C', Old Oak Common fish empties due at 8.41 pm and in charge of a (Swansea) Landore crew. The Neyland men were booked away at 8.51 pm and due in at Neyland at 12.35 am. This was the return working of the engine of the previous days 3.50 pm fish train
6.50 pm Class 'A' Mail and Passenger to Paddington
Carmarthen engine and men, Monday to Saturday inclusive. Neyland engine and men Sundays only. This train carried a Post Office van to Bristol, although until at least 1952 the van ran to Paddington.
7.50 pm Class 'C' Parcels to Cardiff due at 2.45 am
Carmarthen engine and men, the return working "off" the 10 am Cardiff Parcels due Neyland 5 pm.
8.50 pm Class 'B' Passenger to Johnston arriving at 8.50 pm.
Return working by Milford Haven men of the branch train. Normally this ran between Milford Haven and Johnston where it made a connection with trains to and from Neyland. The branch train provided this service whilst the main line train ran to Milford Haven. (See the 2.30 pm working above.)

Recollections are also that Neyland enginemen worked all the freight trains in and out of Neyland. As the timetable did not always provide the opportunity to change over trains en–route it appears that some turns involved riding "on the cushions" to or from the point when they took over the train working. In total it appears that in the 1950's Neyland had seven passenger turns, five parcels / fish turns, and seven freight turns. In addition there were four pilot turns – two each at Neyland and Haverfordwest and at least three spare shed turns at Neyland. Where the time on these turns did not occupy a normal eight hour day the men undertook shed duties.

The first driver and fireman came on duty at about 4 am (known as "early shed"). They took engines that had arrived at Neyland and needed to face in the opposite direction to the turntable where they also took water. In addition they also prepared engines required for duty that morning. These included the engine for the Llandilo Junction goods and usually a 63xx, the Haverfordwest pilot, a tender engine either a 63xx or 22xx, the Neyland pilot turn, usually a pannier tank engine, and often No 3654 although on occasions 'Prairie' tanks were also observed on this work.

The driver and fireman normally started work one hour before the booked departure time of a passenger train to enable them to prepare the engine. In winter months they booked on duty 30 minutes earlier as this enabled the engine to be coupled to the coaching stock and provide heat as necessary. Neyland was code '167' and 'NEY' in G.W.R. days with this designation painted on the running plate in the usual GWR position. In BR days Neyland engines carried '87H' on a plate attached to the smoke box door.

Main Line Services Operated by Neyland Engines –Winter 1958/9

Turn	Engine type	Days	From	To	Train	Men
NEY 1	County	TThS	Swansea	Cardiff	12.40 Carmarthen – Cheltenham	CDF 258
		TThS	Cardiff	Neyland	1035 Kensington –Neyland	LLY 258 NEY 307
NEY 2	County	M–S	5.20 Milford	Cardiff	5.20 Milford – Paddington	NEY 306 LLY 100
NEY 200	County	M–F	4.35 Neyland	Felin Fran	4.35 Neyland – Paddington	NEY 307 LLY 334
NEY 201	County	M–S	8.00 Neyland	Carmarthen	8.00 Neyland – Paddington	NEY 300
		M–S	Carmarthen	Neyland	6.20 Newport – Neyland	NEY 300
		M–S	2.30 Neyland	Carmarthen	2.30 Neyland – Paddington	NEY 303
NEY 220	43XX	M–S	Carmarthen	Whitland	8.55 Paddington – Pembroke Dock	NEY 308
NEY 221	43XX	MWF	Carmarthen	Whitland	8.55 Paddington – Pembroke Dock	CARM 330
		MWF	6.50 Neyland	Carmarthen	6.50 Neyland – Paddington	CARM 330

The curving side of the shed is well emphasized in this 1930's official view. A smoke pall also hangs over the town but there did not ever seem to have been any complaints from the residents. As can be seen, the principal constituent of the depot was timber and it must be no small wonder that it did not catch fire at some time over the years. According to several staff though, it was a close run thing on a few occasions&..!

NRM GWR B.Box 161/20

Engines allocated to Neyland

1921 (20)
756, 1427, 2622, 3303, 3315, 3326, 3378, 3382, 3408, 3422, 3432, 3453, 3454, 4352, 5379, 5394, 5395, 5396, 5397, 5398.

1934 (20)
2618, 3011, 3397, 3400, 3435, 3437, 3447, 4311, 4331, 4340, 4352, 4356, 4382, 4399, 5347, 6310, 6315, 6336, 6345, 6389.

1947 (19)
3654, 3447, 4358, 5310, 5353, 5357, 5368, 5372, 5392, 6347, 6355, 6371, 6389, 7306, 4937, 4957, 4997, 5929, 7816.

1950 (21)
3654, 1001, 1009, 1020, 4358, 5310, 5353, 5357, 5368, 5372, 5392, 6347, 6355, 6371, 6389, 7306, 4908, 4957, 4982, 4997, 7816.

1956 (45) Now including the sub depots at Whitland, Pembroke Dock, Milford Haven and Cardigan.
1001, 1020, 1027, 1029, 1601, 1611, 1637, 2220, 2228, 2229, 2263, 2283, 2288, 3654, 4654, 4699, 5748, 8738, 8739, 9652, 9714, 4132, 6105, 8102, 8107, 4519, 4550, 4556, 4557, 4558, 4576, 4579, 4594, 5513, 5520, 5549, 5550, 5324, 5357, 5372, 6347, 7306, 7318, 9318, 5903.

1961 (40) – again included the sub depots.
1014, 1020, 1027, 1613, 1648, 1666, 1669, 2220, 2283, 3624, 3639, 3654, 3678, 4654, 4699, 8738, 8739, 4107, 4122, 4159, 5193, 6114, 6125, 4557, 4558, 4569, 5520, 5549, 5550, 5357, 7306, 7318, 7320, 7340, 6610, 6623, 6627, 82008, 82042, 82044.

Inside the single road shed looking to the double road section and in the direction of the station on July 7 1958. Two engines, a 63xx and a 22xx repose in the sunlight. A suitcase is next to the door leading to the clerk's office. The water column was fed via an underground pipe from the hydraulic building. The gloomy interior made the work of the fitters and shed staff more difficult and the general working conditions would not be permitted by current health and safety regulations. Several proposals were made to replace the antiquated building but it remained until the end of steam in 1963. .

R.M. Casserley

A private owners coal wagon belonging to Messrs. Baldwins stands in the mileage siding used by the local coal merchants. Behind the coal wagon was the shed foreman's office and to the left the drivers cabin. Recorded as allocated to Neyland in 1936 were 'Aberdare' 2–6–0 No. 2640, Ex 'ROD' 2–8–0's Nos. 3002, 3006, 3009, 3010, 3011 and 3015, 'Bulldog' 4–4–0 Nos. 3382, 3435 and 3447, and 'Mogul' 2–6–0's' 4340, 4363, 4399, 5371, 6302, 6309, 6310, 6331, 6385 and 6391. May 31, 1936.

Authors Collec.

A superb study of 1020 'County of Monmouth' ready to come off shed at Neyland and in seemingly ex–works condition.
P.J. Kelley

The oil gas retort building with a tar wagon in the siding. According to an old plan, just beyond the gas works towards the Rock sidings there had at one time been what was referred to as a signal box. Its size though suggests it was more likely a ground frame which may have controlled the entry to Rock sidings and the turntable. The provision of a ground frame was necessary where the sidings were too far to be controlled from the signal box. With advances made in mechanical signalling the function of this ground frame was taken over by Neyland signal box. The Mogul 2–6–0 is on No 5 siding used to form up the 4.35 pm parcels to Cardiff.

Brinley John

Utilities – Water Supplies

To provide water for the station buildings and the railway owned houses, engine shed and other facilities, the GWR. built a reservoir on a hillside at Westfield Mill and a pump house constructed on ground close by the railway line from Johnston to Neyland. This pump house was 36 foot by 12 foot with a curved corrugated roof. It housed two vertical boilers and a vertical engine. Outside was a coal store served by a lorry that delivered coal from Neyland. Water flowed by gravity to Neyland through a pipeline which followed the track bed and which from time to time sprang leaks due to the movement of trains along the line. At Neyland the water fed the hydraulic building and the water cranes used by the locomotives. The water was not filtered or treated and with rising health standards was unsuitable for drinking water. In the 1930's a satisfactory supply was obtained for the town by a pipeline from a reservoir in the Preseli Hills. The GWR entered into an agreement with Neyland Urban District Council on 25 March 1939 for the council to supply the station and yard with a minimum of 47,000 gallons every 24 hours. It must have exceeded this amount as correspondence from the Chief Mechanical Engineer's department Swindon to Neyland UDC dated 25 March 1943 sought the council confirmation that it intended to restrict the supply to 68,000 gallons per day. On this basis the railway stated that it would bring into use the Westfield Mill plant which was not suitable as drinking water and accordingly it would be necessary to connect the station with the council's drinking water supply. With the Westfield Mill plant in operation the amount to be drawn from the council would be far less than the 68,000 gallon maximum.

Water cranes supplying the locomotives were provided between the two lines to the turntable when sited at the Rock and at the bottom end of the sheds. Inside the sheds were two further watering points. When the turntable was re–sited near the hydraulic building in 1939, a water crane was provided between the entry road and the line to the turntable. which was capable of supplying engines on either line.

Gas

The gas works and gasholders were constructed early in the station's history appearing on a plan attributed to 1863. There were two separate buildings one for coal gas and the other oil gas. The coal gas building was 44 feet by 18 feet wide with a curved roof having a maximum height of 26 feet. In the building was a bank of 5 compressors, a meter house with a capacity of 3600 cubic feet per hour, purifiers a coal store, and 2 retort benches. There was also a tar well 21 feet in diameter and 9° feet deep. Outside this building was an over head tar tank 28 feet long with a diameter of six feet and with a connection for a travelling railway tank wagon which could be filled from the siding running past this and the oil gas–house. The two buildings were 36 feet

The gas works built by the GWR with the oil gas retort house to the right and behind the coal wagons. The coal gas retort house is behind the three "loco" coal wagons . The tank behind the first coal wagon was used to store tar, a by–product of gas production.

NRM GWR B.Box 161/23

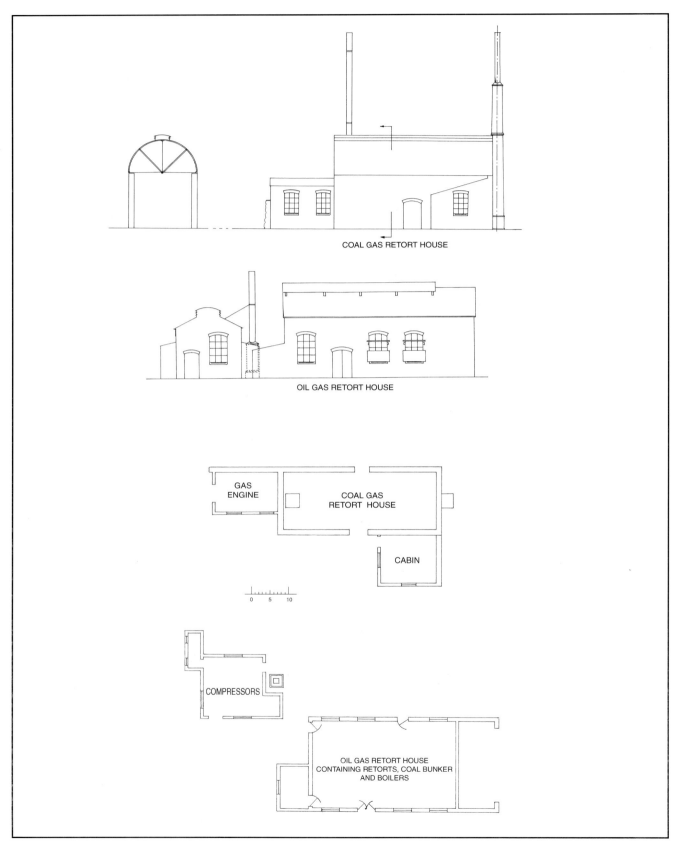

COAL GAS RETORT HOUSE

OIL GAS RETORT HOUSE

GAS ENGINE

COAL GAS RETORT HOUSE

CABIN

0   5   10

COMPRESSORS

OIL GAS RETORT HOUSE
CONTAINING RETORTS, COAL BUNKER
AND BOILERS

was a fixed hand crane capable of lifting 30 cwt. at a 12–foot radius.

The oil gashouse measured 53 feet by 18 feet and a height of 27 feet. There was a cabin at the rear of the main building used as a mess room. The oil house contained a low–pressure gasholder with a capacity of 2,000 cubic feet. The building housed four compressors, a meter house capable of supplying 1,200 cubic feet per hour, two vertical boilers, a retort bench, coal bunker, condensers, scrubbers, and two underground oil tanks both of six foot diameter one 20 and the other 21 feet long. Outside were high–pressure oil gas reservoirs two of four–foot diameter one 17 and the other 20 feet long.

The gas works supplied gas to the station buildings, yard lights and railway owned houses as well as the South Wales Hotel. Gas was not generally available to the other homes or businesses because the Pembroke Dock Gas Company had not fulfilled its prospectus commitments. The GWR. at the behest of Neyland U.D.C. agreed to supply gas to the Pembroke Dock company and did so until 26 September 1927 when the G.W.R. leased to the Council certain land and the gas works. As part of the agreement the council had to supply oil gas to the railway. This obligation resulted in an annual loss to the council and they were released from it by an agreement of 3rd December 1934. This provided for the council to pay an annual sum of £40 for a maximum 10 year period commencing 1 January 1935, or shorter, if the GWR. ceased to use oil gas upon their trains west of Llanelly. This annual payment was the subject of correspondence, with the council seeking to be released but the outcome is not recorded. The gas works continued to supply town gas until a pipeline from Milford Haven came into operation in 1939.

A report in 1910 of the staff employed by the Locomotive, Carriage and Signal department's records that of the 79 men at Neyland, three men were employed in gas manufacture. On the hillside near to the Iron Bridge a house was provided for the manager of the gas works which was occupied in 1938 by Mr Williams. One of the men employed at this time was Mr Tom Evans a Welsh Rugby International who on the closure of the gas works obtained employment on the railway at Neyland. Coking coal came from the South Wales coalfields and was shunted into the gas works sidings by the Neyland pilot engine.

The 1926 coaching programme shows that the 7 pm perishable and milk train from Neyland to Cardiff General conveyed a gas tank wagon, known by the railway telegraph code as a cordon, as far as Llanelly. Its return working is not shown. This working suggests that Neyland UDC were no longer supplying the GWR with oil gas. The working of cordons was a feature of Neyland into the 1950's supplying gas for the stoves in the guard's compartments of coaching stock.

The two Gasometers were at the Johnston end the yard with Neyland woods behind.   NRM GWR B.Box 161/24

A 56xx 0–6–2T stands on the holding road with the departure line immediately to it's right. In later years this class of engine was stationed at Neyland and used on the station truck goods to Neath. Immediately in the foreground the stack of used engine brake shoes awaits collection. The turntable is immediately beyond the hydraulic building and which housed two stationary boilers. One of these was continuously kept in steam to provide hot water for boiler wash outs. It was a job for the cleaners to look after the stationary engine and was often a useful first experience at raising and maintaining steam.

Brinley John

Chapter 6
THE TRAFFIC DEPARTMENT

Station Master

During the post war years, the Station Master's duties were to roster the guards to cover the booked train workings and also for special workings, holiday and sick absences. This was done in consultation with the men's trade union representatives. He also supervised the men under his control seeing to conduct and disciplinary issues and dealt with interviews for vacancies he was authorised to fill. The Divisional Office at Swansea held the staff personal records. He had to answer all correspondence concerning the running of the station – apart from the engine shed. As an experienced man he would be well versed in the rules and regulations being on call to deal with any problems which might arise. His normal hours were 9 am to 5 pm but he often called in for an hour in the early evening. He worked Saturday mornings but was not on duty on Sundays. Christmas was the time he could expect to earn overtime because of the extra parcels and postal workings that required supervision. During holidays, a relief stationmaster was organised by Swansea but if no one was available then the station clerk covered his absence.

Economies were being sought by the GWR in the late 1930's and as stationmaster posts at smaller stations were dispensed with the duties were combined with another location. Accordingly the Neyland post holder of the time, Mr. Winter, took over responsibility for Johnston station. In practice he would spent most of the day there, leaving the clerk in charge at Neyland. On returning later that afternoon he would deal with any paperwork or matters arising. This arrangement continued with Mr. Winter's successor, and whose name is unfortunately not reported, but who came from Saundersfoot. After he took early retirement the arrangements continued during the initial tenure of his successor, Mr. Jones. However the separate post at Johnston was later resurrected, it is said after an incident at Johnston involving a missing barrel of oil. Railway Detectives based at Fishguard investigated the disappearance following a claim made against the company. The barrel was eventually discovered in the checker's cabin being used as a seat!

The stationmasters from 1856 were Messrs: H. Bessant, W. Halford, W.I. Gray, W. Davies, J.W. Berry, H.A. Hare, W.E. Winter, 'A.N. Other', D. Jones, E. Dummer and finally leading up to closure, G.W. House.

Station Porters

There were two porters and, if the positions were filled, two additional lad porters. The shifts varied over the years but were typically: 7 am to 3 pm and 3 pm to 11 pm. On arriving at the station the early shift porter had to go to the signal box to collect the keys to the station building. He then opened up and if necessary lit the gas lamps both in the station building and on the platform. Next he checked to see if the late turn porter from the previous evening had left any messages which required follow–up action. He then telephoned the signal box to enquire as to the running of the first passenger train of the day and when it might be expected. If there was sufficient time before its arrival he made a start on the daily tasks. The fire in the stationmaster's office was prepared and lit and this office cleaned. After this the Booking and Parcels offices were cleaned. A fire was prepared and lit in the Booking Office as well as in the Booking hall. The Booking hall and Ladies Waiting rooms were cleaned but a fire was not lit in the latter because it saw little use.

The porter issued tickets until the clerk arrived and met all the passenger and parcels trains, collecting tickets, assisting passengers with any luggage and collecting parcels. Parcels received were taken to the Parcels office where they were booked in the Ledger. Outgoing parcels and luggage in advance would be taken to the train by the porter and handed over to the guard.

The porters were also responsible for watering of the water tanks of lavatory fitted incoming coaching stock. Modern coaches were fitted with an external pipe which allowed the water in the reservoir to be replenished at platform level by use of a hose–pipe. A lot of the older GWR design coaches though were not equipped in this manner and the watering of the coaches became a two man operation. One man then had to climb on to the roof and insert a hosepipe into the reservoir whilst the other stayed on the platform and turned the water supply on and off. Lad porters were not supposed to climb on the roof because it was a potentially hazardous operation especially in wet or icy conditions. However this requirement was not always adhered too. On one occasion a lad porter fell from the coach roof breaking an arm and a shoulder blade and was off work for many weeks. This incident in common with other 'minor accidents' was dealt with locally without the need for an enquiry by the Divisional Superintendent at Swansea. This avoided and questions being raised about unauthorised practices and a black–mark on the record of those concerned.

The lad porters would assist in collecting tickets and meeting trains. A principal duty was the collection of tail lamps from the coaching stock held in the various sidings. These were taken back to the station, cleaned, their wicks trimmed and if required filled with paraffin, the supply being contained in a 50 gallon drum in the lamp hut on the platform. They labelled coaching stock using paper destination labels that were stuck on to the windows of the coaches in a prominent position. Because there was little goods traffic at Neyland there was no designated goods porter these

The rear of the signal box with the engine shed beyond. The up main line ran immediately in front of the 'box. Following the General Strike of 18/19 August 1919, it was recorded in GWR Minutes that, "...Station master Mr. Davies was awarded one guinea gratuity for performing duties in the signal box in recognition that he remained on duty throughout although subjected to abuse by an angry and threatening crowd." Also R. Jones, Foreman, who did spend duty at Neath for three days, was awarded two guineas when his weekly wage was £2 15s. J. W Wager, acting Shed Foreman at Neyland for, "...looking after the engine sheds at Neyland and Pembroke", was also awarded two guineas when his weekly wage was £3 10s. The record of the events for those days also stated that the 10.50 am and 9.15 pm Paddington to Neyland trains were combined for part of the journey with services destined for Penzance.

duties being undertaken by the lad porter. Another duty that often fell to the lad was to change any gas mantles in the offices and in the lamps on the platform. After trains had arrived and terminated he would walk through each coach closing windows and checking for any personal effects which had been left behind.

Besides the daily routines including sweeping the platform and keeping the station tidy there were other tasks which were under–taken from time to time including keeping the fire buckets topped up with sand and painting the white line along the platform edge. This was a safety measure introduced during the Second World War to assist passengers during darkness in not stepping beyond this line and running the risk of falling on to the track.

Unlike a number of other stations a Porter's room was not provided and instead the staff made use of the parcels office. In the late 1940's only one set of wet weather clothing was provided for the porters and was supplied to fit a man of medium build. This situation was not remedied until after Nationalisation.

The routine of the afternoon shift was similar to the early turn in meeting trains, and, after the Clerk had finished work, selling tickets. The station was closed after the arrival of the last passenger train known to the railway men as 'The

Cork'. This was due in at 10.30 pm, and its unofficial title lay in the heyday of Neyland's Irish boat traffic. After the last passengers had left the station, the porter extinguished the station and platform lights and locked up the station, returning the keys to the signal box.

Station Clerk

In the early 1920's there had been three clerks – subsequently reduced to two and then by 1929 reduced to one. At this time the clerk was not permitted to work on a Sunday as this entailed overtime payments. His rates being more expensive than that of the first class porter and checker who took it in turns to man the booking office on alternate Sundays. The clerk commenced duty on Monday at 7.30 am, in order to complete the books with Sunday's figures and balance the cash. He then ensured that the cash was placed in the travelling safe on the 8.00 am train. He had an hour lunch break at mid–day and a half–hour tea break in the afternoon and finished work after booking the mail which left at 6.30 pm. On Tuesdays through to Saturdays he booked on at 9 am and finished after the mail with the same meal breaks as a Monday. On Wednesday he took his half–day in the afternoon. Interestingly in 1929 the rate books for calculating charges from when the station had been called New Milford were still extant. During this period a single milk churn was sent daily by Mr. Davies who brought it to the station, occasionally he also dispatched rabbits.

About 1940 the clerks' post was abolished when Neyland and Johnston reverted to having separate stationmasters but subsequently due to the pressure of work the position was restored. There was also a senior clerk at Neyland in the early 1950's. He was under the control of the stationmaster and was assisted from time to time by a junior clerk, a post filled by a school leaver. The senior clerk worked 7.30 am to 4 pm or from 10.30 am to 7 pm alternate weeks on a Mondays to Saturdays inclusive basis. A half–day was taken each week either on a Wednesday or Saturday afternoon which he alternated with the junior clerk. When working a half–day this shift was from 7.30 am to 12 noon.

The junior clerk normal hours were 9 am to 5 pm and in 1953 the starting salary at aged 16 was £151 per annum for a 42 hours working week. The junior clerk duties were to assist his senior and at Neyland he would also learn the full range of station duties, passenger, parcels and goods, unlike at larger stations where the work was sufficient to warrant men who specialised in one of these areas of work. Each week he wrote out the pay bill for the operating side and which entailed entering the details for between 55 to 60, people including their PAYE tax code. These comprised: 12 passenger guards, 14 goods guards, 17 carriage cleaners, three signalmen, a Relief Signalman, three shunters, a Relief Shunter, Mrs. Harrison – Crossing Keeper at Westfield Mill, two porters and one lad porter.

Once a week he would visit the local Post Office to purchase stamps to stick on the National Insurance cards, a cheque for this being received from the Operating Superintendents office at Swansea to cover this outlay. He did not though undertake many ticket sales and which were the province of the senior clerk and the leading porter, but otherwise he assisted in all other duties including the 'Coal sales to staff scheme', for those in railway service prior to 1948.

It was the responsibility of the senior clerk to order wagon loads of coal from Swindon for sale to staff. An invoice accompanied the wagon and which was hauled free of charge. The clerk would then work out the cost per ton. In addition he calculated the cartage charge from the station to each man's home for the amount they had purchased and raised an invoice. The coal was sold to the men, including those who had retired from railway service, at a preferential rate. In an average year this could involve between 12 to 14 wagonloads delivered to Neyland. Additionally, and on average twice a year, he ordered from the Permanent Way Divisional office at Neath, wagon loads of old railway sleepers cut into blocks. In the same way as for coal he worked out the costs and raised an invoice; the lorry driver collecting the amount due and paying this over to the clerk.

Lost property was a significant area of work simply because all trains terminated at Neyland. Aside from the lad porter the carriage and wagon cleaners would also walk through the coaches and remove items left behind. Umbrellas and books were the commonest items, and occasionally clothing and money. These were handed to the clerk who entered each item in the lost property register and stored them until claimed or until the end of the stipulated period when they were sold, the proceeds being recorded. In the event of their owner claiming them, the item was sent by rail to the nearest railway station to the claimant, together with an invoice raised at Neyland to cover the cost of the carriage. The local station that sent a credit note to Neyland but retained the money collected.

Luggage sent in advance was another significant area of work during the holiday season and another seasonal traffic was sugar beet. Wagon loads were sent to the sugar beet factory for processing, farmers being encouraged to use the railways by the Government who subsidised the transport costs by providing vouchers which involved the clerk in special invoicing arrangements.

Each day the monies collected from all sources had to be totalled and balanced against records and then put into a leather bag. This bag was placed in the travelling safe and dispatched in the care of the guard of the 6.50 pm service. The safe had arrived earlier that day on the 10.30 am passenger train. Travelling safes were substantially built wooden trunks and were inscribed to show the stations they worked to and from. In this case Neyland to Swansea. Every four weeks a return was made to Swansea to account for all tickets sold and which also showed the ticket stocks on hand. The return also accounted for lost property, parcels, demurrage, coal sales to staff receipts, and even receipts from the pennies collected from the station toilets.

At the year–end he had to balance the pay bill and prepare the certificate of tax deduction, form P60 for each employee.

The senior clerk post at Neyland in the 1950's was attractive because it involved working every other Sunday for payment at time and three–quarters rate. The work involved split shifts: 5.30 am to 12 noon and 5.30 pm to 7 pm. This was necessary to cover the one arrival and one departure. The job though was shared with the leading porter who was specially trained in booking office work and was the subject of an inter–trade union agreement. The Sunday work involved elements of both portering and clerical work and this shared arrangement was more cost effective than employing both men each Sunday. Thus the clerk watered the coaching stock, lit the station fires and unloaded the newspapers. On the alternative week the porter issuing tickets. Only on Sundays did newspapers arrive by train. The clerk or porter off loaded them from the overnight train from Paddington that arrived at 5.50 am and which was often longer than the arrival platform. He made use of a

5938 'Stanley Hall' heads a line up of engines including on the turntable, 5030 'Shirburn Castle'.

Paul Chancellor

sack truck to carry the 25 bundles each weighing half a hundredweight from the train to the Booking Hall. Here he cut the stings of each bundle and placed them round the seats to aid sorting and to assist the newspaper deliveryman who, with his family, descended on the waiting room between 7 to 7.30 am. They used the Booking Hall to organise their paper rounds. For this help the clerk or porter had free papers. For the rest of the week the newspapers were taken off the train at Haverfordwest and delivered by lorry to Neyland.

For the purpose of levying and collect demurrage the senior clerk, or if he was too busy, the junior clerk went round the yard each day and recorded the running number of each wagon in the demurrage book. From these details it was possible to determine how long each wagon had been in the yard. A levy was then calculated and charged where the wagon had been delivered and remained in the possession of the consignee for more than three days. Most demurrage at Neyland was levied on the coal merchants and who preferred to bag the coal straight from the coal wagon and onto their lorry rather than off-load to the ground, bag it and then reload it on the lorry. As a consequence and also because of the small scale of their operations they were in no hurry to unload their wagon. Naturally the demurrage

charge was unpopular and difficult to collect. The result was that a compromise arrangement was adopted informally, whereby the levy was charged only after four or occasionally five days and in return the merchants paid any dues promptly.

The work of the clerks could also be subject to unannounced audit visits, conducted in the 1950's by Bill Morris the auditor based at Carmarthen and described as a "real gentleman". Mr. Morris would arrive by train and bang on the booking office window. He would then announce that he was going to Warlow's cafe, which was situated on the station approach road, and that on his return if the money was not correctly accounted for there would be trouble. This gave the clerk ten minutes to rush around the station yard in order to recover any unauthorised "subs" he had made to the men in advance of their pay, and regularise his books. This gesture by the auditor was a recognition that such practices went on but not for the personal gain of the clerk. All other irregularities were rigorously pursued and including a number of clerks in the West Wales area covered by this auditor who were found to be defrauding the Railway. One ploy was for a cash sale to a far-flung and therefore expensive destination to be recorded as a local fare and for the clerk to pocket the difference. A pre-printed ticket could not be used as it would have to be accounted for in stock checks and instead the fraudster would use a 'blank–card' ticket, writing the destination in by hand. To counter this the auditor was provided with the actual tickets collected at destination stations and which he then compared with the issuing station's records. Less serious was one of the clerks who unofficially assisted in the operation of a football

---

G.W.R General Appendix to the Rule Book 1936

Standard Whistle Codes

Main Lines   1 Whistle
Relief Lines   2 Whistles
To or from Platform Loops 2 Whistles
Branch Lines 3 Whistles
Goods Lines 4 Whistles
Bay Lines   2 Short Whistles
To Engine Sheds   4 Short Whistles
Yards, to or from   1 Crow
Crossover Road
     Main Line   1 Crow and 1 Whistle
     Relief Line   1 Crow and 2 Whistles
In Siding, clear of Running Lines   3 Short Sharp Whistles

For crossing operations whistles should be used made up of a combination of the whistle for the road upon which the driver is standing or running and the road to which he wishes to be transferred, for example

	Whistles
Main Line to Relief Line	1 pause 2

---

sweepstake run by one of the staff by deducting the stake money from the weekly wage of the participants. In return the clerk was given a free entry.

Rent was collected for the railway housing by a deduction from the weekly wage of men in railway service. Those men or their widows who had retired called at the station weekly and paid the rent to the clerk who acknowledged receipt by signing their rent card. He then accounted for the money in his records.

Every pay day the clerk determined the pay due to each man by reference to the hours worked and the rate per hour together with any other payments to which he was entitled. This information was entered on the pay bill. One copy was retained and the other sent to Swansea for checking by another clerk at Divisional Office. This pay bill showed the breakdown of the coins and notes required for each man and also the total amount. If the net wage was £10 or more then he received a £5 note, some £1 notes and the balance in coins. The money was sent from Swansea in the

Travelling Safe and the pay packets were made up at Neyland. The money did not arrive until 10.30 am and as the men collected their wages at 2 pm time was short – the other booking office duties continuing at the same time. Each packet was sealed only when the money received matched the pay packet totals and if money was left over, or a pay packet was short, each packet had to be emptied out and checked until the discrepancy was found. If a man was unable to collect his wage it was placed in the safe and an entry made in the unclaimed wages register. He had to sign this register on collecting it. As salaried members of staff the clerks were paid monthly, however each fortnight they received an interim round sum payment made without any deductions with the balance after stoppages at the end of the month.

When the senior clerk was on holiday his duties were covered by a relief clerk. Whether he undertook all the jobs depended on the character of the relief man. Whilst some did the time consuming month end balances, others would leave it, much to the disgust of the resident clerk, on his return to work.

One incident involving a clerk resulted in a report made to the Divisional Superintendent. It appears that during a slow Saturday morning this un–named individual harvested some cockles along the waters edge and then used the kettle in the guard's room to boil them. He was though caught in the act by a guard from Bristol clearly none too pleased about the likely taste of his tea.

Signalmen

In the late 1940's until at least the mid 1950's the signal box was opened continuously Mondays to Saturdays on a three shift pattern, 6 am to 2 pm, 2 pm to 10 pm and 10 pm to 6 am. On Sundays two short shifts were worked 9 am to noon and 10 pm until the last train had cleared the block section. Neyland, in common with other signal boxes was given a classification and therefore a rate of pay in accordance with the amount of work required of the signalman in a given period. This work was measured by the number of lever and instrument movements and also telephone calls required for the pattern of traffic. In this way Neyland was a Class 4, whilst Johnston was a higher rate of pay at Class 3 and due to it being a busier location as the junction for the branch line to Milford Haven

The signalmen were under the day to day control of the Station Master but were also answerable to the District Signal Inspector, then Glynn Griffiths who was based at Whitland. In the 1950's they were; Billy Rees, Bertie Mends and Mr. Phillips. In the period 1948 to 1957 Bill Chamberlain a district relief signalman was based at Neyland and worked directly to Glynn Griffiths. Bill was authorised to operate any of the 37 signal boxes in the district.

The original signal box had been situated between the up and down main line and close by the top end of Neyland engine shed, it was replaced in 1919. Neyland's

Standard GWR fittings on this wooden post 'stop' signal and which acted as No. 46, the up starter. Originally a fixed distant had been located under the stop arm but this was removed at the time the station became controlled from a single signal box.. (See appendix 1.)

P.J. Garland / Roger Carpenter

final signal box was situated between the up main line and the siding leading from the turntable. Neither Neyland or Johnston had line side apparatus on which the signalman would place or collect the token and the practice at Neyland was for the signalman to hand out the token to the fireman of up trains by leaning out of the front window of the box. For down trains he left the box and crossed over the running lines by a wooden walkway to collect the token whilst standing at ground level. Unlike at some stations, Neyland was not provided with a treadle, activated by the wheels of a passing train, which caused a bell to ring at the station to warn the platform staff of an approaching train. Instead they had to rely on their knowledge of the train service, alterations or additions reported in the weekly notices, or messages from the signalman. The omnibus telephone circuit serving Neyland 'box reached as far as Carmarthen as well as extensions to the parcel office, engine shed and Johnston station master's office.

Access to the 'box was from an ash path that led from the Barnlake ferry footpath passing by an old building that stood on the embankment behind the signal box. This building was used by the railway workers to store their cycles under cover. It had formerly been rented from the railway and used as a smokehouse and later for the manufacture of boxes. The entry into the signal box was through the doorway that faced the engine shed. A megaphone was provided to aid communications with other railway men. Detonators were of course supplied although it was not until the 1950's that lever detonator placing was provided.

Weekly notices were received showing alterations to the working timetable and were delivered to the box by either a porter or the stationmaster. Care and maintenance of the box and its equipment was the responsibility of the Signal and Telegraph Department whose men were based at Haverfordwest.

As Neyland was a terminus it was provided with a fixed distance signal on the approach. Officially the speed of an approaching train should also have been reduced to no more than 5 m.p.h. by the time it was approaching the platform.

Movements along the running lines were controlled by the signalman and required co–operation between him and the locomotive crew. To assist in communications the crew used the locomotive whistle to blow a set pattern this code related to a particular movement.

The arrival platform was not signalled for departing trains but was instead provided with a backing signal from which any one of three routes could be taken. These were to the Loco shed, Down main or Down siding. In an emergency a train could depart from this platform but this entailed clipping and padlocking of the facing points. On the occasion of the Queen's and the Duke of Edinburgh's visit in 1955, the Royal Train departed from the arrival platform under these arrangements.

Lamp man

The signal lamps were attended to on a weekly basis by the District Lamp Man and who earlier in the 1940's had been based at Neyland. Later these duties were carried out by a man from Johnston. His duties were to ensure that the wick in each lamp was properly trimmed and that there was sufficient paraffin in the reservoir to enable the light to burn for seven days. In the 1940's a typical week involved: Monday – out on the 8.15 am from Neyland as far as Whitland. Then walk from here to Cardigan Junction and on to Clynderwyn filling up all lamps en–route, trimming the wicks and cleaning the spectacle glass in order that the light would be visible. A stick was carried which had been split at one end and into this was placed a lighted match to assist in re–lighting the lamp. Four boxes of matches were supplied to the lampman each week. He returned to Neyland

43xx No. 4358 taking on water at Neyland. The 'Moguls' were regular visitors to the station for several decades and were to be seen on a variety of workings. The houses in Cambrian Road overlook the site and were where many railwaymen lived, including before his marriage, Bill Morgan of 'Behind the Steam' fame.

Authors Collection.

by train arriving after 4 pm. Tuesday – departure and arrival as for Monday, the lamps between Sarnau and St. Clear were covered. Wednesday - all the lamps at Neyland were maintained. Thursday – Haverfordwest. Friday –Johnston. Saturday – Milford Haven.

An oil can holding 1$^{1/2}$ gallons was carried on his round. Each signal post had to be climbed in order to remove the lamp and carry it to the ground where it was cleaned filled and trimmed. A couple of spare lamps were carried to be used if necessary and any spares or oil he required was ordered on his behalf by the Station Master at Neyland and took up to 14 days to arrive. The lampmans work, was spot checked by the signal inspector who, if dissatisfied would make a report to Neyland's stationmaster.

Shunters

In the 1950's there were three shunters. The head man was Fred John and after he progressed to goods guard, Reggie Thomas. The other Shunters were Ivor Lloyd, George (Jock) Wright, and Freddie Harrison, who also later progressed to a goods guard post. There was also a relief shunter, George Seaton but who spent most of his time working away from Neyland. They normally covered their own holiday or other absences by working rest days and overtime, but occasionally had assistance from a goods guard. The shunters worked shifts based on 6 am to 2 pm and 3 pm to 11 pm with the head shunter overlapping both men on an 8 am to 4 pm routine.

The shunters cabin stood in front of and at the top end of the engine shed. It was of brick construction with a slate roof. Inside there was a gate for a coal fire and a hob either side. There were seats but no table and the building was gas lit.

Although originally classified as goods shunters the men in fact dealt with very few goods vehicles most of the work at Neyland being passenger coaches and 'brown vehicles' all of which had screw couplings. Although slightly

out of context it may be worth recounting that in the final years when rumours began to circulate of a run down at the station and possible redundancies, the men quickly realised that if they remained classified as goods shunters their jobs were at risk. This was because any goods guards who might also be made redundant were classified as being in a senior post and could then drop down a grade and claim a goods shunters job. With the approval of the Divisional Office at Swansea they made out a case to be re–graded as passenger shunters, which was accepted and so prevented any redundant goods guards from taking their jobs.

Passenger Guards

At Neyland the passenger and goods guards came under the control of the stationmaster. Goods guards normally came from the ranks of shunters whereas passenger guards came from the porter grades. Whilst goods guards were trained to act as passenger guards the converse was not the case. A number of men who also later became passenger guards had their first taste of the work in the form of summer relief turns, of which Neyland had its share. Such temporary posts were advertised internally and staff then had to apply for them. Many of the Neyland guards had in fact originated from nearly Milford Haven and simply because the staffing levels were greater at that station. A local arrangement also ensured that substantive goods guards were exclusively allowed to apply for every fourth vacancy for a passenger guard vacancy.

Guards' duties varied over the years not least by the alteration in the time that the services ran even if the basic pattern were retained. Recollections suggest that at some time in the 1950's there were 12 men formed into two links with the senior men having four turns:

Top Link

The premiere job was the 8 am Neyland to Paddington passenger train which the Neyland guard worked throughout, booking off at Paddington about 4 pm and going to lodge in the railway hostel at Old

Oak Common. The guard booked on at again at Paddington the following day, reported to the station inspector, and then worked the 8.55 am passenger to Milford Haven and booked off at Neyland. This duty was also well paid, with each turn attracting 16 hours pay as well as lodging allowances and spending money. A Neyland guard worked the service on Mondays, Wednesday and Friday opposite a Paddington guard who was in charge of the train from Neyland on Tuesday, Thursday and Saturday. Locally the Paddington man had lodgings in Cambrian Road overlooking the station.

8.55 am Fishguard Harbour to Paddington parcels train.

For this service, the Neyland guard travelled as a passenger on the 8 am London train as far as Clarbeston Road. On the subsequent arrival of the 8.55 am from Fishguard he took charge of this and worked it as far as Cardiff before booking off and going to his lodgings. The following day he worked back to Neyland with the 6.50 pm Swindon to Neyland parcels. This turn was operated on Mondays, Wednesdays and Fridays from Neyland. The service also picked up four empty newspaper vans at Carmarthen which were worked through to Cardiff and also occasionally conveyed horseboxes conveying Irish racehorses frequently with a travelling groom.

4.35 pm Neyland to Paddington parcels train.

This was another double home turn to Cardiff alternating days with a Paddington man. The service left Neyland generally with eight parcels vans and for destinations as diverse as the West of England, Bristol, Cardiff, Nottingham, Sheffield, Birmingham and Paddington. The Paddington vans being placed in the middle of the formation to ease re–marshalling en–route. In to the 1950's this train is recalled as carrying a substantial amounts of rabbits, indeed it was not unusual when the service

arrived at Haverfordwest for as many as eight platform trolleys to be piled high with boxes of rabbits requiring to be loaded by the station staff. To avoid a late departure, the guard would also assist with this task. Further rabbit boxes would be picked up as the train proceeded up the line. Because the parcel vans were going to different locations it was also essential for the guard to supervise the loading to ensure the consignments were stowed in the correct vehicle. This turn was Mondays, Wednesdays, and Fridays and returning the following day.

9.55 am passenger train which was worked to Milford Haven via Johnston and thence to Paddington.

On this duty the Neyland guard left the train at Carmarthen and then worked a train to and from Llandilo. Back at Carmarthen he waited the arrival of the 11.55 am Paddington – due to arrive at Milford at 6.57 pm and which he worked as far as Johnston. A Neyland goods guard then took charge of the train to Milford and then with the same coaching stock and engine worked to Clarbeston Road to make a connection with the 3.55 pm Paddington to Fishguard Harbour and then back to Neyland arriving at 10.30 pm.

Bottom Link

2.30 pm Neyland to Paddington passenger train.

The Neyland man worked as an assistant guard as far as Whitland where he left the train. His next job was on the 3.50 pm milk train from Whitland to Kensington as far as Swindon where he booked off and went to his lodging. The following day he returned to Neyland booking on at Swindon and working from there on the 1.55 pm Paddington passenger arriving at Neyland at 9.35 pm. This service was known to generations of Pembrokeshire railway men as the "Cheap". The name harking back

57xx PT No. 4654 attached to the Neyland shunters truck, possibly No. 41739 and which was for some time allocated to the station. The guards van is standing in No. 7 siding, part of the complex known as the pontoon sidings. May 25 1963.

E. Wilmshurst 1556

to the previous century and the 1883 Act of Parliament.

4.35 pm Neyland to Cardiff Parcels

Worked on Tuesdays and Thursdays returning the following day on the 10 am Cardiff to Neyland parcels. This turn had a Saturday as a rest day and was shared with a top link men as described earlier.

7.50 pm Neyland to Cardiff parcels

The Neyland guards worked this on two turns. One working away on Mondays, Wednesdays, and Fridays and the other turn worked Tuesdays, and Thursdays. They men were in charge all the way to Cardiff where they booked off and went to lodgings. The next day the guard worked a trip to Barry and return and then back home as an assistant guard on the 1.55 pm Paddington from Cardiff due at Neyland 9.35 pm.

The 7.50 pm parcels normally commenced from Neyland with five vehicles of which four were parcels vans. The train then picked up any fish traffic at Johnston and which could be just boxes of fish or full loads, extra vans being attached to the rear of the train. Milk traffic was also picked up at Whitland and other parcels vans en–route so that by the time the train reached Cardiff it was not unusual to have 20 parcels vans in its formation. All the vans were vacuum fitted and capable of running at passenger speeds but occasionally some of these were 4–wheel vehicles and in consequence the speed of the train had to be reduced. Aside from the initial four vans, the formation also included a brake 2nd passenger coach and was booked as a passenger working between Carmarthen and Ferryside. This provided a service for late night revellers. At the Carmarthen stop, from 10.26 pm to 10.55 pm the fireman changed the lamp on the engine from the class 'C' head–code carried as a parcel train to the 'B' head–code signifying a passenger train. (On occasions also the Control office at Swansea would extend the passenger working from Ferryside to Llanelly to get a passenger home who had missed his train.)

8.55 am Fishguard Harbour to Paddington parcels

Shared with a top link guard and covered on Tuesdays and Thursdays out bound, returning on Wednesdays and Fridays.

3.50 pm Milford Haven to Severn Tunnel Junction fish train returning on the 1.55 pm Paddington to Neyland as an assistant guard. The duties now were to help ensure parcels traffic was put off at the correct destination and not under or over carried.

Spare turns

In addition there were spare turns, but the mail trains to and from Neyland was a double home turn for Swindon and Bristol guards. The Summer timetable brought extra trains and work on the Pembroke Dock branch with 2 turns these being:

7.30 am Pembroke Dock to Shrewsbury as far as Llandovery working back from here on the 12.00 Shrewsbury to Pembroke Dock.

8.30 am Pembroke Dock to Birmingham as far as Cardiff returning on the 11.35 am passenger – a relief service to the 11.55 am Paddington to Neyland. On the 8.30 am service the engine was changed at Whitland with a 'Hall' class engine working light from Fishguard.

At this time Pembroke Dock had two passenger guards together with a porter guard and shared the branch line workings with Whitland men. One of the Pembroke duties was the Pembroke Coast Express as far as Cardiff.

At Neyland the guards, including those from other depots, booked on and off duty in the guards' room. They were first required to read the notices on any temporary speed restrictions together with any other information affecting the running of the train. The guard then went to his train where he took the running number of each coach and its tare weight, which were entered in his journal. As he walked along the outside he visually checked that the coaches were correctly coupled including the connections for the vacuum brake, train heating and the electrical connections. Next he moved inside the train and walked through making sure everything was in order from functioning toi-

lets to any light bulbs which required changing. With the co–operation of the driver he then carried out a brake test in all brake compartments. On the last brake compartment in the formation he removed the vacuum hose and by listening he could ensure it was functioning correctly. Once he was satisfied that he could obtain the correct vacuum he then went up to the engine. Here he took the driver's name, the number of the engine, and again recorded these in his journal. In return he gave the weight of the train and the number of vehicles and also reminded the driver of any changes to the booked pattern of working. The journal was used throughout the journey to record delays whether the fault of the engine, station staff, signals, speed restrictions or other factors. It also recorded the number of passengers and the addition or reduction to the number of coaches or vans en–route. A journal was completed covering the whole journey but in addition a separate journal was also completed for each operating division the train either passed through. Journals were thus completed when working a train for London covering: –

Swansea Division –Neyland to Pyle. signal box
Cardiff Division – Pyle to St Brides
Newport Division – St Brides to Severn Tunnel West signal box
Bristol Division – Severn Tunnel West to Swindon
London Division – Swindon to Paddington.

The journals were also produced in different colours, Blue for up and Red for down trains. The actual journal which was a single sheet of paper completed on both sides, was handed in at the end of the journey. At Neyland they were placed in a box kept for the purpose in the guards room.

On coming on duty the guard carried a pocket watch, whistle, two different carriage keys, one each for the old and new style carriage locks then in use, a red flag, a green flag and a hand held lamp capable of displaying either a red, green or white light. He also carried all the service timetables appertaining to the working of the service, which together with the flags were usually carried in a leather bag supplied.

In the guard's compartment of the coach or van there would be a desk and seat and by this a letter rack used for the internal railway correspondence which the guard sorted en–route and then handed over to a responsible person as it reached its destination, obtaining a signature if required. No record was carried which recorded the parcels being carried or their destination other than for valuable parcels, which had to be signed for on being handed over. Instead he was required to make a mental note and check the brake vans frequently to ensure that parcels were not over–carried. Bullion was regularly traffic in substantial wooden boxes to and from the banks at Haverfordwest and required two men to handle them as they usually contained coins. The boxes were put into the wire cage in the guards' van.

Tickets inspections were carried out by travelling ticket inspectors. These men were based at Swansea and normally joined Neyland trains at Whitland or Carmarthen. They would leave a train at a convenient station and board a service going in the opposite direction and then inspect those tickets. In this way they could check the tickets on four or five trains during their turn of duty. At Carmarthen it was the regular practice for a female cleaner to join a London bound train to undertake any necessary cleaning duties and particularly the toilets. Sometimes a travelling porter also joined at Carmarthen to assist the guard in handling parcels traffic and acting under the guards' supervision. This was a regular practice on the 1155 am Paddington.

Knowledge of the route over which they were working was a requirement of any guards job and they were tested every two years. This knowledge comprised an understanding of the location and position of each signal box on the route as well as catch points, station layouts and speed limits. The location of signal boxes was required in case of an emergency, the location of catch points to ensure that no derailments occurred during shunting movements, and station layouts because of shunting manoeuvres. Some knowledge was required of the location of signals but not to the same extent as the driver or fireman. A Neyland guard working a train to Paddington could pass some 180 signal boxes on his journey.

Porter Guard

This duty which appears to have ceased in the 1950's involved a porter who booked on at Neyland at 2.00 pm and off at 11.0 pm. He undertook portering duties until the departure of the 8.50 pm local passenger on which he travelled to Johnston. Here he either took over the duties of guard on the 1.55 pm passenger train to Milford or travelled as a passenger. Then acting as guard he was in charge of the return working to Clarbeston Road which departed Milford at 9.05 pm. Arriving at Clarbeston Road at 9.21 pm the train made a connection with the 3.55 pm Paddington to Fishguard Harbour passenger train. His train then departed Clarbeston Road at 10.17 pm arriving at Neyland at 10.46 pm. Later this job was taken over by a Neyland goods guard. Passenger guards in the late 1940's and 1950's included :– G. Price, R. Alder, T. Thomas, D. Morgan, F. Scurlock, W. Walters, G. Palmer, D. Laugharne, F. Phillips, W. Mathias, V. Rees and G. Rees.

Goods Guards

Before being appointed in this role each man had to study the rules and was then tested on them by an Inspector based at Whitland. This examination lasted about two hours and if successful the candidate went to Swansea where he was subject to a further examination on the rules by a second Inspector. This man then made a report to the District Inspector, who if satisfied, passed him suitable to do the job. On appointment, the guards were provided by

the local Stationmaster with a pocket watch, journals, rule book and appendices, detonators, a red and a green flag, wet weather clothing and a hand lamp – all of which had to be signed for by the guard.

The guards' workings were of course determined by the working timetable and the actual running of the trains. In the early 1950's these were only single home turns and the distance a guard worked was determined by the running of both his train and that of the goods coming in the opposite direction. There was a supposed booked hand–over point where the guards exchanged trains and worked back to their home station. However it was often impossible to achieve this because one train might be delayed by circumstances such as exceeding their booked shunting time at a station en–route or the late running of a preceding train. Conversely a service might run earlier than its booked timings because of a lack of freight traffic. To account for this, the control office at Swansea were regularly advised of the progress of each train by the signalmen along the route. Control would then contact the signalman to arrange a suitable location where it was possible to bring both trains into loops or sidings. The signalman would then also relay this information to the crew and the revised change over point. Relief would also be needed on occasions for a guard who might have already worked his booked hours and was unwilling to continue on overtime. Swansea Control office in arranging relief would also have to take into account the availability of a train, passenger or goods, on which the guard could journey home. Often as not he would travel back as a "passenger," i.e. without carrying out any duties. The need to provide relief guards was taken into account in the staffing levels of station like Neyland with spare turns booked each day to cover this eventuality. On the spare turns, if not called upon to take over a working of either a passenger or goods train, the man would carry out basic housekeeping duties including cleaning out the brake vans, maintaining the lamps and seeing to the all important stove including ensuring there was an adequate supply of coal on board. He did not though top up the sand boxes and which was the responsibility of the carriage and wagon examiners. Additional equipment in each van included a brake stick to assist in pinning down the brakes of wagons and vans, and a shunting pole to assist in coupling or uncoupling the three–link couplings. In similar fashion to the passenger guards, goods guard's recorded in the journal; the running number of the wagon or van, the tare weight and by reference to the waybills placed under a spring clip on each vehicle, its destination. These journals were single white sheets. Completed journals were handed in when the train reached its destination and which at Neyland was in a box in the guard's room. These were later sent to Swansea for analysis. In the 1950s, except for special workings, all goods trains to and from

Neyland were worked by Neyland based guards.

The rosters of guard's was drawn up by the stationmaster each week in consultation with the Local Department Committee (Trade Union Representatives). One of the requirements being to have a spare guard available every three hours to cover sick leave and any emergencies.

Communications between the guard in his brake van and the engine crew was by means of hand or lamp signals the code of which was based on the rule book. The following observations are based on the 1958 working timetable: –

1.00 am Neyland to Llandilo Junction Class 'J'

This often ran engine and brake van to Clarbeston Road. Here it picked up empties which had come up from Fishguard Harbour. The Neyland guard worked the train at least as far as Carmarthen Junction and occasionally as far as Pembrey or Ferryside where he changed over with the guard of the 9.50 pm Swansea Eastern Depot due into Neyland at 5.17 am.

12.30 pm Neyland to Milford Haven class 'K'

This train took the empty fish vans to Milford for use next day. They were left in the sidings where an engine of the Milford Haven Docks company worked them down to the dock sidings and the fish market. They were loaded the next day and worked out on one of the fish trains. The guard worked the 3.20 pm fish train to Carmarthen and then worked the class 'J' 5.55 pm Carmarthen Junction to Neyland arriving at 8.48 pm.

5.50 am Neyland to Llandilo Junction class 'J'

This train ran to Johnston where it picked up wagons and vans left in the down siding and took them to Milford Haven. The guard then worked this train as far as Whitland, changed over and brought back the 9.20 am Carmarthen Junction to Neyland due at 1.32 pm

7.30 pm class 'J' Neyland to Carmarthen Junction

The train was worked to Milford via Johnston and departed here at 9.50 pm with a full load of coal empties, which were put off at Carmarthen Junction for distribution on other services. The return working was the 1.15 am Carmarthen Junction due Neyland at 3.38 am. On arrival at Carmarthen Junction, the guard and engine crew left the brake–van on the main line and shunted the empties into the sidings before turning the engine on the triangle at the Junction and going back on to the van. The shunter would then direct them to the siding or sidings where they made up the train to a maximum of 35 loaded coal wagons. On the return journey some of the wagons were put off at Whitland, Clynderwen, and Clarbeston Road. The maximum load out of Haverfordwest was 28 and often the remaining wagons would be put off at Johnston leaving the engine and brake van to return to Neyland.

11.35 pm Neyland to Duffryn Yard class 'J'

This was often engine and brake van to Haverfordwest where a train was made up containing coal empties, empty fertiliser vans, and loaded vans Because their was no shunter on duty the guard carried out these duties. The back working was on the 9.30 pm Duffryn Yard to Neyland due at 7.52 am with the exchange taking place at Carmarthen Junction.

5.25 pm Neyland to Neath (Station Truck Goods)

This called at the stations en route conveying a variety of small consignments and also potatoes in season. When the train arrived, at say Whitland, it stopped in the platform to enable the station staff to unload or load. The vans were placed in a set order so that traffic for stations beyond Neath would be placed next to the guard's van, then traffic for Llanelly and Carmarthen in the middle then Neath with Swansea vans next to the engine. This enabled the vans to be dropped off or picked up with the minimum of shunting. The guard's return working was on the 6.10 Llandilo Junction to Neyland due in at 12.13 with the change– over booked to take place at Whitland.

The names of guards recalled in the 1940's and 1950's include; – D. Evans, J. Waller, G. Nicholas, I. Lewis, W. Kent, W. Lawrenny, J. Harrison, F. Harrison, F. Jenkins, D. Huddleston, J. Griffiths, G. Hughes, F. John, P. Stokes, W. Vaughan, C. James, G. Talbot, and A.E. Cronin.

Carriage and Wagon

The carriage and wagon department staff was divided between carriage cleaners and repairers. The carriage cleaners' tasks appear not to have altered over the years although the number of men and the turns of duty varied. At one time 16 men were employed working under a chargeman, then Ronald Hay, with the foreman Mr. Davidge based at the Neath Divisional Office. The day to day supervision of the cleaning activities and the conduct of the men was the responsibility of the Neyland Stationmaster. For many years there were three turns of duty, 6 am to 2 pm, 8 am to 4 pm and 2 pm to 10 am. Each had a maximum of eight men on duty, the numbers and hours dictated by the pattern of train workings and the available layover period of the coaching stock.

In later years the shifts were altered to just the first two referred to above and with up to 10–12 men per shift. These included, Cyril Bevan, Steve Thomas, Walter Rees, Billy Stuart, Tommy James, Jack Griffiths, Ivor John, Paddy Ryan, and Albert John, with Gilbert John as chargeman.

As far as the work was concerned, when a train came into the arrival platform and the passengers had disembarked, the pilot engine first drew the coaches out beyond the Iron Bridge and then pushed them into the siding next to the arrival road. The carriages were then cleaned inside and out including all brass work. The toilets were also dealt with, the towels replaced and toilet paper provided as necessary. Once a month the outside of the coaches was washed down (termed "skivving"), with an acid based substance to remove stubborn dirt and then rinsed with clean water. This chemical was not applied to the windows. Whilst the outside was being cleaned, men inside the coaches removed all the seat cushions and brushed them clean before replacing them. No vacuum cleaners were provided, just dusters and brushes. For the outside cleaning, there were buckets and long handles on which detachable brushes were fixed. Chamois leathers were not provided other than on one occasion, – the visit of the Royal train in the 1950's. No 'Brasso' or other proprietary product was provided to clean the brass work and instead crushed sand was used. The procedure here was to first lay a handful of sand on top of the rail that the pilot engine was working and once the wheels of the engine had passed over it several times the sand then had the consistency of fine flour. This was then placed into a saucer and some water added to form a paste. This was applied to the brass – a set of stepladders was of necessity provided, and once the paste had been rubbed off and polished, gave a finish equal to any commercial product. The sand was obtained from the sand furnace by the engine shed.

Neyland	Passenger	Receipts		Parcels			Milk		
Year	Tickets	Receipts	Season	Forwarded	Received	Receipts	Gallons	Cans	Receipts
1925	41454	5018	156	3915	5782	703			
1926	33601	4302	53	3199	4787	523			
1927	31708	3686	151	2709	5148	520			
1928	28977	3383	129	2560	5222	544			
1929	30249	3492	132	2517	5605	547			
1930	28960	3259	99	2425	6226	532			
1931	25837	3077	88	1890	6484	385			
1932	20788	2475	108	1587	6984	321			
1933	17256	2246	101	1359	9092	283			
1934	15295	1992	88	1398	8901	312	1059	140	6
1935	15583	2130	68	1285	8789	127	4005	534	20
1936	15605	2136	60	1459	8442	129	4701	476	23
1937	13640	2314	59	1413	9800	126	5029	541	25
1938	9601	2108	54	1446	9745	115	509	48	2
1939	8787	2241	48	1259	9790	113			
1940	10117	4086	40	1127	8852	75			
1941	13897	5441	35						
1942	20612	6238	39						
1943	24613	11186	32						
1944	21252	9500	25						
1945	22843	12280	12						
1946	15640	9007	32						
1947	12385	7225	17						
1948	8203	6157	18						
1949	7790	4965	60						
1950	7537	4298	156						
1951	6348	4079	157						
1952	8081	4308	143						
1953	7450	3673	110						
1954	7609	3497	84						
1955	7439	3630	76						
1956	8424	3818	144						
1957	8831	3985	146						
1958	8140	4055	102						
1959	6991	4138	78						

enabled the coaches to be cleaned from ground level. Water taps and hose pipes were provided alongside the siding next to the arrival platform and at also at sidings 7 and 8. In addition to the carriage stock, Neyland was responsible for cleaning the fish vans. These arrived in the early hours of the morning and were also berthed in sidings 7 and 8 One man being detailed to hose them out and make them ready. On the next day they were taken over to Milford and on to the fish market sidings there. The following day they were loaded and worked away, subsequently to work back on a repeating cycle. Parcels vans were swept out and the outside cleaned. The Royal Mail van was only cleaned on the outside, as for security reasons the men were not allowed to enter the vehicle. From 1959 and on a daily basisSundays excepted, a man was also detailed to Milford to clean out the sleeping car as no carriage cleaners were based at that station.

The carriage cleaners' cabin was divided internally into two separate rooms, half also being occupied by the Chargeman carriage and wagon examiner. A gas ring was provided for boiling water and cooking and the cabin was gas lit. Benches were placed around the walls and a long table provided. Steel lockers were available for cleaner's to keep their personal belongings and it was the practice of the men to remove the head of their long handle brush for safe keeping. The men booked on and off in the cabin completing a time sheet which the Chargeman handed

Plastic bags were used to collect the rubbish from the coaches and which were then burnt at a spot near the carriage and wagon cabin which was located close by the arrival platform. The carriage destination boards carried just below the roof guttering were not removed from their brackets but were cleaned in situ. Long handled brushes

The Traffic Department

Goods and Livestock		
Year	Wagons Forwarded	Amount £
1925	5	4026
1926	2	3501
1927	3	2929
1928	2	3082
1929	1	3091
1930	2	3479
1931	2	3189
1932	0	2772
1933	2	2847
1934	2	2544
1935	1	2625
1936	0	2223
1937	0	2695
1938	1	2782
1939	20	3409
1940	36	5608

After 1960 until figures for Neyland were included with those of Haverfordwest. s a comparison also, Milk dealt with at Johnson and Haverfordwest was as

Milk Receipts	Johnston			Haverfordwest		
Year	Gallons	Cans	Receipts	Gallons	Cans	Receipts
1925		8477	952		5462	633
1926					1760	237
1927					2156	294
1928					5168	702
1929					3638	215
1930					5054	204
1931					4386	170
1932					4451	188
1933					7513	290
1934	9343	1208	51	83954	9375	336
1935				1869	203	12
1936				3587	378	22
1937				10794	1074	67
1938				7382	720	49
1939				2588	274	18
1940				6	1	N/A

In Tons the following details are recorded for Neyland (Neyland details were included within Haverfordwest station details from 1943.)

General Merchandise				
Year	Carted Forwarded	Received	Not–carted Forwarded	Received
1925	148	723	1132	782
1926	112	626	168	670
1927	119	617	149	589
1928	85	641	200	767
1929	90	739	159	981
1930	102	674	150	863
1931	77	659	140	722
1932	65	611	64	780
1933	72	647	90	771
1934	64	587	84	639
1935	77	612	67	622
1936	58	507	60	334
1937	66	676	54	477
1938	98	798	105	408
1939	130	1187	108	369
1940	933	282		
1941	436	1290		
1942	750	2545		

Coal and Coke (tons)		Other Minerals	
Year	Not Charged – received	Forwarded	Received
1925	3745		174
1926	803		2931
1927	2510	96	212
1928	3053	303	368
1929	3497	170	126
1930	3196	153	1375
1931	2764	139	473
1932	2791	154	52
1933	3029	207	65
1934	3221	435	122
1935	3313	327	270
1936	3266	137	440
1937	2897	91	288
1938	2833	117	230
1939	2564	207	239
1940	2182	21	72
1941	1967	12	1231
1942	1980	113	531

over to the Stationmaster who in turn passed it to the station clerk to work out wages and make the necessary payment each Thursday. Stores were kept in a building by the end of the cabin and it was the chargeman's job to obtain supplies from the travelling stores van which arrived on Thursday each week as part of a regular passenger working. For wet weather cleaning, staff were provided with a mackintosh.

The carriage and wagon examiners, more commonly known as 'wheel–tappers' were on duty each of two shifts, 6 am to 2 pm and 2 pm to 10 pm. It was their job to check incoming coaching stock, wagons and vans and to report any faults. For this purpose they prepared a card on which the fault was recorded and which was then handed to the chargeman fitter (repairer). A fitter and his mate were likewise on duty on each of the two shifts. These cards were –.

Red – This meant the fault was too serious to allow it to be in service until it was rectified.

Green – The fault was minor and was not detrimental to its safety in traffic. For the purpose of repairing vehicles a siding was available next to the former cattle dock and known as the Hospital siding. The points controlling access to this were padlocked, the key being held by the chargeman repairer. The cabin for the repairers and mates was on the former cattle dock and was equipped in a similar style to that of the cleaners. Some of the names recalled were: Examiners, Charlie Evans and Cecil Macken, Repairers, Dick Gwyther, Billy Evans and Billy Bond.

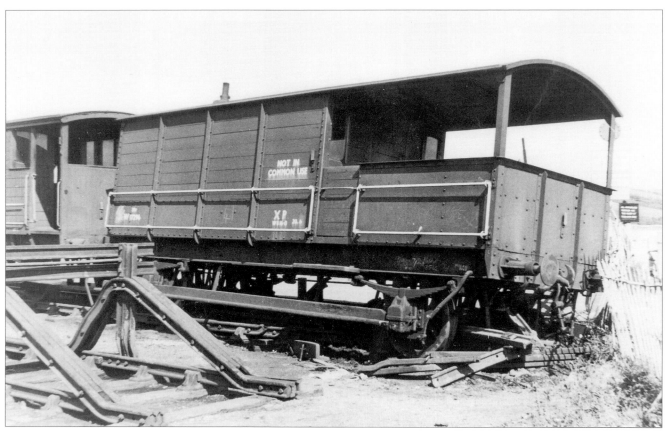

W17296 in trouble! Accidents will happen , this the result of a misunderstanding between the shunter and the crew of the pilot engine when 'Fly Shunting' coaching stock into a siding already occupied by the two vans seen. The buffer stop has been demolished but at least it prevented the van from continuing on through the fence and onto the road leading to the slip–way and the ferry at Hobb's Point! Prior to October 1907 shunters at Neyland were reported as working 60 hours per week, but from that time their working day was reduced from 10 to 9 hours. The wages of a head shunter which had also been 25/– per week but were increased to 28/–, whilst an under shunter wages were increased from 20/– to 24/– per week. A shunters job was potentially hazardous and the minutes of the GWR record the following at Neyland;– 15th September 1909 – J Davies sprained back lifting steel spring and off work three weeks and five days. In recompense for lost wages awarded £2 10 2d. 8th October 1912 – D M Lloyd sprained ankle descending from a brake van and received 3s 7d.

Alan Morgans

Chapter 7
WORKING THE STATION

At Neyland the shunter's worked closely with the driver and fireman on the station pilot. The early pilot duty was booked to start work at 6.00 am and if the shunter had not arrived, the crew took the engine off shed and over to No 5 siding where the fireman coupled to the shunter's truck. Next they proceeded to the middle road, the name given to the line next to the arrivals platform, ready to start their day's work. At one–time shunter's truck No 41817 was allocated to New Milford and later 41739 was at Neyland.

Shunting accidents occurred from time to time and generally involved the station pilot propelling a wagon or carriage so hard that it came into violent contact with another vehicle or the buffer stop. Normally there would be no damage but when a coach was roughly handled one consequence was to damage the cells of the batteries. It was though often possible to effect a temporary repair and thus avoid having to explain away the accident, by calling out the duty carriage and wagon repairer. Less easily covered up were the occasions when the vehicle hit the buffer stop so that these moved backwards and away from the end of the track. On at least one occasion the buffer stop ended up on the road leading to the Hobbs Point ferry slipway! Such was the camaraderie amongst the men however, that minor accidents were never reported to the Divisional Office thus avoiding awkward questions and a blemish on the record of the man at fault.

The pattern of passenger and goods trains varied little over the years other than for modest alterations in the timetable. It is reasonable to conclude then that the method of operations at Neyland in the 1950's had not altered significantly since the loss of the Irish traffic.

All passenger, parcels and mail trains coming to the Terminus were signalled into the arrival platform, their progress and anticipated arrival reported by the signalman who informed the shunter and pilot crew when they would be likely to be required. The station pilot would then wait in the middle road next to the arrival line. After the arrival had come to a stand, the pilot engine would gently come on to the rear vehicle and the shunter would couple up. Normally he would then walk the length of the train and uncouple the train engine assuming the fireman had not already done this – as was the custom of the Neyland and Carmarthen men. This allowed the pilot engine to draw the stock away and the train engine to go to shed.

The exception to this procedure was the first train to the station on the morning shift, 'The Mail', a service paid for by the Post Office but which also conveyed passengers. On this train the Mail Van arrived at the front of the train coupled to the locomotive tender. The pilot first removed the rear passenger coach, either a brake composite or brake 3rd, and fly shunted it to the middle road, the shunter riding in the guard's compartment. This was not an authorised move; the rulebook dictating that the engine should remain coupled to the coach at all times, but was ignored because it saved both time and effort. Upon returning to the coaches, the shunter then uncoupled the mail coach from the rest of the train and with the pilot coupled to the almost complete formation this was then pulled clear and shunted forward onto the previously removed brake vehicle. Finally the mail coach was collected and placed at what was now the front of the train. The train engine would now leave the platform and the complete formation would be removed again and placed in a suitable vacant siding ready for the attention of the carriage cleaners. This performance was necessary as it was a requirement that when the train left Neyland the Royal Mail van would again be coupled next to the train engine.

Later in the day after the 4.25 p.m. passenger train had departed, the mail train stock was drawn from the middle siding by the pilot engine and placed in the departure platform. This manoeuvre normally took place about 5.00 p.m.

A similar pattern of movements was made by the pilot engine in dealing with parcel trains, except that there was no need to remove the brake van providing there were other like vehicles amongst the formation. The placement of brake vans within a train's formation was governed by rules and regulations, which limited the number of coaches or vans placed behind it. The calculations were based on the number of wheels, which followed the brake van.

Certain passenger trains arriving at Neyland had only a short layover before returning, in which event the pilot engine would remove the coaches from the arriving engine and place them straight away in the departure platform. The auto train that came from Fishguard consisted of a 48XX (later 14XX) class 0–4–2T tank engine and trailer. Because Neyland was not signalled for passenger trains to depart from the arrivals platform, after depositing its passengers, it too moved under the protection of the backing signals along the arrivals line and then forward into the departure platform. This manoeuvre did not entail the assistance of the pilot engine.

Goods trains arriving at Neyland when a shunter was on duty, used the arrivals line and came to a stand adjacent to the shunter's cabin. They were then uncoupled behind the train engine. Whilst this was taking place, the pilot engine ran down the middle road until it reached the points where it switched to the arrivals line. It then reversed direction and moved slowly onto the goods brake van - the guard in the meantime having secured sufficient

285 miles and 26 chains from Paddington – measured by the original route through Gloucester. Coaching stock of the 'Mail train' is stabled in the middle road. The arrival platform had lost its overall roof in the 1930's.

Roger Carpenter

wagon brakes to hold the weight of the train. The van was then uncoupled from the train and coupled to the pilot engine, which drew it down the running line and propelled the van into one of the sidings, which lay adjacent to the arrival platform. Here the shunter uncoupled it and put the brakes on. (Surprisingly despite the practice of fly–shunting a passenger brake vehicle, fly shunting was not common practice with the goods brake vans.) The pilot engine then returned to the remainder of the wagons and shunted them to the various sidings according to space or traffic requirements.

When no shunter was on duty and no pilot engine available, an arriving goods train would run into the arrivals line and pass the shunter's cabin before coming to a halt. After the points had been changed, the engine pushed the vehicles back into the third road at Barnlake. Here the guard applied the van brakes and after removing his personal belongings, locked up the van. He also pinned down the brakes from a number of the vehicles which had formed the train. The engine then went to shed. This procedure was normally only necessary at night. Subsequently the

early turn shunter and pilot engine coming on duty had the task of shunting the vehicles to their correct sidings as their first job after dealing with the mail and parcels trains.

In the 1950's Neyland received or dispatched only a modest amount of goods traffic and consequently very few wagons were seen here. Goods trains were still time–tabled to run to or from Neyland but in practice mainly carried wagons or vans bound for Milford Haven. At Johnston the vehicles were set down in the long siding next to the arrival platform and frequently the train then ran to Neyland as a light engine or with only the guard's brake van attached. In the up direction the engine or engine and brake van ran to Johnston were it picked up the traffic for Milford Haven and took it down the branch. At Milford it set down the train and sometime later took another train out and up the line to Carmarthen Junction yard.

Passenger trains ran to fixed formations week by week depending whether the summer or winter timetable was in operation. The formation was varied to accommodate the fluctuation in traffic and this was controlled by the issue of weekly notices from the Divisional Office at

Swansea. Neyland kept spare coaches that could be used to augment existing formations or form up an extra train. These were normally stored in the Barnlake sidings although for a short time use was made of the sidings at the NATO quay. Later this practice was stopped by higher authority as the jetty was owned by the Ministry of Transport to whom rental would have to be paid to use the facility. Accordingly the points leading on to the quay were padlocked, the key being held in the station master office.

Each day except Sundays a shunter had to go to all the sidings where coaching stock was held as well as the platform lines and record the type and running number of each vehicle. These details were handed to the head shunter who had to telephone the control office at Swansea with the information and then send a written note in confirmation. In practice it was usually the lad porter who collected the note from the head shunter and arranged for it to be sent through the railway's internal post service.

The formation for passenger trains during the winter months was generally three coaches although this increased to five vehicles for the summer months. In all cases as the trains moved up country further coaches were added and the converse applied in the opposite direction. It was not unusual for Paddington bound trains to add coaches at Whitland, from the Pembroke Dock branch, Carmarthen and Swansea High Street. Because trains reversed direction at Carmarthen and Swansea it was necessary to ensure that a coach with a guards compartment was correctly placed in the formation for the reasons previously described. As a consequence of the additional portions being added, trains arriving at Paddington may have had 12 coaches or more including three to four brake vehicles.

Neyland's sidings were sited at three locations. The Rock, Barnlake, and those by the station, known as the Pontoon. Next to the arrivals platform was the middle road and between this and the Pill were a series of dead end sidings. The first of these was capable of holding three coaches and was known as the machine road. This name originated from the wagon weighbridge, which was originally provided but had been removed. The brick built hut, which formally housed the weighing machine, was subsequently used to store blanks used at the end of the corridor connections. Next to the machine road was the goods siding with a platform on which was a lock up shed and a hand operated crane. By the 1950's this saw little use. Further over was a short siding known as No 4 siding, and beyond this was 'New Found Out' siding, the origins of the name being lost in the passage of time. Further down the site there had formerly been four looped sidings but later two of these were converted to dead end's and fitted with stop blocks. Stop blocks were also erected at the end of No's 5 and 6 sidings. The remaining two loop sidings. No's 7 and 8, were treated as if they were dead end sidings. It was possible for a train to depart from both 5 and 6 but not from 7 or 8. The 1950's NATO quay was constructed

The backing signal at the end of the arrivals platform complete with its 'cash register' and which allowed for any one of three number of routes, down sidings 31, down main 28, or loco shed 34, to be selected.

P.J. Garland / Roger Carpenter

adjacent to No 8.

Because of the curvature of No 5 siding, buffer–lock could sometimes occur here when shunting passenger stock. This required some ingenuity to remedy without resorting to calling out the carriage and wagon fitters. The procedure was for the pilot engine to move the offending vehicles hard against the stop block to compress the buffer springs to the further extent possible. This allowed the shunter to go underneath the buffer housing and draw out the cotter pin that held the buffer in place. The pilot engine then drew the vehicles apart and with it the trapped buffer out of its housing allowing it to fall to the ground. With a gap now available between the offending vehicles the shunter had to be lift and manhandle the heavy buffer back into its housing, this was not an easy task because of the weight. The vehicles were then pushed together and the buffers compressed as much as possible to allow the cotter pin to be refitted.

Sidings 7 and 8 were used exclusively to berth fish vans (bloaters) which arrived six days a week and were cleaned in these sidings before being sent on the following day to Milford Haven – (Sundays excepted). Fish vans, which could not be accommodated in 7 or 8 were held in the Rock sidings. The fish landings at Milford Haven dictated the number of fish vans required and the shunter at Milford Haven would telephone Neyland signal box to specify his requirements. This information was relayed to the Neyland shunter who made up a train to suit Milford's requirements.

'Slopers Siding' and 'The Third Road' were the names given to the two long sidings, which ran parallel to the main line and lay between it and the Pill side. They formed long head shunts and were joined by a turnout at the Johnston end before terminating at a stop block.

Wagon loads of household coal arriving were always placed in the goods siding where the coal merchants bagged the coal direct from the wagon on to their lorry. The goods brake vans were normally placed in 'New Found Out' against the stop block and out going wagons or vans were shunted and coupled up to these. In this way a train was made up ready for departure. If the shunter's had finished work for the day before a goods train departed, they left a message for the guard in the guard's room to advise him of the siding in which his train was stabled together

with the number of wagons and vans and their destinations. The shunter also saw to the waybills, which he placed in the spring clip on the wagon or van ensuring that they showed their destination. If they were being returned empty then they wrote 'M/T' as short hand. These were normally destined for the sidings at Carmarthen Junction to be held ready for onward distribution. As far as can be established only one 'Toad' was inscribed Neyland and was not in common use, instead being frequently used on the fish empties working between the Terminus and Milford Haven.

The parcels train at 4.35 p.m. always left from No 5 siding where it had been formed up during that day. This was often a lengthy train and on occasions the whole of this train could not be accommodated in this siding and so the surplus stock was placed on the middle road. Shortly before the booked departure time the extra stock was collected by the train engine before drawing forward and backing down on to the vehicles in No 5 siding and when after coupling up the train was able to depart. The 7.50 p.m. parcels departed from the middle road but was formed up in one of the pontoon sidings.

The mail train was drawn out of the bottom end of

Viewed from the Iron Bridge, the lines in front of the signal box reading right to left are: – Up Main Line, Down Main Line, Middle Road, No. 5 Siding, No. 6 Siding, No. 7 Siding – containing vans, No. 8 siding, and which afforded access to the Nato Quay post 1955. September 20, 1962.

Roger Carpenter

The coach destination board reads, 'Paddington Newport Cardiff Swansea & Neyland'. Neyland railwaymen must have taken pride in being recognised along with these important towns and cities. Later though the terminus was replaced by the anonymous 'West Wales'. The 'concertina' coaching stock was introduced in 1906/7. They were 70 foot long and built up to the maximum loading gauge width of 9 foot. The need to recess the doorframes into the coach sides produced a ripple effect when viewed from certain quarters. This bellows–like feature gave rise to the name concertina after the musical instrument of the same name. When built they were used on the more important services including those between Paddington and Neyland. The brake coaches of the design remaining in service long after the other types had been withdrawn. In 1901 the GWR had coaches especially built for the 'New Milford Boat Trains'. These coaches were of an innovative design having a centre corridor and an open plan seating arrangement. They were used on the 6.25 pm Neyland to Paddington and the 4.25 pm Paddington to Neyland. The coaches were amongst the first with electric lighting and the first equipped with what subsequently became the GWR standard emergency communication system. However the novelty of the open plan seating arrangement did not find favour with the travelling public and was not repeated by the GWR.

R.C. Riley

the middle siding by the pilot engine and placed in the departure platform to await the arrival of its locomotive ready for its 6.50 p.m. departure. Again due to the length of the train and with the mail van marshalled at the front, this vehicle would often stand off the end of the platform causing some difficulty for the GPO staff when loading. After complaints, it was the practice to leave a trolley at the spot where the mail van normally stood and so assist access.

Full details of the traffic carried in the earliest days cannot be clearly established but in the period of the Irish traffic it involved a substantial trade in livestock, particularly cattle but also horses. General merchandise would have also featured to and from Ireland as well as like goods for Neyland and its hinterland. Household coal was also a

dominant traffic from the South Wales coalfields as well as loco coal for Neyland's engine shed. Coal also arrived for use at the gas plant.

Passenger Trains.

The actual number of passenger trains to or from Neyland, including local trains and those destined beyond Carmarthen showed little variation over the life of the station and this despite the loss of the Irish Ferry service. What did alter though was that gradually more trains from beyond Carmarthen ran to or from Milford Haven instead of Neyland and which instead saw a corresponding increase in local trains making a connection with the Milford services.

In the 1920's auto trains were in frequent use although a decade later the only auto service was a single

An interesting collection of coaching stock viewed from the fish platform with the former site of the fish market in the middle distance and next to Westfield Pill. The vehicles were probably stored and able to be called upon to supplement trains at periods of sudden demand. Although in truth it must be admitted that such spare capacity was hopelessly uneconomic, it is all so different from today's 'take it or leave it service'.

NRM / GWR B. Box 161/26

Viewed along 'New Found Out' siding with the Nato Quay in front and to the right. Barnlake sidings are in the far distance. A Gas Tank – 'Cordon' is against the buffer stops in No. 5. This and No. 6 had once been through lines. Sidings 7 and 8 are virtually empty but would normally be used for the cleaning and inspection of fish vans. Brinley John

daily train from and to Fishguard Harbour. Additional trains were of course run to meet special needs or seasonal traffic.

Passenger Trains	To Neyland	From Neyland
1867	4	4
1888	7	7
1905	7	7
1924	8	9
1938	10	9
1947	10	10
1954	11	11
1963	8	8
1856	**Express Fare**	**Ordinary Train**
First Class	£3 2s 9d	£2 10s 0d
Second Class	£2 4s 0d	£1 17s 10d
Third Class		£1 3s 0°d
1901	**Single**	**Return**
First Class	£2. 3s 6d	£3 14s 9d
Second Class	£1 7s 2d	£2 7s 6d
Third Class	£1 1s 8°d	
1928	**Single**	**Return**
First Class	£2 14 s 4d	£5 8s 8d
Third Class	£1 12s 7d	£3 5s 2d
1952	**Single**	**Return**
First Class	£2 17s 2d	£5 14s 4d
Third Class	£1 18s 1d	£3 16s 2d

Sleeping cars are known to have been in use between Paddington and Neyland for much of the early part of the 20th Century and despite the loss of the Irish traffic. First class sleeper vehicles known to have been used to Neyland prior to 1928. In 1928 three coaches Nos. 5140 to 5142 and to diagram J10 were introduced to use between Paddington and Neyland. Although as built accommodation was only provided for 3rd class passengers, one vehicle was later rebuilt and provided both 1st and 2nd class sleeping accommodation whilst the remaining two were rebuilt eliminating the seating accommodation and increasing the 3rd class sleeping compartments from three to eight. The G.W.R timetable for summer 1930 advertised 1st class sleeping accommodation was available on the 9.25 p.m. Paddington to Neyland and on the 6.30 p.m. Neyland to Paddington. It also promoted what it termed limited 3rd class sleeping accommodation on the same trains. A supplementary fare of 15/– in addition to the 1st class fare of £2 14s 4d single or £5 8s 8d return was levied, whilst for 3rd class the supplement was 6/– on top of the £1 12s 7d single and £3 5s 2d return fares. The sleeping car arrived on the down mail and the attendant working a double home turn had lodgings in Neyland booking on in time for the departure with the up mail departing at 6.30 pm.

When the daily sleeping car service to and from

Below: 4962 'Ragley Hall' of Goodwick arrives with the 10.35 am Cardiff parcels, due at Neyland at 5.00 pm. To the left are the 'Rock' sidings and to the right, 'Barnlake'. The line immediately next to the train known as 'Slopers'

E. Wilmshurst 1554

Neyland was withdrawn is not clear but it may have been shortly after the end of the Second World War. Thereafter sleeping cars only ran to Neyland on Sundays and as far as Carmarthen the other nights. The position changed in 1959 when a daily service commenced to run to and from Milford Haven, which at this time was developing, into an important oil refining centre.

Mail

From the earliest days trains conveying mail reached Neyland and departed as follows: –

1867			
Paddington	8.10 pm	New Milford	6.50 am
New Milford	5.00 pm	Paddington	4.35 am
1888			
Paddington	9.25 pm	New Milford	6.50 am
New Milford	5.00 pm	Paddington	2.15 am
1905			
Paddington	9.15 pm	New Milford	6.38 am
Gloucester	5.35 am	New Milford	11.25 am
New Milford	1.00 pm	Paddington	11.45 pm
New Milford	6.30 pm	Paddington	3.30 am
1924			
Paddington	9.15 pm	Neyland	6.45 am
Gloucester	5.25 am	Neyland	11.25 am
Neyland	12.40 am	Hereford	?
Neyland	6.40 pm	Paddington	3.30 am
1938			
Paddington	9.25 pm	Neyland	6.18 am
Neyland	6.50 pm	Paddington	3.25 am
1948			
Paddington	9.25 pm	Neyland	8.37 am
Neyland	6.50 pm	Paddington	4.20 am
1958			
Paddington	8.45 pm	Neyland	6.33 am
Neyland	6.50 pm	Paddington	4.40 am
1963			
As per 1958			

Parcels Trains

Parcels traffic was heavy on a Wednesday with consignments arriving for the local shopkeepers including Palethorpe pies and sausages from Harris' at Calne in Wiltshire. Parcels were recorded in a book and signed for either on collection or on delivery. Before World War 2, the

Cartage service was provided by Mr. Reece. Originally he had used a horse and cart but latterly employed a lorry. He was paid per item carried and with his contracted area encompassing Neyland and the surrounding environs. At this time Mr. Lamb was the cartage agent for Haverfordwest and Mr. White for Milford Haven. Later, parcels were delivered by a railway lorry based at Haverfordwest the driver collecting any monies and obtaining signatures. In the 1950's the charges recalled were 2/6d, collected at the station, and 5/– delivered. Amongst parcel traffic recalled were young chickens in boxes and turkeys sent up the line at Christmas time. Boxes of homing pigeons were also sent away for release with their baskets marked Return to Neyland' on the reverse of the label. Boxes of pigeons were also received and were released by the porter on duty.

1926 the following parcels trains worked to or from Neyland: –

8.55 pm Paddington due at 7.50 am
Siphon 'G'.
70 Foot parcels van.
Non gang–way Siphon 'C' originating from Bristol on the 6.05 pm attached at Cardiff.
Non gangway brake van originating from Treherbert.
5.   Brake van Manchester London Road working from   Crewe on 1.10 pm to Pontypool Road and going forward on 4.40 pm to Swansea.

12.35 pm Cardiff due Neyland at 6.22 pm
Non gang–way Siphon 'F' Cardiff General.
 Non gang–way van third Cardiff General.
Non gangway 8 wheel brake van Cardiff General
Non gangway Siphon, Merthyr.
5.   Siphon 'G', Mountain Ash.

2.20 pm Neyland to Paddington due 4.20 am
Siphon 'G' to Wolverhampton.
Brake van to Manchester London Road.
Non gangway Siphon 'H' to Birmingham (Midland)
        Detached at Cardiff and on by 10.42 pm thence. *(It had worked down on the 12.35 pm Cardiff to Ney–land but is shown as working to Fishguard Har– b o u r . How it reached Neyland is not clear.)*
4.   70 foot parcels van to Paddington.
5.   Siphon 'G' to Cardiff.
6.   Brake van to Paddington *(Worked to Neyland by 5.25 am Gloucester)*
This train also conveyed fish trucks Milford Haven to Treherbert and Maerdy and to Bridgend

7.00 pm Neyland Perishable and Milk to Cardiff due 1.32 am which conveyed:
1.   Fish truck Milford Haven to Llanelly.
2.   Gas tank wagon to Llanelly.
3.   Non gangway van to Cardiff.
4.   Non gangway brake van to Treherbert.

With the photographers back to the arrivals platform, the TPO coach standing on the 'middle road' has been re–marshalled to be at the head of the service when it is time to depart at 6.50 pm. The site of the original 40' turntable had been just beyond the coaling stage and with the curve of the engine shed noticeable alongside what is the arrival line.

Brinley John

5. Siphon 'G' to Mountain Ash.
6. Non gangway Siphon Johnston to Cardiff.
7. Non gangway Siphon to Merthyr.
8. Non gangway van third to Cardiff.
9. 8–wheel brake van to Cardiff.
10. Non gangway van to Swansea High Street.

In **1938** the trains were, Paddington 8.55 pm due
Neyland 6.53am and Cardiff 12 Noon due Neyland 5.00
pm formed;
Rear Siphon 'G'.
2. Brake van (Collett 1935 stock).
3. Brake van (40 foot Dean stock).
4. Third brake (Non gangway clerestory).
5. Siphon 'G'.
6.   Siphon 'G'.
Brake composite 68 foot
Siphon 'G'

Neyland 4.35 pm to Paddington 2.25 am
Neyland 7.45 pm to Cardiff 1.55 am

1948
Paddington 8.30 pm to Neyland 8.37 am
Cardiff 11.30 am to Neyland 5.10 pm
Neyland 4.35 pm to Paddington 3.25 am
Neyland 7.30 pm to Cardiff 2.13 am
1958
6.50 pm Swindon #due Neyland 7.35 am
10.00 am Cardiff due Neyland 5.00 pm
Neyland 4.35 pm to Paddington 3.20 am
Neyland 7.50 pm to Cardiff 2.45 am
*# In earlier years this was a working from Paddington to Neyland but the working of parcels trains program for 1958 shows that only a Siphon 'G' 1186 or 2780   from Paddington arriving at Swindon off the 2.20 pm Paddington parcels. The 6.50 pm working picked up other vehicles en–route but only the following were booked to arrive at Neyland: – sx Brake van Cardiff to Neyland attached at Carmarthen off 6.00 pm Canton parcels
sx Parcels van Cardiff to Neyland
sx Van   Bristol to Neyland
Siphon G   Paddington to Neyland*

Surprisingly despite the number of parcels services running analysis of the actual number of parcels handled reveals these services must have been almost empty when arriving at or leaving Neyland. Indeed the average number of parcels forwarded each day in the 1920's was nine and in the 1930's four - this based on trains running six days a week throughout the year. Parcels received averaged 16 each day in the 1920's and 26 in the 1930's. This does not take into account the additional services which were run in the period immediately prior to Christmas. Throughout the two decades two parcels trains arrived and two departed each day on six days. A major service with apparent limited traffic. Bearing in mind also that some parcels would arrive via the guard's compartments of the passenger trains. The only conclusion then must be that these services terminated at or commenced at Neyland purely from the perspective of operational convenience and where there was room to stable and re–marshall trains. The GWR would certainly have been quick in removing or reducing such trains if necessary and so additional revenue was no doubt gained from parcels collected or destined for intermediate stopping places.

Goods Trains

Details can be found in the relevant appendix but the following gives an overview:–

1867
Arrivals (3)
7.15 am Ex Swindon 6.00 pm. Runs as required.
3.00 pm Ex Carmarthen Junction 11.00 am.
5.20 pm Ex Paddington 11.40 pm. 'Irish Goods'.
 Departures (3)
 6.30m to Carmarthen Junction 10.05 pm
10.00m to Paddington 3.10m. 'Irish Goods'.
 5.30m to Swindon 6.30 pm. Runs as required.

1888
Arrivals (2)
1.35 pm Ex Carmarthen Junction 9.15 am.
5.20 pm Ex Gloucester 6.10 am Irish Goods.
Departures (2)
9.00 am to Paddington. 3.55 am 'Irish Goods'.
12.30m to Paddington 8.25m 2nd 'Irish Goods'.

1905
Arrivals (4)
8.00 am Ex Margam Junction 11.05 am 'K'.
10.20 am Ex Neath 1.20 am. 'K'
12.45 pm Ex Carmarthen Junction 'K'.
3.20 pm Ex Paddington 12.15 am 'E' (express goods).
Departures (4)
5.05 pm to Neath 2.15 am 'K' (station truck goods).
9.15 pm to Tondu 6.45 am 'J'.
11.00 pm to Neath 8.25 pm 'K'.
11.30 am to Paddington 2.35 pm 'Irish Goods.'

1924
Arrivals (7)
5.55 am Ex Carmarthen Junction 2.45 am 'J' (return

Neyland goods)
6.35 am Ex Neath 10.15 pm (station truck goods).
7.15 am Ex Duffryn Yard 10.45 pm. 'H'.
2.35 pm Ex Carmarthen Junction 8.50 am 'J'.
5.30 pm Ex Cardiff Goods 10.30 am 'E'.
6.30 pm Ex Carmarthen Junction 2.10 pm 'K'.
9.00 pm Ex Carmarthen Junction 5.45 pm 'K'.
Departures (7)
5.20 am   to Llandilo Junction 12.05 pm 'J'.
9.30 am   to Carmarthen Junction 3.30 pm 'J'.
11.15 am to Haverfordwest 12.10 pm 'K'.
1.00 pm   to Carmarthen Junction 6.55 pm 'J'
5.15 pm   to Neath 3.25 am F (station truck goods).
8.20 pm   to Duffryn Yard 6.10 am 'J'.
10.30 pm to Carmarthen Junction 1.45 am 'J'.

1938
Arrivals (7)
7.10 am Ex Swansea Eastern Depot 9.25 pm class 'H'.   6.20 am to Llandilo Junction 2.36 pm.
7.35 am Ex Cardiff. 9.45 pm class 'E'.
7.55 m Ex Cardiff. 5.00 pm class 'H'.
10.55 am Ex Duffryn Yard. 11.30 pm class 'J'.
4.05 pm Ex Carmarthen Junction. 8.35 am class 'J'.
8.20 pm Ex Cardiff. 8.20 am class 'E'.
9.40 pm Ex Carmarthen Junction. 5.30 pm class 'K'.
Milford Haven
6.40 pm Ex Carmarthen Junction 2.10 pm class 'K'.
Departures (6)
6.20 am to Llandilo Junction 2.36 pm class 'J'.
8.17 am to Carmarthen Junction 4.17 pm class 'J'.
1.25 pm to Carmarthen Junction 7.35 pm class 'E'.
5.20 pm to Neath class 'K'.
8.35 pm to Duffryn Yard class 'J'.
11.50 pm to Carmarthen Junction 2.34 am class 'J'.
Milford Haven
None

1948
Arrivals (7)
3.52 am Ex Carmarthen Junction   12.27 pm class 'J'.
5.52 am Ex Swansea Eastern Depot 9.25 pm class 'H'.
6.09 am Ex Cardiff 5.00 pm class 'H'.
7.53 am Ex Cardiff 9.45 pm class 'E'.
8.12 am Ex Duffryn Yard 9.30 pm class 'J'.
3.25 pm Ex Carmarthen Junction 8.30 am class 'J'.
10.00 pm Ex Carmarthen Junction 6.30 pm class 'K'.
Milford Haven   (1)
6.08 pm Ex Carmarthen Junction 3.10 pm class 'J'.
Departures   (6)
5.20 am to Llandilo Junction 3.45 pm class 'J'.
9.10 am to Carmarthen Junction 3.54 pm class 'J'.
1.00 pm to Milford Haven 1.55 pm class 'K'.
5.15 pm to Neath class 'K'.
7.45 pm to Carmarthen Junction 12.27 pm class 'J'.
11.50 pm to Duffryn Yard class 'J'.

1953

Arrivals (7)

12.37 am Ex Llandilo Junction 6.00 pm class 'H'.

3.17 am Ex Cardiff 6.10 pm class 'F'.

3.38 am Ex Carmarthen Junction 1.15 am class 'J'.

5.52 am Ex Swansea Eastern Depot 9.50 pm class 'H'.

7.12 am Ex Duffryn Yard 9.30 pm class 'J'.

1.37 pm Ex Carmarthen Junction 9.05 am class 'J'.

9.55 pm Ex Carmarthen Junction 6.30 pm class 'J'.

Milford Haven (1)

6.18 pm Ex Carmarthen Junction 3.15 pm class 'J'.

Departures (7)

12.01 am to Duffryn Yard 8.46 am class 'J'.

1.00 am to Llandilo Junction 5.14 am class 'J'.

6.20 am to Llandilo Junction 1.42 pm class 'J'.

9.10 am to Carmarthen Junction class 'J'.

12.50 pm to Milford Haven 1.35 pm class 'K'.

5.15 pm to Neath 3.56 am class 'K'.

7.30 pm to Carmarthen Junction 12.27 am class 'J'.

1958

Arrivals (7)

12.13 am Ex Llandilo Junction 6.00 pm class 'H'.

3.17 am Ex Cardiff 6.10 pm class 'F'.

3.38 am Ex Carmarthen Junction 1.15 am class 'J'.

5.17 am Ex Swansea Eastern Depot 9.50 pm class 'H'.

7.52 am Ex Duffryn Yard 9.30 pm class 'J'.

1.32 pm Ex Carmarthen Junction 9.20 am class 'J'.

8.48 pm Ex Carmarthen Junction 5.35 pm class J

Milford Haven (1)

6.27 pm Ex Carmarthen Junction 3.00 pm class J

Departures (6)

1.00 am to Llandilo Junction class J

5.50 am to Llandilo Junction class J

12.30 pm to Milford Haven 1.15 pm class K

5.25 pm to Neath class J

7.30 pm to Carmarthen Junction class J

11.35 pm to Duffryn Yard class J

Milford Haven Departures (1)

12.30 pm to Carmarthen Junction 3.22 pm class J

It must be noted that again these were the booked workings and take no account of any seasonal or other extra traffic workings.

The volume of goods traffic to or from Neyland was very small. If no traffic originated at Neyland the engine and brake van worked to Johnston where it picked up any traffic and preceded to Milford Haven. In a similar vein, trains booked to Neyland often had no traffic other than for Milford Haven by the time they reached Johnston. Here they left the Milford traffic in the down siding and went to Neyland light engine. Latterly, the only significant traffic for Neyland was coal principally for the engine shed but also for domestic consumption. The statistics show that on an average day one 10–ton load of household coal arrived and it is estimated that five 10–ton wagons of locomotive coal would have been required daily.

Viewed from the water, and the fish vans are in sidings 7 and 8 for cleaning and inspection by the carriage and wagon staff.

Desmond Davies

The South Wales Hotel separated by the trees in the Hotel gardens from Neyland station. The disused Ice factory building stands on the Barnlake side of Westfield Pill. A number of boats are moored near to the site of the railway pontoon. Construction work has commenced on the Nato Quay – see Cahpter 9, but no railway lines have been laid. The former marine factory would have occupied the foreshore near the old hulk that is next to what appears an old ferryboat.
Roger Worsley

Chapter 8
THE CHIEF CIVIL ENGINEER'S DEPARTMENT

The Permanent Way

The P.W. Inspector covering Neyland was based at Clynderwen and was also in charge of the routes to Fishguard, Milford, and Pembroke Dock.

In the middle 1950's there were six men in the permanent way gang at Neyland including the Ganger Tommy Griffiths. He had the responsibility for looking after approximately 16 acres of ground in Neyland and the single track mainline as far as Norton Bridge near Rosemarket, a total of seven track miles. The track, line side and verges beyond Norton Bridge were the responsibility of the gang based at Johnston. Another gang at Milford Haven covered this branch line.

The gang also maintained the various officially recognised walking routes around Neyland for the railway men. They looked after all track except that inside the engine shed and on the turntable deck which was the responsibility of the locomotive department. The sidings in the vicinity of the former cattle dock unusually retained the original inside keyed chairs until closure. As was common GWR practice the sidings in the yard were laid with rail downgraded from running lines.

The maintenance of the stop blocks were also the responsibility of the gang. In practice very little work was necessary other than as a result of a shunting accident. The gang did not maintain the automatic train control ramps and associated equipment, which was the responsibility of the Signal and Telegraph department.

A task before the onset of winter was to dig a trench down 10 inches on each side of point rodding so that if snow fell it settled below the rodding and did not foul its movement.

After snowfall the gang would apply salt to the point rodding and signal wire pulleys to prevent them freezing solid. This task was of necessity repeated frequently and copious amounts of salt were applied, being taken around the lines and sidings in buckets. A summer job for the gang was to dig a fire break around their storage area to ensure that if a fire broke out it could be more easily be contained. During late February of March the gang removed the fishplates cleaned them, and applied a black tar oil before replacing them. This allowed for easier expansion and contraction and so avoided fractures.

The ganger was assisted by the sub–ganger and by packers and linesmen. The gangs normal hours were 7.15 a.m. to 4.45 p.m. Mondays to Fridays, although previously their working week had also included a Saturday morning. On a Sunday it was common practice to work overtime on track renewal, ballast replacement or work in connection with the civil engineer anywhere in a district covered by the local Inspector. It is recalled that when the line through Whitland was upgraded this included laying 300 feet lengths of rail which were welded to form lengths of 900 feet incorporating expansion joints. This involved a sustained period of weekend working with the job starting on Saturday evening and two or more gangs working 12 hours or more in shifts. This took its toll on the men who were then not in peak condition ready to start their normal work the following Monday morning.

The basic tools of the gang were key hammers, long handled spanners and box spanners that incorporated a handle on top. They also used a hand auger to drill the sleepers and which required three men to operate it. In this period there was no crane to assist in the normal day to day work or for

Snow on the West Wales Coast is unusual. The date is unknown but is prior to the removal of the train shed extension in the 1930's

Simon Hancock

Three wagon turntables formally gave access to the two lines leading down to the pontoon. Opposite the GWR sign, and which reads, " No Thoroughfare – Trespassers will be Prosecuted – By Order", was a capstan, formerly used to haul wagons of coal to the tip on the Pill side. On the right a former broad–gauge bridge is stored pending an alternative use.

NRM / GWR B.Box 161/28

more substantial work such as the replacement of crossovers, lengths of rail and sleepers. Instead these operations were carried out using a combination of brute strength and technique bearing in mind that a crossover weighed a ton and each sleeper in excess of 1 cwt. To move a length of rail or a sleeper the gang used long handled grippers (looking like large tongs), the load being shared between two or more men. Heaving bars were used to move the rail into its final position.

To move their equipment around the yard and on the main line the gang used a non–motorised trolley. This had limited application and whilst capable of moving sleepers the bed of the trolley was not long enough to carry a length of rail. Where use of this trolley was impractical material was delivered by railway wagon to the required site and then off loaded to wait a suitable time to carry out the work. Where

ballast was involved this had to be shovelled off the wagon because bottom discharge wagons were not available.

After setting the gang their various tasks, the sub ganger regularly walked the section to Norton Bridge. He took with him a key hammer with which he tapped home any loose wooden keys, which held the rail in place against the sleeper chair. He also took a yellow flag and a supply of detonators in the event of a major fault in the track. He also kept an eye on any length of rail, which was wearing badly or unevenly or was out of gauge. To check that the track was level he placed three boards at intervals. An experienced eye enabled him to determine any defects, which were subsequently remedied. He also made use of a track gauge to check that the rails were the correct width apart. This incorporated a spirit level.

The gang worked closely with the signalmen at Neyland and Johnston and when they required occupation of the single running line for example to repair a broken length of rail then the line had to be closed. As with many aspects of railway work rules and regulations were not always followed to the letter. An example being the rule which laid down that no work was to be carried out on the line until a train leaving either Johnston or Neyland had reached the other station – was often ignored because it was impractical to observe. With a train in the section between these two points on average every 30 minutes very little work could have been done if it were strictly followed. Instead when work was to be undertaken mid–section this would commence as soon as a train had passed. However other rules were strictly observed for safety, such as during certain operations when a look out men was provided to warn of an approaching train. The look out was required to carry and use a whistle and red and green flags. In poor visibility or at night a hand lamp capable of displaying these colours was used instead of the flags.

When fog descended the gang provided a fog–man to man the fogging hut by the down distant signal outside Neyland. The first task being to check that the signal lamp was alight. If this could not be verified from ground level he had to climb the signal ladder to seek confirmation. Whilst on duty he was required to place detonators on the rail which exploded when the wheels of an engine passed over them. This indicated to the locomotive crew that they were passing the distant signal, and to reduce speed and be prepared to stop at the next signal. Detonators were only required to warn trains arriving at Neyland and the fog–man had to have knowledge of the train service to ensure that the detonators where removed before the passage of a train from Neyland. Failure to do so would result in bringing the train to a halt. Once an up train had passed the detonators were placed back on the rail. The fog hut was not provided with a phone to contact the signal box or any indication of an approaching train. Instead it was up to the man on duty to listen out for an approaching train and by the nature of the sound and from their knowledge of the timetables, to recognise in which direction it was travelling. The hut was provided with a coal–fired stove to boil a kettle and a bench seat but otherwise was very rudimentary.

The ganger's cabin was situated beyond the former gas works. Inside there was a table and wooden benches. No wash basin or toilet was provided. A coal fire heated the cabin and there was a hob, which was used to boil a kettle of on which to cook food. The fire was kept a light all the year round for six days each week. The first duty each Monday being to light the fire. Next water was collected in a bucket, holding about four gallons, from a barrel which collected the rainwater off the cabin roof via shoots. This was boiled to provide hot water for washing at the end of the day. Drinking water was collected from the shunters cabin. Personal effects were stored in lockers whilst tools and equipment were stored in a large shed by the cabin which also housed two large vices. By the cabin was a large stone grinding wheel used to sharpen the scythes and hooks. The gang had another hut just beyond where the new road bridge spans Westfield Pill and where were stored jacks. When it was necessary to set temporary speed restrictions the warning boards came by rail from Whitland. The main PW storage area was situated at Clynderwen but a supply of rail and sleeper chairs was kept at Neyland.

At one time painters, bricklayers, masons, maintenance staff and their Inspector were based at Neyland but were also later moved to Clynderwen.

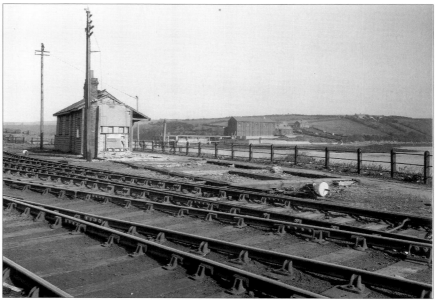

Inside keyed chairs within the sidings at Neyland, some of which would survive until closure. There were a number of restrictions on locomotives at Neyland, the Sectional Appendix stating that Barnlake Sidings Nos 1 & 2 beyond clearance at Johnston end were banned to the following classes, 70xx, 10xx, 79xx, 78xx, 42xx, 72xx, 73xxx and 70xxx engines. All locos were also barred from the coal stage road beyond the entrance to the coal stage, and also from the arrivals platform to No. 3 pit road – direct. Finally there was a restriction on the 82xxx class from using all of the 'Traders Sidings'. The building was originally used by the Trawl Company but was then derelict for many years. NRM / GWR B.Box 161.27

Chapter 9
THE END OF AN ERA

Nationalisation at first brought little change to the railway at Neyland, true the locomotives and rolling stock may have slowly started to sport a differing livery and insignia whilst the paperwork also was gradually changed, but externally matters continued much as before. The aspirations and promises a change from private to public ownership was supposed to deliver, destined largely to remain unfulfilled.

But changes were afoot and the corporate ideal would take place. As far as Neyland was concerned these ideals were first mooted consequent upon the announcement of the 1955 British Railways modernisation programme, one aspect being a plan to introduce diesel traction to replace the steam engine. Accordingly, there would also be a significant reduction in the number of locomotive depots that would be required and with it hoped for reduced operating costs. A foretaste of these occurred locally in 1958 with the issue of a questionnaire to all staff in the various locomotive departments at Neyland, Milford Haven and Pembroke Dock. Much of the information that was gleaned would already have been known within each depot but a centralised return yielded the following insight ;–

144 Forms returned.
114 Married men, 30 Single men

Age Groups	Number	Length of Railway Service (Years)	Number
16–20	7	1–5	19
21–25	14	6–10	24
26–30	13	11–15	32
31–35	13	16–20	13
36–40	25	21–25	18
41–45	16	26–30	3
46–50	17	31–35	5
51–55	9	36–40	11
56–60	22	41–45	13
61–65	8	46–50	6
Total	**144**	**Total**	**144**

From contemporary records it seems clear BR were plan-ning to site a new diesel depot at Whitland and were trying then to gauge the social implications this would have on the other communities affected. Because the railway were still the largest employer in the Town, Neyland Urban District Council were understandably concerned about the impact on the local economy if a depot was built at the new location. Accordingly, a meeting was arranged with Mr K.W.C. Grand, General Manager of the Western Region at Paddington on Monday 5th May 1958. There a deputation from the local council accompanied by the constituency MP, Mr Desmond Donnelly made their case. They argued that as steam traction would still be in use for a considerable period the existing

Places of Residence	Number	Housing	Number
Neyland	107	Employees Owning a house	67
Milford Haven	14	Council House	30
	3	Railway House	10
Haverfordwest	3	Private Landlord	18
Johnston	3	**Married Men**	
Burton	2	Families with children	76
Sardis	2	Total number of children	161
Llangwm	2	Families with children at primary school	35
Rosemarket	2	Secondary School	13
Others	6	Grammar School	7
Total	**144**	**Single men with dependants**	**23**
		Number of dependants supported	**25**

depot at Neyland could continue with its original function. They also pointed out that as a result of recent expenditure the depot was now in better condition that at any time in the previous 20 years and in their view there was also sufficient room to construct a diesel depot nearby without detriment to the existing steam service.

Opposite page;

May 19th, 1961, and 1020 'County of Monmouth' stands at the head of the 2.30 pm departure to Paddington. The engine and crew taking the train as far as Carmarthen. The extreme curvature of the platform meant the crew could not ses the guards signal to depart and this was relayed to them by a porter.

J.S. Gilks

The Nato Quay and complex of sidings and which due to the restricted nature of the site contained some complex pointwork. These sidings were provided with the intention of forming a railhead for military traffic but despite a not inconsiderable investment by the Government they remained largely unused. At one time there had been a proposal to operate a car ferry from the new quay at Neyland to Ireland – shades indeed of years earlier, but BR were seemingly unwilling to make part of their own land, and which have been necessary for the service, available.

Desmond Davies

The Milford Haven branch train at Neyland. This was the 7.05 pm Johnston to Neyland working that had originated from Milford Haven at 6.30 pm. It returned at 9.00 pm leaving Johnston at 9.25 pm for Milford Haven. The service also provided Neyland passengers with a connection at Johnston off the 11.55 pm Paddington to Milford Haven train. The windows visible in the side wall of the station building front the guards room, although since the train shed had been removed many years earlier there was no protection for arriving passengers from the elements.

H.C. Casserley

Former ROD 2–8–0 No. 3010 depicted at Neyland sometime during the early 1950's – note the early BR crest on the tender, and seemingly having recently been overhauled. This engine was at the time allocated to 87G, Carmarthen, but had also at one time been a Neyland engine.

R.J. Buckley

Driver Ken Cannings in charge of No. 1020 'County of Monmouth' having just arrived at Neyland in August 1960. Notice also the coach destination board on the stock stabled in the middle siding.

B.P. Hooper

The case was also made of the potential social consequences to the community and the economic impact on the town should the existing depot close. Additionally that Neyland had long been a centre of recruitment for other regional depots and that Whitland did not have sufficient houses or school places to accommodate the railway staff and their families that might be displaced from Neyland.

Regretfully there is no record of the Western Region response although it would appear the local delegates were assured that a final decision had not then taken place. Subsequently the Council had further correspondence with Mr. Grand's successor, Mr J R Hammond and were further assured that they would be consulted before any decision was taken. The impression being given that although some dieselisation might take place it would be some years ahead, 1967/8, before any decision on the future of Neyland's engine shed would be made. It was also suggested that although the locomotive department would inevitably be reduced it might be possible to retain the location as a booking on point. In light also of prospective industrial development BR would not be stampeded into a decision.

But with the benefit of hindsight this was little more than appeasement, for on 8th February 1960 and seemingly without any further consultation in the local area, Neyland UDC were advised that BR did indeed intend to construct their new diesel depot at Whitland although this would not be brought into operation for same years, the dates 1967/8 being suggested. BR continued that due to the forward timescale, detailed planning of the new depot would not necessarily commence for some time and so it was too early to say what arrangements would be made for the staff affected.

In 1960 the suggested timetable may well have been indented to be genuine but elsewhere matters were moving more rapidly, for co–terminus with the decision the general economic position for the railways was far from good and economies were urgently sought. Indeed by the end of the 1950's it would be fair to say that road transport was in the ascendancy and with the local rail situation bleak both as regards this road competition and also affected by dwindling ferry receipts. Accordingly Pembrokeshire could not escape cost cutting measures, the first of these when the railway operated passenger ferry service between Waterford and Fishguard was withdrawn and which brought to an end a service that had begun a little over a hundred years previously initially from Waterford to Neyland.

However, a welcome development was the construction of oil refineries on the banks of Milford Haven.

The Royal Train at Neyland on August 6th 1955. The service had been worked to the terminus by two ex LMS 8F's arriving at 7.25 pm. The Royal Party were greeted by hundreds of well wishers upon their arrival and which included the Station Master, Mr. Humphrey together with a number of retired railwaymen and their families and also widows of former staff. Elaborate decorations cover the station buildings and which were no doubt intended to mask what was otherwise a visual embarrassment to the Western Region. This was part of a tour which included visits to Haverfordwest, St. David's, Milford Haven, Pembroke Dock and Neyland. The tour concluded with a return to Neyland but departure by sea on the Royal Yacht.

Simon Hancock

The remains of the jetty and site of the fish market.

NRM / GWR B.Box 161/25

Material for the first refinery brought in by rail although subsequently it was largely road hauled, even if later still the movement of petroleum products in rail tank–cars delivered significant revenue. Neyland enginemen and guards had hoped to provide the crews for the petroleum traffic but in the event other depots were allocated the work.

A further blow was a decline in the share of fish traffic to just 10,000 tons and the lowest rail hauled figure recorded.

Matters now move away from the local scene and to 222 Marylebone Road with the appointment of Dr. Richard Beeching as Chairman of the British Railways Board. The results of his review are well known and need not be repeated, although as far as Neyland was concerned there was considerable relief that the reshaping report did not include proposals to reduce the status of either the station or threaten closure of the line from Johnston. Any such relief though was destined to be short lived for early in 1963 it

was announced that Neyland Locomotive Depot would indeed be closed and shortly afterwards that BR would seek approval to withdraw all rail services between Johnston and Neyland.

Understandably this was a bitter blow to the town and Neyland UDC immediately launched a campaign in an attempt to reverse the decision. Additionally they sought a postponement of the plans to close the engine shed, this even before the outcome of the Transport Users Consultative Committee hearing on objections to the line's closure was known.

Locally, what the council was also aware of, was that a proposal had been made by a consortium of three Irish shipping companies to develop Neyland as a terminal for a proposed new car ferry service probably to Rosslare. It was planned to use a vessel 275 feet in length having a beam of 47 feet and a draught of 12 feet 6 inches and capable of accommodating 80 average size saloon cars together with 400 passengers. At Neyland though access to BR owned land was essential as it was proposed to use the Nato Quay for embarkation. The consortium thus anticipated BR would allow them to rent or purchase the necessary space for ancillary offices, car parking and a restaurant. A new pontoon would also be constructed close to the existing ferry pontoon to allow the ferry to berth at all states of the tide. It was envisaged that between 35–40 jobs would be created locally together with a further 50 for the boat crew and which included 14 relief men. The ship would also take fuel at Neyland although repairs and overhauls would be carried out at either Milford Haven or Pembroke Dock. Regretfully in the event the proposal failed, and simply because BR would not consent to the consortium having access to the land required. BR being concerned that their own

1027 'County of Stafford' near the turntable. In the background is a 'WD' 2–8–0, which class were frequent visitors also to Neyland in the BR period.

Paul Chancellor

marginally profitable steamer route between Fishguard and Rosslare was likely to have been seriously affected by the competition of the new service from Neyland.

Returning though to the local railway situation, and a deputation from the Neyland UDC met Mr. R. C. Hilton, WR Divisional Manager, at Cardiff on 2nd September 1963 and to make a case to postpone the closure of the locomotive depot and also to outline its objections to the permanent closure of all the railway establishments at Neyland. The deputation reiterated the arguments made in 1958 and went into detail as to how complete closure of the line would have a devastating effect on the economy of the town. They claimed that BR had not taken notice of proposals made by its own employees based at Neyland that would have resulted in a reduction of operating costs. These included changes to the passenger guard rosters and the current inefficient use of locomotives. They claimed that BR had not sought to exploit the traffic potential of the line and illustrated their case by reference to the railways failure to tender for the renewal of the school children contract. They also pointed out that no attempt had been made to encourage patronage when the technical college opened in Neyland and which served the whole of Pembrokeshire.

In response, Mr Hilton accepted that Neyland had not been included in the original reshaping plan but that a re–appraisal using more up to date information clearly showed that there was no case for retaining the Neyland service. He further pointed out that the closure of the depot was unconnected with the closure of the line because it would not be required even if the line remained open. With the introduction of the diesel multiple unit service west of Swansea, diagrams had been introduced to give the best possible use of men and machines and he was satisfied that it was better to have a depot at the centre of operations and not at the periphery.

There was perhaps one small concession, for realising the very real human problems that existed he had agreed to a number of turns being based at Milford Haven and which were available for the Neyland men. Accordingly it was announced that the position after the 9th September 1963 was that steam locomotives in the West Wales area would be reduced to just four based at Carmarthen. With regard to the financial position he give the following information on the line from Johnston to Neyland ;–
Revenue attributable to the line £733 per annum,
Direct costs – terminal £5174 with movement costs £6750. He also explained that alternative employment was available for most of those displaced albeit not in the locality and in so far as passengers services were concerned adequate alternatives were available. He also stated that on the freight side it was not BR's policy to jettison remunerative traffic but a more efficient and economic service could be given to customers by reducing the number of centres handling goods and from which then goods would be delivered by road to their final destination.

The deputation asked Mr Hilton to reconsider the decision but he was unmoving, stating he was satisfied that all factors had been considered and the closure proposals were justified.

The end was now inevitable and the last steam hauled service, a passenger and mail train, departed on Sunday 8th September 1963 behind 6984 *Owsden Hall* in charge of Driver George Morgan and Fireman, Cedric Smith.

The following day 114 jobs were lost when the locomotive depot was closed. About 20 drivers or guards though were relocated to Milford Haven to work the train services from there. For the remainder it was a sad time. Some took early retirement whilst others transferred to railway jobs elsewhere, but a significant number of the younger men who were unable to transfer were made redundant. The reason for this was simple, Neyland was just one of many locations where staff were no longer required and accordingly there was a finite limit to the vacancies that were available.

Westfield Pill and viewed up–stream with the Nato Quay appearing as if it is brand–new in the evening sunshine. The pontoon has been removed and in place of 'The Tube' is a new ramp for the Neyland to Hobbs Point Ferry.

Desmond Davies

Neyland Staff "shot" by Magazine

As Goods Guard **Jack Harrison** came off duty at Neyland recently our *Magazine* representative was on the spot to take this cheerful picture of him (*right*). He has been a railwayman for 23 years and, like so many of his colleagues, is a keen gardener.

Just when Leading Porter **Fred Edwards** showed a parcel in need of repair to Station Master **G. W. House**, the camera clicked again; snapped cleaning the window of a diesel multiple unit was Carriage Service-man **J. Griffiths** who supports the local rugby team.

Prepared to pose for a picture was Junior Clerk **Peter Lewis** who has completed his first year's railway service. (*bottom right*)

NEYLAND MEN

Left: *Perhaps somewhat ironically it has proved impossible to locate a better copy of the Western Region Staff Magazine for 19161 and which included this delightful piece on some of the staff. Nowadays viewed perhaps as propaganda, at the time such items – a different location was featured each month, produced a welcome morale booster at a time when modernisation and change was being felt throughout the system.*

Lower Left:

Staff outside the Carriage and Wagon Cabin and featuring, (back–row) L–R, Jack Griffiths – Goods Guard, Cyril Bevan – C & W, Albert John – C & W, Alfie White, Reggie Townsend, (front–row), Tom Thomas – Porter Guard, and Ivor John – C & W but later became a Shedman.

Western Telegraph

Lower right:

Staff outside the Booking Office in 1951, (back–row) L–R, Tommy James – C & W, Cyril Bevan – C & W, Steve Thomas – C & W, Jack Griffiths – Goods Guard, Gilbert John – C & W Chargeman but who had started as a carriage cleaner (see also top view on page 78), (front–row) L–R, W. (Billy) Stewart – C & W, Albert John – C & W, M. (Paddy) Ryan – C & W, and Walter Rees – C & W.

Western Telegraph

For the present though the station remained open although now only with the status of an unstaffed halt. A DMU shuttle service operating to Johnston where connections were made with trains to and from Milford Haven. But despite the setback behind the scenes the UDC were still fighting and continued to canvass support both locally and further afield to prevent a complete closure of the line. The council also retained a barrister to argue their case at the TUCC hearing at Tenby in October 1963. Other interested parties, including regular railway users who would suffer hardship if the closure took place, supported this case.

Despite these efforts though, the TUCC conceded the case for closure. The next stage coming on 4th November 1963 when BR issued a letter announcing that from Monday 2nd December 1963 the goods facility at Neyland would be withdrawn in favour of Johnston and Milford Haven for "full load" traffic and Milford Haven for coal and coke. Facilities for handing in and the collection of parcels and freight "smalls" would though continue to be available at Neyland.

Undaunted Neyland UDC still continued to press for the line to be retained. In correspondence with the Ministry of Transport in January 1964 it drew attention to earlier assurances given by BR that no accommodation difficulties would arise at Milford Haven station because of additional traffic following the run down at Neyland. The Council though claimed that time and again these assurances had proved to be worthless. The letter added that complaints had also been made to the Area Manager that "smalls" and passenger rated parcels traffic was being operated from Johnston instead of Neyland even though Neyland station remained open. It was as if a deliberate policy was in place to deny the station of both customers and revenue. Finally, it said that steam locomotives were still reaching Neyland once or twice a day and using the turntable and this despite the assurance given that steam engines would not need to operate west of Carmarthen

6984 'Owsden Hall' on the last scheduled steam hauled passenger train departing Neyland on Sunday September 8th 1963. The service was the 6.20 pm to Paddington and in charge of Driver George Morgans and Fireman Cedric Smith.

Western Telegraph

when BR had made it's case for closing Neyland locomotive depot.

The voice now though was left unheard and despite the protestations the last passenger train, a 3–car DMU, left Neyland on Sunday 14th June 1964. The set was driven by Hilliard James and with Jack Harrison as guard.

There were rumours at the time that BR was considering using Neyland as the terminal for ore imports, possibly up to 20,000 tons per day being distributed by rail to Port Talbot, Newport and possibly Cardiff. However nothing came to fruition.

Following the closure the level crossing gates between Neyland and Johnston were locked in favour of road traffic and Westfield and Upper Rosemarket Crossing keepers' lodges sold and became private residences. Lower Rosemarket Lodge was demolished. At Neyland the

An unidentified 'Hymek' diesel waiting at Neyland for its turn of duty. The head–code displayed. '3F17', refers to the 6.40 pm parcels from Swindon, and so the return working may well have been on '3A40' the 3.35 pm Neyland to Paddington parcels.

Brinley John

The last passenger train to leave Neyland on June 14th 1964. Driver H.V. James in charge accompanied by Guard J.E. Harrison. DMU's had first appeared in this part of West Wales in 1959 when they began to operate between Bristol and Milford Haven. They only saw use at Neyland for the final few months of service consequent upon the closure of the engine shed.

So ended 108 years of railway service to the Town.

Aurora Imaging 709420

The very last day of service and closure of the 'engine house' – as it had been called on the earliest plans of the station. The Shed Foreman Hilliard Jones, shakes hands with driver Arthur Evans. Behind are (L – R), Fred Griffith – Driver, Cyril Shortman – Clerk, Edward G. 'Teddy' Morgans – Driver, Victor Rowe – Driver, William L. James – Driver, Sidney Lloyd – Driver, William Bryant – Fireman, and Charlie Evans – Carriage and Wagon Examiner. September 1963.

Alan Morgans

demolition gang arrived in 1965 and razed the station building and other railway structures except for the signal box and the Iron Bridge. For a time a guards van was used as an office for the selling of surplus equipment and materials. The track though between Neyland and Johnston still remained but at the Johnston end was now used to store wagons surplus to requirements.

Despite having lain moribund though for almost two years, there was a renaissance in May 1966 when the line was reopened to allow construction material to be transported to the former station site and which was being used as a base for the construction material for an oil refinery in the area. It was destined to be a temporary resurgence for this traffic ended in May 1968 and afterwards the signal box was demolished and the track lifted back to Johnston. After more than 100 years Neyland was no longer connected by rail to the outside world.

Subsequently the Iron Bridge was removed in 1972 whilst the track bed found a new use as a cycle and footpath. It was though to be nearly 20 years before the land at the former station and yard was redeveloped into a marina, the area being known as Brunel Quay. Notice boards have been placed around the site giving details of the former railway activities including the maritime trade to Ireland. Indeed, railways lines remain visible in the marina site on what was the former Nato Quay and ancient bridge rail on which broad gauge trains ran to Neyland now find use as fencing at the quay. The former station masters house is also still in use as a private residence as are the railway built houses in Lower High Street and Railway Terrace.

Brunel's involvement is also commemorated in one other way, a statue having been erected as a fitting reminder that it was his decision to build the South Wales Railway line to Neyland Point and which had then given birth to the town of Neyland.

Sandra Parker

Appendix 1
Signalling at Neyland

The first signal box at Neyland probably dated from about 1881 previous to which operation was principally on the 'time–interval' system with signals and points operated by 'Policemen' but without interlocking of any sort. Accidents therefore were a feature of the early days, perhaps surprisingly few, considering the conditions of working. Several are known of though, including when a 'pilot engine' arriving at Neyland ran into a siding colliding with some stationary trucks, and another when the 'Up Mail' service left the station but travelled a mile on what was the down line simply because the points had not been properly set. Two others occurred in 1886 and 1867. In the former year a late running train derailed on the reverse curves between Westfield Mill Crossing and New Milford when a 6–wheeled coach jumped the rails. The situation was made worse by the driver's attempt to stop the train by reversing his engine. Nine passengers sustained minor injuries. Finally in 1867 an overloaded cattle train left New Milford but stalled on the steep bank before reaching Johnston. The crew decided to take part of the train forward whilst the guard protected the rear although unfortunately another train collided with the rear van before this could be accomplished.

Such situations were by no means uncommon, the staff at fault often dismissed as a result. In reality though what was really needed was a means of operating whereby 'block–working' was introduced allied to the interlocking of points and signals. This was a message the Board of Trade had been promoting for many years but it would not be until the latter part of the 19th century – the exact date is unknown, when such modernisation would reach Neyland.

Accordingly co–terminus with the opening of the first signal box it is likely that modern operating practices were slowly introduced. This first box 'Neyland Station' ('New Milford Station' until 30–8–1906), and which can just be seen in the view on page 44, appeared to have been a brick and timber affair. It is believed to have contained 20 levers and was to Signalling Record Society classification '3'.

Expansion of the station and its facilities meant an additional signal box was required and 'Neyland East' was opened in 1892. It contained 13 levers and was likewise known as 'New Milford East' until the 30–8–1906. The type of construction is not known. It is believed also it may have been around this time that block working was completed to Johnston.

Of somewhat indifferent quality but an interesting view none the less depicting what was then the new footbridge for the Barnlake Ferry and also baulk road and a slotted post signal. The signal itself would appear to a contemporary Westinghouse design and is the only view located to give a possible hint then that the early signalling at the Terminus may well have been provided by a contractor rather than the GWR. Standard GWR fittings did of course appear in later years. The scene was recorded

'Neyland East' closed in 1910 but a new timber ground–level 'box contained just 5–levers was opened with the same name in 1917 and to SRS type 21.

Changes to operating requirements in 1919 again resulted in alterations and around July 1919 the original 'Neyland Station' signal box was closed to be replaced at the same time by a new 'Neyland West'. This was to type 7D and is the structure depicted in the various illustrations. It was renamed 'Neyland' from 3–4–1932 following the closure of the small 5–lever 'Neyland East'. The 'west' box would survive until closure and latterly contained a 46 lever frame at 4–inch centres with vertical tappet 3–bar locking. It ceased working on 14–6–1964.

Appendix 2
Mail Train Formations

The coaching stock formation was recorded as
Circa 1913–1924

9.15 pm Paddington
70 foot parcels van
50 foot ocean mail brake van
Post Office sorting van
Mail van
70 foot third class passenger coach
70 foot third class passenger coach
70 foot first class passenger coach
Van third
The first 2 vehicles worked back on 3 pm Neyland and were detached at Swindon. They were forwarded on to Paddington by the 5.10 pm Penzance. All the other vehicles worked from Neyland by the 6.30 pm train which also conveyed a Siphon G to Cardiff.

1924

9.15 pm Paddington
Van Paddington to Neyland
Post Office parcels van Gloucester to Neyland
Mail van Paddington to Neyland
Van Paddington to Neyland
Brake van Paddington to Neyland
Composite sleeping coach Paddington to Neyland

Composite coach Paddington to Neyland
Van Paddington to Neyland
All these vehicles worked from Neyland on the 6.30 pm Neyland.

1929

9.25 pm Paddington

Post Office stowage van	Paddington to Neyland
Siphon G	Cardiff to Neyland
Brake van	Paddington to Neyland
70 foot third passenger coach	Paddington to Neyland
Composite sleeping coach compartments trailing)	Paddington to Neyland (First class
Composite coach	Paddington to Neyland
Van third	Paddington to Neyland

All these vehicles plus another Siphon G worked from Neyland on the 6.30 pm train.
As can be seen these were passenger trains, which also carried a post office vehicle.

In the **1950's** the 6.50 pm Neyland to Paddington carried a Post Office stowage vehicle as far as Bristol either No 815, 816, or 817. In addition it picked up a sorting carriage at Carmarthen detached at Bristol either No 796, 848, or 849. The Neyland stowage van arrived at 6.50 am on the 1.05 am Bristol passenger and mail train.

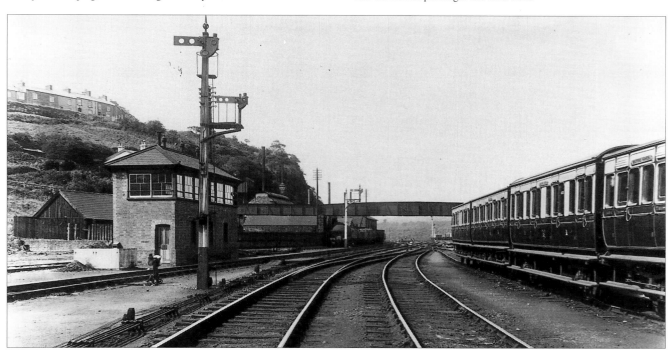

Above; Probably taken in the early years of the present century, standard GWR signal fittings appear to now be the norm. The bracket arm is nos. 22 and 27 in the frame. Interestingly the carriage destination boards proclaim 'Milford Haven'.

Barrie Jacobs

Previous page: – The duty signalman passes the token to the fireman of 7829 'Ramsbury Manor' at the head of the 8.00 am to Paddington on 25 May 1963 and which was due to arrive in London at 3.10 pm. The 'box was 32 feet 6 inches by 11 feet 9 inches and contained a frame of 46 levers. Token working to Johnston being to configuration 'C' – coloured green. The door visible within the end wall was used solely to gain access to the locking frame, a similarly positioned door at the opposite end leading to a set of internal stairs which rose to the operating floor. The 'box had at one time been manned continuously on the standard three–shift pattern although in later years traffic on nights was sparse and the duty man was able to catnap on a cushion purloined from one of the passenger coaches.

E. Wilmshurst 1557

Appendix 3
Goods Trains

1867 Service Timetable gives the following insight:

Down Trains

4.10 am Express Goods Swindon to New Milford (continuation of 11.45 pm Paddington)

To take all through perishable and important goods for Cheltenham and South Wales and from Gloucester to take forward full loads of cattle and perishables for stations at which it calls and for Ireland via New Milford. Trucks intended for this train must in all cases be placed consecutively. To take station truck from Gloucester and from London to New Milford. To pick up cans of milk at Awre Junction, Chepstow and Portskewett on Sundays for Newport and Cardiff passenger station. To call at Port Talbot and Swansea Valley Junction to put off meat or block tin from London only. To make up a full load at Carmarthen Junction. To leave Gloucester at 7.30 am on Sundays and work forward traffic brought in by 12.40 am ex Paddington.

4.45 am Gloucester to New Milford

To do station truck work only as far as Gowerton. To work the gunpowder van on Tuesdays and Fridays and not to do any shunting at intermediate stations.

Station Truck No 34 ex Cardiff, No 33 ex Bridgend and Nos 63, 130, 151, 152, 153, 154, 155, 156, 157, 173, 174.

To pick up station truck No 198 at Newport brought in by the 7.30 am ex Pontypool Road. Not to exceed load of 33 from Gowerton, Llanelly and Pembrey so that Kidwelly may be able to put seven trucks on the train daily making the load from there up to 40 trucks. To change engines and guards at Neath. To shunt to Neath goods shed platform if necessary. At St Clears and Clynderwen the train must shunt into the goods shed to put

in and take out goods unless they can be put off and taken on in separate truckloads. Also to shunt into Haverfordwest goods shed if required but as far as possible Haverfordwest goods and also goods for St Clear must be kept in separate trucks and put off in truck loads to avoid exposure and risk of pilferage by night on platforms. The guards to see to this at the different stations along the road. This train (when necessary) must take on general traffic from stations that cannot be worked away by other trains up to a limit of 20 wagons. Train to be started from Neath without shunting trucks into siding order. Train to be marshalled where convenient. Station trucks only to be taken on at Landore. Trucks for Clynderwen, Clarbeston Road and New Milford only to be picked up at Gowerton. Trucks in the goods shed at Llanelly for this train to be formed in station order by the yard engine. To call at Severn Tunnel Junction to pick up station trucks. The 7.00 pm guards to assist in transfer of goods at Neath when train is late.

4.55 am Swindon to New Milford (continuation of 12.40 am ex Paddington)

To convey general goods traffic and empties and empties for Cirencester and stations on the Gloucester line where timed to call and for South Wales proper. Traffic for Brimscombe on this train must not be detached en route. To call at Newnham when required to pick up trucks of fruit and to call at Ely paper mill siding when required to pick up paper for Cork. To take on at Stormy, trucks for Carmarthen and west thereof. To call when required at Port Talbot and Kidwelly to put off trucks of tin from London only. Aberdare wagons must not be put on this train. Trucks for Pembrey on this train to be put off at Gowerton to go on from there by subsequent train. Trucks for Johnston and Milford to be put off at Haverfordwest to go on from there by S.T. train.

6.20 pm Bristol to New Milford via Severn Tunnel

Assorted freight, parcels and passenger stock at Neyland in what is probably a late 1940's or early 1950's view. Despite the apparent prominence of freight vehicles seen in several of the views throughout this book, it must be recalled that after the loss of the Irish Ferry Traffic and Fishing fleet freight vehicles seen at Neyland were largely those held for other destinations.

Author's Collec.

To convey through traffic for stations in South Wales any traffic for Aberdare and Hereford district to be put off at Severn Tunnel Junction.

Up Trains

8.00 am New Milford to Gloucester – Mondays only
Empties may be sent by this train to Gloucester but not for Bristol.

9.00 am Express New Milford to London
To take full loads of Irish goods, perishables and cattle only from New Milford for London. Load to be limited to 23 trucks of goods or 25 of cattle to Cardiff and 30 beyond. To make up full load, if necessary, with important traffic for Reading and London, also take pigs for Birmingham as far as Newport. On Mondays to call at Llantrisant when required.

12.30 pm New Milford to Gloucester and London Express
To take cattle and full loads and perishables from stations at which it calls for Reading and London. Not to be delayed at stations shunting out traffic. To take trucks (full loads) from Clynderwen to Carmarthen Junction. To call at St Clears on Thursday for pork traffic and for cattle on first Tuesday in each month. Trucks for north of Newport to be put off at Landore for 5.00 pm ex Swansea to take on, Great Western empties for east of Pyle, not to be put off on this train. To take meat when required from Johnston to Carmarthen Junction. To call at Kidwelly and Pembrey when required for Gloucester and London trucks and for dead meat for London.

3.00 pm New Milford to Bristol via Severn Tunnel Junction.
To be limited to 20 trucks from New Milford. To take general and Bristol traffic but must not be loaded with traffic from main line stations east of Severn Tunnel Junction. All Bristol traffic from stations at which it calls to be kept back for this train. This train to take loco. coal empties from New Milford for Briton Ferry. All local trucks to be put off at Carmarthen Junction to go on from there by 9.35 pm and 11.30 pm trains and from Carmarthen Junction upwards this train is to take on trucks for beyond Pyle only. To call at Ferryside and Gowerton for cockles or Bristol traffic only. To call at Pembrey, Briton Ferry and Port Talbot for Bristol traffic only. To put off at Cockett, trucks for Swansea and the Vale of Neath to go on by 9.35 pm ex Llanelly Dock, the trucks in question must be marshalled in station order when put off at Cockett. Station Truck Nos. 195 and 196.

5.15 pm New Milford to Neath
To leave New Milford with station trucks and goods only. Each station from Johnston to Clynderwen to wire New Milford daily by 5.00 pm what empties are on hand and a special to be arranged to clear whenever there are not less than 20 empties at the stations in question. All empties and London trucks for South Wales stations east of Neath, except trucks of general goods traffic and cattle to be put off at Dynevor. Goods for Loughnor must be put off at Llanelly to go on by 7.00 am from Llanelly Docks.

In 1903 it is recorded that the total goods tonnage was 20242 and in addition 37 wagons of livestock were transported. The modest number of livestock wagons may be due to the policy having changed so that most of the cattle were slaughtered in Ireland and the carcasses shipped over. After the Irish trade had been moved to Fishguard the decline in goods traffic was at first not as marked as might have been thought. In fact the figures for 1913 show 25 wagons of livestock but an increase in total goods tonnage to 27424 tons. However following the First World War with the growth of mechanised transport the goods traffic declined markedly so that by 1923 the total was 7829 tons with only 11 wagons of livestock. (See also statistics on pages 105/6.)

The Service Timetable for 1905 shows further development in Neyland's goods traffic

Down Trains

1.20 am Neath to New Milford
Engine to be out at 12.15 am to form the train. To clear Neath of down line goods shed traffic the Landore and Swansea traffic to be put off at Landore relief sidings and the other traffic from Neath and Dynevor sidings for stations west of Landore. To leave Llandilo Junction sufficiently light to clear Kidwelly

6.40 am Newport to New Milford
To take all through perishable and important goods for South Wales and for Ireland via New Milford. Station Trucks Nos. 28,29,30,49,90 and 194 from Llanelly. Trucks intended for this train must in all cases be placed consecutively. To take on traffic from Cardiff any traffic brought in by the 10.20 pm ex Reading and 10.50 pm ex Paddington for stations west of Cardiff. To call at Port Talbot Swansea Valley Junction and Gowerton to put off meat and black tar from London only. To call at Llandilo Junction when required to put off traffic for the Llanelly line only. To make up a full load at Carmarthen Junction.

8.30 am Carmarthen Junction to New Milford
To take traffic for stations where timed to call Station Truck No 211. The engine to be out at 8.00 am, shunt out the wagons to go on by its train.

9.00 am Cardiff to New Milford
To be worked by engine and guard of 3.25 pm Trawl Fish train from Old Milford. To be loaded with traffic west of Neath only. To run through passenger road at Neath. To take on at Landore, relief sidings and Llandilo Junction traffic for Carmarthen Junction and beyond only. To call when required at Swansea Valley Junction to put off trucks only for Cardiff. To call at Landore and Llanelly for water only. To call when required at Loughor for Old Milford coal. Advice of departure and loading of this train to be wired from Carmarthen Junction to Johnston.

11.25 am Alexandra Dock Junction to New Milford (12.50 am ex Paddington) to convey general goods traffic and empties for South Wales Station Trucks Nos. 89, 340. To call when required at Port Talbot to put off traffic from London only. Swansea Valley Junction, tin from London to be put off at Neath and to be sent forward by first available train. Trucks for Pembrey on this train to be put off at Llandilo Junction to go on from there by subsequent train.

6.00 pm Neath to New Milford
To leave Neath punctually, whether the marshalling can be done or not, To call at Dynevor station when required to put out petroleum and station goods. This train must be confined to station truck work, cattle, and perishables, and any other urgent traffic. Trucks in the goods shed at Llanelly for this train to be formed in station order by the yard engine. To take coal trucks or urgent traffic from Haverfordwest when required.

3.35 pm Pontypool Road to Carmarthen Junction
To convey traffic for stations where timed to call and Ice traffic from Cardiff for New Milford to be put off at Carmarthen Junction to go on by 10.30 pm ex Tondu.

10.30 pm Tondu to New Milford
To take trucks for stations west of Landore. An advice by wire to be sent from Tondu to Neath stating how many trucks there are in the train for beyond Landore so that an engine may b provided to assist from Neath to Cockett. To call at Port Talbot to pick up only. Not to take trucks for Port Talbot, Briton Ferry, or South Dock Swansea via Eastern Depot. To pick up at Carmarthen Junction traffic put off by the 3.35 pm ex Pontypool Road. To put off trucks for Kidwelly and Ferryside at Llandilo Junction, for Sarnau and St Clear at Carmarthen Junction and for Clynderwen and Clarbeston Road at Whitland, to go on by the 11,20 am ex Neath and 8.30 am ex Carmarthen Junction.

Up Trains

11.30 am Express New Milford to London

To take full loads of Irish goods, perishables, and cattle only form New Milford to London. Also to take trucks of pigs for Birmingham as far as Cardiff to go on by 8.30 pm Cardiff to Birmingham and traffic for the Birkenhead and Manchester Districts to be put off at Newport, to go on by the 7.40 pm Newport to Pontypool Road. To take trucks of hides when required, Swansea to Cardiff. To call when required at Port Talbot passenger station for consignments of copper and yellow metal for stations beyond Manchester. An advise to be sent by wire from Port Talbot to Neath, when this is required, and enginemen and guard to be advised at Neath. To call at Cockett to put brakes down only.

1.30 pm New Milford to Bristol (Temple Meads)

Station Trucks Nos. 448,449, to Neath, 450. On Tuesdays, Thursdays, and Saturdays this train must leave New Milford with a load of not more than 6 wagons so as to be able to clear traffic from stations between Johnston and Carmarthen Junction. On other days it will leave New Milford with a load of not more than 16 wagons. To take on at stations New Milford to St Clear inclusive, livestock, perishables, Bristol traffic, and G.W. empties (to be put off at Carmarthen Junction.) and to make up a load with trucks for Vale of Neath line. To place trucks in up line siding at Clarbeston Road for 11.00 pm goods. Cattle for Ferryside and Kidwelly may be sent by this train. From Carmarthen Junction. up the train must take on traffic for beyond Pyle only, but must not take on trucks for main line stations East of Severn Tunnel Junction. To call at Ferryside, Kidwelly, Pembrey and Gowerton for cockles or Bristol (Temple Meads) goods shed traffic only. To call at Pembrey for cockle traffic for Vale of Neath line. Traffic for Bristol East Depot, on this train from stations West of Landore to be put off at Neath to go forward by 12.15 am Landore to Bristol East Depot, except livestock for stations served by 8.50 am Bristol East Depot to Didcot, which must be taken to Temple Meads when train is running in time to catch 8.00 am thence to East Depot. To call at Briton Ferry and Port Talbot for Bristol (Temple Meads) goods shed traffic only

2.45 pm Express New Milford to London

Station trucks Nos. 447, 457a. To convey through cattle traffic, also traffic for Reading, Acton, and London only from Carmarthen Junction. Llanelly, Landore, and Port Talbot. To put off at Carmarthen Junction trucks with Irish goods for South Wales and West of England to go forward by the 6.00 pm ex Carmarthen Junction. Cattle traffic from Haverfordwest and Clynderwen to be worked by 1.30 pm. New Milford to go forward by 2.45 pm. London traffic from Neath be worked to Port Talbot by 6.50m goods. Haverfordwest, Clynderwen and Whitland to wire before 12.30 pm particulars of cattle trucks for the 2.45 pm to pick up at Whitland so that loading can be arranged or a second engine provided. To convey traffic for Didcot and beyond, also traffic from New Milford and stations west of Landore where the train calls for Birmingham and South Staffordshire, to be put off at Port Talbot for the 8.45 pm Neath Junction to Worcester. This traffic must be taken on next to the engine and a wire sent to Port Talbot giving number of wagons. Stations sending Birmingham and South Staffordshire traffic on this train must wire Port Talbot, so that the 8.45 pm Neath Junction may be kept for it. Trucks to go by this train to be marshalled in following order :– Acton trucks first, then Paddington, then Reading.

Special Cargo Train

When a special cargo train is run with surplus traffic after the departure of the second Irish goods the loading from New Milford to be wired Carmarthen Junction, and trains to be amalgamated with 6.00 pm from Carmarthen Junction if practicable.

3.25 pm Trawl Fish Train, Old Milford to Paddington

The maximum load for one engine is 100 wheels and if there are more than this number a second engine must be provided to work to Carmarthen Junction When the traffic necessitates the running of two trains, the 3.25 pm must start punctually with traffic for all stations except London and run as far as Gloucester, the second train to leave at 4.00 pm with London traffic only running via Badminton. When a second train is run a telegraphic advice must be sent to Haverfordwest, Whitland, Carmarthen Junction and Carmarthen. When an assistant engine is required Old Milford must advise New Milford by 11.00 am and the second engine must leave New Milford at 1.45 pm. When a second train is required, Old Milford by 12 noon and a guard and van must be provided to work with the 1.45 pm engine. Old Milford must wire Gloucester daily, the number and destination of the wagons for Gloucester and beyond. Bristol fish to be put off at Cardiff to go on by 9.33 pm train. Fish for London must be formed together and as far as possible must be loaded in vacuum brake vehicles. Every possible effort must be made to work this fish train punctually. Engine and guard to return from Cardiff working a special express goods next day. No fish will be conveyed from Old Milford by the 12.55 or 6.24 pm train, but the whole of the fish must be forwarded by the special fish train.

4.00 pm Trawl Fish Train, Old Milford to Paddington (RR) Via Badminton

This train will convey London and West of England traffic only.

5.05 pm New Milford to Neath

Station Trucks Nos. 443, 444, 445, 451, 452, 452a, 453, 454, 455, 456, 457, 458, 459, 460. This train to be limited to 20 wagons and be confined to station truck work, cattle and perishables and any other urgent traffic. To shunt into goods shed at St Clears to put in and take out goods, unless they can be put off and taken on in a separate truck loads.

5.35 pm New Milford to Old MIlford (RR)

When this is required to run a telegraphic advice to be sent from Old Milford to New Milford not later than 2.30 pm.

9.15 pm New Milford to Tondu

To take traffic for the Lynfi and Ogmore line and Port Talbot and Briton Ferry and make up with local traffic. To clear Johnston of up line traffic and put trucks except cattle for 11.00 pm ex New Milford off at Haverfordwest for that train to take on. To take on at Pembrey empties for L and O line only. These trucks to be shunted in readiness for 9.15 pm pick up. To call at Briton Ferry when required for Tondu trucks only.

11.00 pm New Milford to Neath to work local traffic.

To clear Haverfordwest of up line trucks. An advice to be sent to New Milford by 7.00 pm what trucks there are to go on. On weekdays, empties for Cae Duke to be put off at Loughor. To run on to Briton Ferry when required, leaving Neath with Briton Ferry trucks only. To call at Swansea Valley Junction when required to put off traffic. To call when required at Dynevor Sidings to take crippled wagons for repairing shops and other traffic for Neath. Train and engine to be relieved as soon as possible on arrival at Neath, and crippled wagons to be taken to shed by shed pilot. On Sundays, calls as required at Llandilo Junction to put off Cae Duke and Loughor colliery empties. When running late every effort must be made to get this train to Neath to connect with 10.30 am to Tredegar Junc. and if necessary trucks must be picked up un–marshalled, but guards must give full particulars of such cases in their journals. Maximum load for empties Neath to Dynevor 40 empties.

CATTLE SPECIAL NEW MILFORD TO ACTON

This train is to be run when there are 10 or more trucks of cattle for Acton or beyond. Maximum load 20 wagons. Trucks worked on this train to be fitted with screw couplings. To carry E head marks and be signalled by bell code 1–2–1. It is important that the train be got through without delay, and Station masters and Station Inspectors must take steps to ascertain the actual running of the train on receipt of advice from New Milford, and personally see the train through their respective stations. As the times for starting this special will be uncertain the following table is a guide to the time that should *not be exceeded* in running between stations and at which the train calls for water and examination :–

Driver Sid Lloyd and fireman, long term Neyland resident pannier–tank No. 3654 complete with shunters truck and 'A' class headcode! August 8, 1950.

Brinley John

Running times:

New Milford – Carmarthen Junction	1 hour 30 minutes
Carmarthen Junction to Landore	1 hour 20 minutes
Landore to Cardiff	1 hour 28 minutes
Cardiff to Severn Tunnel Junction	39 minutes
Severn Tunnel Junction to	30 minutes
Stoke Gifford to Swindon	1 hour 10 minutes
Swindon to Reading	1 hour 15 minutes
Reading to Acton	58 minutes

Time to be occupied at under–mentioned stations:

Carmarthen Junction	10 minutes
Landore	10 minutes
Cardiff	10 minutes
Severn Tunnel Junction	10 minutes
Stoke Gifford	10 minutes
Swindon	10 minutes
Reading	10 minutes

Trawl Fish Traffic from Swansea

When the two Trawl trains ex New Milford are run, Swansea traffic to be marshalled at South Dock High Level as under; – Gloucester and Midland, Paddington, Reading, Swindon, Bristol, Cardiff, Landore transfer. When one train only is run it must be marshalled as under ;– Paddington, Reading, Swindon, Gloucester and Midland, Bristol, Cardiff, Landore transfer.

WORKING OF RETURN KINSALE FISH, CATTLE, AND CARGO SPECIALS. GLOUCESTER AND BRISTOL TO NEW MILFORD

These specials must carry 'F' head marks as far as Neath and 'E' head marks from Neath to New Milford and in making arrangements for their running regard must be paid to the working of the trains into Gloucester and Bristol on the forward journey, so as to allow men sufficient rest before returning. The specials will call only at Cardiff, Neath, Longhor for Old Milford coal, Llandilo Junction (trucks for Llanelly to be put off at Llandilo Junction) Carmarthen Junction and Johnston and must only be loaded with traffic for stations at which they are timed to call, except trucks for Llanelly and stations West of Carmarthen Junction. The trains must be loaded from Gloucester and Bristol with traffic for stations West of Newport only, from Newport, Alexandra Dock Junction and Cardiff with traffic for stations West of Neath and from Bridgend, Stormy, Neath, and Landore Relief Sidings with traffic for Carmarthen Junction, Newcastle Emlyn Branch, Manchester& Milford Railway, and stations West of Carmarthen Junction Trucks for stations West of Carmarthen Junction at which these trains do not call to be put off at Carmarthen Junction to go forward by local trains. Traffic for stations West of Whitland to be conveyed from Llandilo Junction and Carmarthen Junction. Specials returning from Newport and Cardiff to New Milford must carry 'F' head marks, must take on the same description of traffic as the Gloucester and Bristol specials calling at the same stations, and in addition they may take traffic from Newport, and Cardiff for Neath and stations West thereof, and must call at Gowerton and Pembrey, and take from Gowerton the same traffic as permitted from Landore Relief Sidings, and from Pembrey the same traffic as permitted from Llandilo Junction by the Gloucester specials. Specials returning from Carmarthen Junction only to New Milford will carry 'K' head marks, and will take on at Carmarthen Junction empties for New Milford, making up a load with traffic for intermediate stations. To call where required to put off traffic and to pick up trucks for Old Milford and New Milford These trains may be stopped when required at Briton Ferry to pick up and at Johnston to put off steamer coal. Trucks to be in readiness at Briton Ferry to be picked up in one shunt. Time allowed for return specials from Gloucester and Bristol and from Newport and Cardiff to New Milford:

Carmarthen Junction to Whitland 45 min.
Whitland to Haverfordwest   45 min.
Haverfordwest to Johnston   15 min
Johnston to New Milford   15 min

IRISH CATTLE TRAINS
Special cattle trains conveying Irish cattle traffic from New Milford must not be stopped at stations on the journey to pick up traffic. It is important these trains should not be delayed by goods or local traffic.

HAVERFORDWEST FAIR
Held usually on Tuesday in second week of each month.
Haverfordwest tickets to be collected as follows;–
11.00 am Paddington. At Clarbeston Road. On the Monday before the Fair. The Haverfordwest ticket collector to go to Clynderwen by up Mail, and return by 11.00 am. Paddington, assisting in the examination and collection of tickets at Clarbeston Road.
4.30 pm Paddington. In train by Travelling Collector. On Monday before the Fair.
Chief Inspector Elliott to arrange for the necessary assistance in collection of tickets.

12.05 pm Neath to New Milford
This train must run on the Monday before Haverfordwest Monthly Fair, the date of which will be announced in Weekly notice. The train must be confined as far as possible to through trucks, and must not be kept at stations shunting beyond the time allowed. To call at Cockett to set down brakes only.

8.20 am Carmarthen Junction to Haverfordwest
This train will generally run on Haverfordwest Fair days, and special notice of its running will be given. To convey from Carmarthen Junction cattle trucks for Haverfordwest and important trucks for Whitland and Haverfordwest. On return journey this train will leave Haverfordwest at 3.00 pm for Carmarthen Junction conveying cattle from Haverfordwest cattle Fair and calling where required to put off.

9.30 am New Milford to Haverfordwest
To take Haverfordwest trucks only.

3.00 pm Haverfordwest to Neath
To take cattle from the fair, and call where required to put off. Particulars to be wired from Haverfordwest to Landore of any Swansea trucks on this train, and to Neath of any trucks for Vale of Neath. Chief Inspector Elliott to provide two extra men to assist with Fair traffic at Haverfordwest on this date. The tickets of the 1.00 pm and 4.40 pm trains ex New Milford on the Fair day to be examined at Clynderwen and Whitland tickets collected. Three third class compartments to be locked at New Milford in the first coach of 1.00 pm and 4.40 pm trains from New Milford, for the accommodation of drovers returning from Haverfordwest. The 12.25 pm (RR) goods New Milford to Carmarthen Junction not to run.

TRAIN SERVICES FOR LIVE STOCK TRAFFIC
In order as far as possible to prevent delay in the transit of live stock, the following time table has been compiled showing the trains by which stock should be forwarded except on Mondays. Senders must be informed of the time live stock should be at the station to ensure transit by these trains, and that a good transit cannot be given if not received in time for the trains named. From: –

Haverfordwest and Clarbeston Road :–
to Carmarthen and LNWR line   Second Irish
to Llanelly   1.30 pm New Milford
to Swansea   1.30 pm or Second Irish
to Neath and Vale of Neath stations Second Irish
to Port Talbot and R& S B Railway 1.30 pm New Milford
to Stations beyond   First or Second Irish
Note: the First and Second Irish goods trains do not run on Monday and live stock from stations west of Carmarthen Junc. should on that day be loaded up in time for 11.15 am New Milford connecting with the 3.30 pm Carmarthen Junction. On Tuesdays, Thursdays and Saturdays the Second Irish goods New Milford must not be stopped at Johnston, Haverfordwest, Clarbeston Road or Clynderwen for live stock traffic and such traffic must be conveyed by the 1.30 pm goods as far as Whitland to go forward by Second Irish. Senders must be advised of the arrangements by the Station Master of the station named.

The goods trains running after the loss of the Irish traffic from the marshalling instructions of 1913 records the following :–

To Neyland

11.55 am Cardiff – engine a 4–4–0 or 0–6–0 with the load limited to 50 mixed wagons or vans. The engine and the guard return home with this train having previously worked the Trawl fish from Milford Haven.

8.50 am Carmarthen Junction – a 0–6–0 engine with a mixed load limited to 30 wagons or vans to convey traffic for stations at which it was booked to call.

11.45 pm Tondu – booked for a 2–6–0 tender engine and a load of 50 coal wagons and assisted by a 0–6–0 engine from Neath to Skewen and a 2–6–0, Landore to Cockett.

From Neyland

1.40 pm to Carmarthen Junction – a 0–6–0 with a mixed load of 35 and booked to take on traffic at stations from Neyland to St Clear inclusive. Livestock, Perishables, Bristol traffic, G.W. empties to be put off at Carmarthen Junction. Vacuum fitted vehicles to be in the front of the train and to convey station trucks numbers 598 / 59 / 614 / 615a / 629 / 634.

3.20 pm to Haverfordwest and Milford Haven – the fish train engine may be utilised to clear traffic to Milford Haven and to perform shunting required at Haverfordwest.

4.15 pm (Mondays and Tuesdays only) – to Neath booked for a 0–6–0 engine to convey livestock traffic only and to be extended to Cardiff if required. When extended the trains load is to be made up with G.W. open wagons.

4.55 pm to Carmarthen Junction – the engine being a 0–6–0 with a mixed load of 35 and to be confined to station truck work, cattle perishable and urgent traffic. To shunt into the goods shed at St Clear to put in or pick up goods unless they can be put off and taken on in separate truckloads. The train to convey station trucks 600 / 601 / 607 / 609 / 613 / 615 / 633 / 638 / 639.

5.35 pm – Runs as required to Milford Haven.

10.30 pm to Tondu – with a 2–6–0 tender engine and a load of 50 mixed to be assisted by a 2–8–0 and a 0–6–0 engine from Swansea Valley Junction to Skewen. To call at Johnston for salted fish traffic.

The End of an Era

(The train from Tondu would have carried coal and the return workings the empty coal wagons.)

The working timetables from 1938 onwards demonstrates that although the number of trains arriving or departing varied over the years the destinations remained constant. We find that trains arrived from Cardiff and Swansea Eastern depot but there was no corresponding return working. Instead the trains worked to Llandilo Junction and Neath.

The Neath working was remarkably consistent being reflected in the 1888 timetable and still running in 1963 being a station truck goods.

Some details of "Through and Important Local Freight Trains" of the 1930's give the following information

10.45 am Cardiff to Neyland
E head codes to Llandilo Junction and 'H' beyond
Engine category 'D' (68xx)
Booked to call at: Llandarcy, Felin Fran, Llandilo Junction, Carmarthen Junction, Whitland, Fishguard * * Detached at Clarbeston Road for 8.30 pm Carmarthen Junction to Fishguard Harbour, Haverfordwest, Johnston
Neyland. Traffic attached en–route at Felin Fran, Llandilo Junction, and Carmarthen Junction. At each of these locations traffic to be formed with wagons on train. The train was described as terminating at Neyland or Fishguard according to the engine working the train. Feeding trains and connecting trains were shown as :–
Cardiff: Feeding trains;
12.55 am Severn Tunnel Junction to Cardiff
1.10 am Salisbury to Cardiff
3.10 am Banbury Junction to Cardiff
8.40 pm Exeter to Cardiff
9.50 pm Victoria Basin to Cardiff
10.30 pm Paddington to Cardiff
11.30 pm St Philip's Marsh to Cardiff
Felin Fran: Feeding trains:
6.35 am Llantrisant to Llandilo Junction

Connecting trains;
7.40 pm Felin Fran to Tirydail (local train No 9)
Llandilo Junction
Feeding trains:
10.00 am Swansea Valley Junction to Llandilo Junction
12.30 pm Pontardulais to Llandilo Junction
Return of 2.45 pm Llandilo Junction to Loughor.
Connecting trains:
2.00 pm Llandilo Junction to Pembury (2nd trip)
6.50 pm Llandilo Junction to Carmarthen Junction
Carmarthen Junction
Feeding trains:
8.10 am Aberdare to Carmarthen Junction
Pilot ex Carmarthen Town.
Whitland
Connecting trains:
4.55 am Whitland to Tenby
7.15 am Whitland to Cardigan
8.25 am Whitland to Pembroke Dock

5.00 pm Cardiff to Neyland
'H' head code. Engine category 'E' (72xx) to Llandilo Junction, 'D' beyond. Late loaded traffic ex Spillers Mills in reverse order. Booked to call at :– Port Talbot, Felin Fran, Llandilo Junction, Carmarthen Junction and branches including, Clynderwen, Clarbeston Road, and Fishguard, Whitland and branches, Haverfordwest, Johnston and Milford Haven, Neyland. Traffic attached en–route at Felin Fran, Llandilo Junction, Carmarthen Junction, Clarbeston Road. To be formed with wagons on train at the first two locations and at one shunt at the other two.
Cardiff
Feeding trains:
10.00 pm ex Banbury Junction
Felin Fran
Connecting train:
11.30 pm ex Jersey Marine
Llandilo Junction
Feeding trains:

53xx, No. 5324 at Neyland on July 7 1958. The allocation of this engine at this time is interesting, as it is shown in 1958 as being based at Reading, in which case it was almost as far as it was possible to be from its home depot. The spear fencing in the background may well date from the time of the existence of the ticket platform and would have been intended to separate this from the running shed.

H.C. Casserley

141

1.25 pm Severn Tunnel Junction to Llandilo Junction
4.55 pm Llandovery to Llandilo Junction
9.45 pm Tirydail to Llandilo Junction
Connecting trains:
4.30 am Llandilo Junction to Gwaun –cae Gurwen
4.45 am Llandilo Junction to Neyland
5.40 am Llandilo Junction to Tirydail
8.30 am Llandilo Junction to Llandovery
Carmarthen Junction
Feeding trains:
Pilot ex Carmarthen Town
6.50 pm Llandilo Junction to Carmarthen Junction
Connecting trains
5.40 am to Aberayron and Newcastle Emlyn
6.25 am to Whitland
6.40 am to Aberystwyth
Whitland
Connecting trains:
4.55 am to Tenby
7.15 am to Cardigan
8.25 am to Pembroke Dock
Clarbeston Road
Feeding trains:
12.20 am Fishguard to Clarbeston Road

9.45 pm Cardiff to Neyland

'E' head code to Carmarthen Junction, 'J' beyond
Engine category 'D' (43XX).
Formed from Newtown Goods Shed:–
Neyland, Johnston (including Milford Haven), Haverfordwest, Clarbeston
Road (including Fishguard), Clynderwen
Whitland and branches. From Newtown Down side:–
#Whitland and branches, #Clynderwen, #Clarbeston Road (including
Fishguard), #Haverfordwest, #Johnston(including Milford Haven),
#Neyland.
From Newtown Goods Shed:–
Carmarthen Junction and branches (including Station Truck 162 Neyland),
Llandilo Junction.
From Newton Down side:–
Llandilo Junction, Carmarthen Junction and branches.
At Carmarthen Junction to be formed with wagons on train and at
Clarbeston Road at one shunt.
The traffic for Llandilo Junction and Carmarthen ex Down side to be
marshalled on the Brake Van and the wagons marked # to be kept on a
separate road and picked in after the Carmarthen and Llanelly traffic (ex
shed) has been put on the train. On arrival at Carmarthen Junction, the
rear portion of the train with van to be left on the avoiding line until after
departure.
Cardiff
Feeding trains:
11.00 am ex Pontypool Road (steel bar traffic only, Newport to Milford
Haven)
5.25 pm ex Pontypridd
Llandilo Junction
Connecting trains:
4.30 am to Gwaun–cae–Gurwen
5.40 am Mountain Goods
7.00 am to Pontardulais
8.30 am to Llandovery
Carmarthen Junction
Feeding trains:
6.50 pm Llandilo Junction to Carmarthen Junction
Connecting trains
5.40 am Carmarthen Junction to Aberayron and Newcastle Emlyn
6.25 am Carmarthen Junction to Whitland
6.40 am Carmarthen Junction to Aberystwyth
6.45 am Carmarthen Junction to Carmarthen Town
8.50 am Carmarthen Junction to Aberystwyth

10.30 am Carmarthen Junction to Newcastle Emlyn
Whitland
Connecting trains:
4.55 am to Tenby
5.35 am Passenger to Pembroke Dock
5.55 am Mixed to Cardigan
7.15 am to Cardigan
8.15 am Passenger to Pembroke Dock
8.25 am to Pembroke Dock
Clarbeston Road
Connecting trains:
Fishguard Shunting engine No 1
Johnston
Connecting trains:
8.40 am Passenger to Milford Haven
10.10 am to Milford Haven (8.17am ex Neyland)
Conveys Station Trucks:–
149 Cardiff to Aberayron from Cardiff to Carmarthen Junction
152 Cardiff to Aberystwyth from Cardiff to Carmarthen Junction
153 Cardiff to Brynamman from Cardiff to Llandilo Junction
154 Cardiff to Cardigan from Cardiff to Whitland
158 Cardiff to Llandovery from Cardiff to Llandilo Junction
161 Cardiff to Newcastle Emlyn from Cardiff to Carmarthen Junction
162 Cardiff to Neyland from Cardiff to Carmarthen Junction
163 Cardiff to Pembroke Dock from Cardiff to Whitland
170 Cardiff to Neyland from Carmarthen Junction to Whitland

5.20 pm Neyland to Neath

'K' head code Station Truck goods. Engine category 'D'
This train served local stations en–route.
Whitland
Feeding trains:
12.40 pm ex Pembroke Dock
2.05 pm ex Cardigan
Carmarthen Junction
Feeding trains
7.20 am and 9.25 am ex Aberystwyth
11.20 am ex Aberayron
3.05 pm ex Newcastle Emlyn
9.05 pm ex Carmarthen Goods
Connecting trains:
5.40 am Carmarthen Junction to Aberayron
6.45 am Pilot to Carmarthen
11.15 am Whitland to Severn Tunnel Junction
11.20 am Carmarthen Junction to Cardiff
Llandilo Junction
Connecting trains:
5.40 am Llandilo Junction to Tirydail
8.30 am Llandilo Junction to Llandovery
11.30 pm Whitland to Swansea (High Street)
Landore
Connecting train:
5.45 am Landore to Cardiff
Neath
Connecting train:
6.10 am Neath to Aberdare
Conveys Station Trucks:–
3 Aberayron to Cardiff from Carmarthen Junction to Landore
13 Aberystwyth to Llanelly from Carmarthen to Llanelly
169 Cardigan to Carmarthen from Whitland to Carmarthen Junction
356 Milford Haven to Cardiff from Johnston to Carmarthen Junction
357 Milford Haven to Carmarthen from Johnston to Carmarthen Junction
358 Milford Haven to Llanelly from Johnston to Llanelly
360 Milford Haven to Swansea from Johnston to Llandilo Junction
371 Newcastle Emlyn to Llanelly from Carmarthen Junction to Llanelly
372 Newcastle Emlyn to Swansea from Carmarthen Junction to Llandilo
Junction
461 Pembroke Dock to Carmarthen from Whitland to Carmarthen Junction.

Appendix 4
Details from the 1926 Sectional Appendix

NEYLAND

TRAINS ARRIVING AT NEYLAND

Down Passenger Trains must reduce speed to 4 miles an hour in passing the Locomotive Shed.

Trains having on two Engines must be brought to a stand clear of the Points leading to Engine Shed for the leading Engine to be got out of the way, and the Train must be drawn into the Station by the Second Engine.

Down Goods Trains approaching Neyland must come to a dead stand opposite the Gas House.

LOADING OF GOODS TRAINS TO NEYLAND

Goods Trains on arrival at Neyland must, as far as possible, have the different class of vehicles together thus : Cattle Wagons, Wagons containing Empty Fish Boxes, Empty Vacuum Stock, Empty Opens and Wagons loaded with Goods.

GAS TANKS FROM LLANELLY

On arrival at Neyland these tanks must be placed in position for re–charging without any delay, and returned by first authorised available Train. They must not be intercepted at Johnston or elsewhere but worked, direct to home station.

BANKING UP PASSENGER TRAINS NEYLAND TO JOHNSTON

When the Bank Engine is required to assist a Passenger Train from Neyland to Johnston the Station Master or person in charge at Neyland must arrange with the Locomotive Department.

ASSISTING PASSENGER TRAINS FROM NEYLAND

When a Passenger Train requires assistance from Neyland the Assistant Engine should be sent from the Signal Box on to the Train attached to the Train Engine, but when this is not practicable the Train must be stopped at the Signal Box for the Assistant Engine to be attached.

The Assistant Engine must not be allowed to go on to the Train while the Train is standing with the Train Engine attached at the Departure Platform.

When it is not possible to send the Assistant and Train Engines back to the Train when it stands at the Platform to be attached thereto, the Assistant Engine must be placed in the Hospital Siding or kept on the Engine Shed Line (East End) until the Train which it is to assist has come to a stand at the Signal Box.

DOWN SIDINGS EAST AND WEST OF BARN LAKE BRIDGE

No Engine must be permitted to enter the Yard until the Signalman has permission from the Shunter in charge it may do so.

If an Engine is required to move out on to the Down Line, or over the Middle Road towards the Station in addition to the hand signal from the Shunter, the Engine Whistle must be sounded as under, to ensure the Signalman being satisfied everything is clear.

To or from Down Main Line and Barnlake Sidings	2 Whistles and 1 Crow
To or from Middle Road and Down Line, Station end	6 Whistles and 2 Crows

When it is necessary for an Engine or Train to pass over the Middle Road from the Station or from the Pontoon Sidings, the Middle Road must not be fouled until the Shunter in charge has satisfied himself that everything is clear.

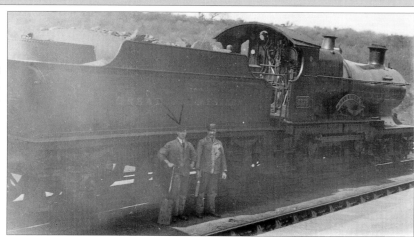

3378 'River Tawe' at Neyland. The Fireman – arrowed, is known to be Terry Morgans, although regretfully the driver is not identified.

Alan Morgans.

ENGINE TURNTABLE

When two or more Engines coupled are travelling to or from the Engine Turntable, a competent Loco. Department man must be in charge of leading and training locomotives.

70–FEET, 72–FEET AND 73–FEET COACHES

Must not be shunted through the connection with the Up Main to the Factory Siding. Vehicles of this description may be shunted from the Factory Siding to No. 1 Rock Siding, and from No. 1 Rock Siding to the Down Main Line, also through the cross–over road Down to Up Main at East end of Yard.

1958 Sectional Appendix;

INSTRUCTIONS FOR USING LEVEL CROSSING OVER TURNTABLE ROAD, NEYLAND.–

 The Lorry Driver before attempting to use the Crossing must contact the Running & Maintenance Depot Foreman or Chargeman to obtain permission, and if practicable the necessary authority will be given. In no instance must the Crossing be used for the passage of the lorry until this permission has been obtained. When, owing to breakdown or other causes, it is necessary for a private lorry to be used, the Neyland Station Master must make such arrangements with the tenant of the Old Sail Loft as will ensure these arrangements being carried out by the Lorry Driver.
A Klaxton Horn is fixed on the Coal Stage in Loco Yard facing towards Signal Box, worked by a push button fixed on a shelf in the Signal Box.
Code.- 3 rings to remind Driver to give whistle signal when clear of points.

Driver Ernie Perry and Fireman Dan James ready to
work the 4.40 pm passenger service to Carmarthen.
Collec. Peter Radford